WEAPONS OF OUR WARFARE

A STORY INSPIRED BY TRUE EVENTS

By Ed Delfin

EAGLE RISE PUBLISHING

EAGLERISEPUBLISHING.COM

WEAPONS OF OUR WARFARE

A story inspired by true events

———————

© Copyright 2021 by Ed Delfin

ISBN 978-1-7367261-3-6

Editors:
William J. Purdy, III
Lauren Humphries-Brooks

Interior Design:
Katie Sanchez

Published by:
Eagle Rise Publishing, Virginia Beach, VA.
EagleRisePublishing.com

Printed and bound in the USA and UK on acid-free paper.
Additional books can be purchased through Amazon.

For Nyree and Rizal

Take hold of the life that is truly life.

FOREWORD

Watsonville, California, is a small farming community rich in history and struggle. This lovely, fertile valley was home to the infamous Watsonville Riots, in which white mobs attacked Filipino American workers in January 1930. It was a cradle of the nascent United Farm Workers Union in the 1960s and beyond, and it later birthed the 1985 cannery workers' strike.

It's also a place that today is steeped in youth violence, a fact that stuns many when I tell them about it. Most of us think the scourge of gangs, drugs and youth violence afflicts cities like Los Angeles, Chicago or Oakland — but certainly not a humble, fertile valley whose apples, blackberries and strawberries feed the nation. Though I have lived in the Pajaro Valley region for years, I, too, had a hard time believing the extent of violence in what should be a serene and peaceful farming region. Then I began investigating this area's gangs and their history — now a two-decade endeavor — and my eyes opened to the tragedy of children killing children, even here, in one of the nation's most picturesque locales.

Ed Delfin knows this world. It's not just the two decades he spent as an officer with the Watsonville Police Department. Or the fact that he spent his teen years here, when, like so many young men, he was tormented by these very gang members. Ed knows this world because he is not just a gang cop — he's also a minister, who lives among and cares about these youth, their families and their community. He backs up compassion with action.

That's why his book is so important. Yes, it's a fascinating novel that stretches from the Philippines to the San Francisco Bay Area and beyond. Yet it's not a typical police catalog of war stories told along an us-against-the-bad-guys plotline. His main character, Dan Bautista, shares his vulnerability, his doubts, fears and aspirations. He brings us directly into this utterly improbable world of farm-town gangs, drug kingpins, even serial killers. And he does it with heart.

Bautista's unlikely friendship with Albert, a drug smuggler who shot a cop, drives home this point. The two met at Bautista's church and were fishing from the Santa Cruz Wharf when Albert finally admitted his crime, committed years earlier.

"Albert and I didn't say much for the rest of the fishing trip. The day started with Albert Gates as a dope fiend with a dark mysterious criminal past. It ended with Albert Gates the convict who'd smoked a cop and lived to regret it for the rest of his life," Delfin writes. Yet he concludes: "Albert and I were friends. Faults, wounds, cuts, scars, tattoos and all."

It's telling that even as he chronicles Bautista's visceral desire to annihilate the local gang leaders, Delfin quotes Friedrich Nietzsche in a cautionary tone: "Whoever fights monsters should see to it that in the process he does not become a monster."

This is the sensibility that infuses his writing with authenticity, nuance and heart.

Ed's own ministry reminds me of what Dr. David Kennedy of the John Jay College of Criminal Justice once said about young gang members: that most of them want to leave that life — they just don't know it yet and they don't know how. Ed has been there to lock up those who don't hear the message to put down their guns, but he's also scrambled down into the trenches to help struggling young men leave that life behind.

We live in a time when many are questioning the role of police. I have friends and family involved in these efforts. But I tell them: don't just imagine — or worse, invent — what you think officers think and feel. I say listen to them, bring them to table and break bread. You might be surprised.

Ed's is a voice that is honest and humbled by self-reflection, a voice that has much to teach all of us about the better angels of our nature.

— Julia Reynolds
Author of *Blood In The Fields: Ten Years Inside California's Nuestra Familia Gang*

PART ONE

---

*When justice is done, it is a joy
to the righteous but terror to
evildoers.*

Proverbs 21:15

CHAPTER

1

0540 Red Bull Day.

Lights from the homes of the early risers were on. Shadows danced as people shuffled from one end of their houses to the other, getting ready for the day. A stray vehicle made its way down the street every so often. The beeping from the garbage truck and its hydraulic fork grinding as it lifted each bin one house after the next was the only noise on the 200 block of Sixth Street.

"Glad I wore my gloves today," I said.

"I should've brought mine. I think I left it in my ride," Carillo said. "I'm feeling it. It's gotta be in the thirties or somethin'. This is cold. California cold."

"I got another pair. One of those tactical ones I never use. It's got 'em plastic bumps on the knuckles in case you end up punching someone. You want 'em?"

"I'm alright."

"Wonder if those knuckle bumps actually work. Seems stupid. Punch somebody with it . . . then what . . . knock 'em out? Leave a mark?"

"Color them black. Call them tactical. That's how they sell everything to cops."

"Genius. It worked. I've got a pair."

"Add a blue line on it. Double the sales."

"Right?"

At one point, the homes on Sixth Street were architectural gems. But that was a long time ago and those qualities had given way to unkempt yards, faded walls, black metal bars on doors and windows, and old cars parked on brown lawns.

A peaceful neighborhood. For now.

Carillo dug his hands deeper in his jacket pockets.

"I'll turn the truck back on and crank the heat up," I said.

"Don't do that. Your lights will kick on, right?"

"Nope. We're good. Fleet fixed it. I can keep my lights off even when the engine is running. It had to get done. It got old sitting in an icebox on surveillance, especially when you're not on point."

Reggie Carillo wouldn't know. He always wanted point. It's the prime assignment on a covert operation. He wanted the best view of the action, the suspect's house, the dope deal, call out what was happening, give the play-by-play to all the other units. He'd die sitting five blocks away from the action mindlessly playing sudoku.

"*Que bueno.* Yeah . . . fire it up. We're ways off from home-boy's pad anyway," Carillo said.

Carillo and I were parked on the east end of the block closest to Walker Street. We were about six houses away from the target's home. Plenty of distance. Our intel told us that there were at least five people in the house: three children, all under the age of six, and their parents, Sergio and Dora.

We wanted Sergio.

At twenty-five, Sergio was already a fully fledged City Hall Watson, CHW, norteño gang member. His allegiance was written in tattoos lining his arms, back and chest.

Sergio had been a City Haller since he was sixteen, giving him almost ten years of work put in. In gang life, Sergio was close to a veterano. He had seen plenty of shootings—that is, he'd been shot at, and on the other end of a gun, multiple times. The goal of operation Red Bull was to take down the top shot callers of CHW and Sergio was at the top.

• • •

The week before Red Bull Day, we'd sent a wired informant, Pequeño, to buy dope from Sergio. It was supposed to be a simple CI buy-walk operation. That is, the confidential informant, the CI, would buy narcotics, then walk.

Buy. Walk. Simple.

The day's instructions for the CI were terse:

Take the $40. Buy dope and get out. We'll be listening on the wire. But make sure the recorder is on. We'll follow you in and out. After the buy, go back to the same place, like the way you did before.

That was the plan.

I'd given that speech to Pequeño at least thirty times.

He parked in front of Sergio's house, and we watched him cross the front lawn to the door. We heard shuffling sounds on the wire as the door opened and Pequeño walked in, out of our sight.

Pequeño didn't bother with the script. Good informants almost never do. Most think they're true artists that shouldn't be constrained. They're confident they can get anything from anybody, and they usually do. Until the time they don't.

But Pequeño went full-improv. The meth deal went off in the first two minutes. Then instead of walking, Pequeño decided to talk about everything from sports to the local baby-mama dramas. The sound of the TV blaring and the silent pauses between Pequeño's blathering made it worse.

They were sitting. Watching a movie.

Buy. Walk. Simple.

I hated prolonged operations that involved any informant. The longer Pequeño was in the house, the more could go wrong: wire batteries die, other people show up and screw the pooch, surveillance units miss an all-important piss-break.

Forty-plus minutes into a simple *buy'n bounce* that was supposed to take five, both voices on the wire shifted, dropping lower and deeper. It was *that* serious tone you know the moment you hear it. Their voices slipped away to a faint, almost inaudible, whisper on the wire. We cranked up the volume but still couldn't hear. At worst these were the faint electronic sounds of an informant getting strangled or knifed by somebody good at it.

My mind raced:

What're they talking about? Is Sergio confessing something? Was Pequeño trying to carve a side deal cutting us out?

Without audio, we had no idea about what was going on in the house. I got ready for a host of scenarios. All bad.

A moment later, we heard the unmistakable sound of a pump shotgun racking. No other sound like it. We held our breath. He'd be gone before we could reach him. If it went like *that*.

"Oh yeah, that's what I need," Pequeño cooed.

"It's badass, homie. Clean too. It's hard to come up on something like this. The kid Gio got this and he said it's totally clean," Sergio said.

"Gio the kid from Bree?"

"You know him?"

"Yeah, he's hooked me up with a couple things, you know? You believe him? He ain't exactly the careful type . . . know what I'm sayin'? I like the kid, but he a kid . . . ."

"He legit. He comes up on all sorta things."

"Don't know, homie. That kid is crazy. He's high. Always high. He just goes on, non-stop. Doesn't care whose house he hits. Hell, he pro'ly break into this house to get this shotty back."

"He'd be dead if that happens." Sergio was right.

Pequeño finagled to buy the shotgun. Despite the ill-advised, off-the-cuff performance, I'd trained him well. He knew we wanted him to buy a weapon, any weapon. Sergio considered the offer.

"Three-fifty! Final offer. C'mon, bro. You know that's a lot of money for that *cuete*," Pequeño said.

Close but Sergio wouldn't budge.

Pequeño knew he couldn't up the price. Overpaying for anything is a red flag in *the Game*. Unlimited access to funds meant a buyer was sponsored by someone, likely as not by the cops.

The deal wasn't happening. Sergio needed a shotgun and he wasn't letting it walk. That was that.

Almost an hour after he walked into the house, Pequeño walked out with two small bindles of crystal meth and no weapons.

• • •

Pequeño's failure to buy the shotgun bought us critical information, nevertheless. We knew the morning of Red Bull Day, the shotgun was in the house. The night before Pequeño called and made one more bid for the weapon. Again, Sergio was having none of it and didn't bother to counter.

The call seemed inconsequential but wasn't. Pequeño confirmed Sergio had the shotgun. This critical fact meant the "Believed to be Armed" box in the Operation Plan got checked.

Hollywood directors get it wrong most of the time when it comes to firearms. They know what they like. They like shiny big handguns mostly. But when it comes to shotguns Hollywood really gets it wrong. Shot for shot, wound for wound, the pump shotgun or worse yet, the auto-loading shotgun is among the most lethal firearms at 100 feet or less ever devised.

During World War I, the German government charged that the American use of shotguns violated the Hague Decrees (pre-Geneva Convention), prohibiting any weapon calculated to cause unnecessary suffering.

Germany even went so far as to send a telegram to the US State Department in September 1918 threatening to execute any American soldier caught with shotguns. The horrific wound damage caused by the weapon terrified German troops so severely military historians suspect some American troops were slaughtered by enraged Germans for using the Winchester Mod 1897 trench broom against them.

The wire told us and Pequeño confirmed a high ranking norteño gangster was holed up in his house with a weapon the German army feared enough to complain about during some of the bloodiest trench warfare ever fought.

Sergio meant to keep the weapon.

We wouldn't be taking any chances.

CHAPTER
2

At precisely 0600 hours, *the snake* composed of CHP search warrant team members crept towards Sergio's house. The nine members were eager and able, and depending on who you talked to, legit operators. For a CHP team.

The morning sun seemed stuck just below the horizon.

The silhouette of the entry team stacked at the front door in full gear was intimidating. Entry would be fast and relentless.

Knowing Sergio was armed with one of the deadliest close-range weapons available changed everything.

The first five in the stack shouldered their semi-auto M-4s as the Breacher crept to the front door carrying the ram, the balance of his breach tools slung on his back. Two guys from the back of the snake walked past the stack and huddled next to the window on the two-three corner behind the front of the house.

Carillo and I languished comfortably in the truck, watching the entry unfold. The heater in my truck was working just fine. I took my gloves off.

The morning silence shattered in a flurry of fist-banging on the front door. Cops have mastered the art of fist-banging. It's nothing like the everyday knock on the door. A sound that says: "We're not asking, we're comin' in."

A voice from the front of the stack yelled: "Police. Search Warrant. Open the door!"

One breath later, the Breacher put the ram in position. He had a compact solid windup style that slammed the ram through the front door on the first huck. We barely heard a thing in the truck.

As the door shot open, the lead operators tossed flashbangs into the foyer. At the same time, one operator posted to the back corner of the house punched a hole in the side window. His partner hurled another flashbang through the broken pane. Moments later, multiple near-simultaneous white flashes were followed by thunderous bangs that shook the entire house and sent little rivulets of dust sifting from the roof gutters.

I'd made sure the truck's windows were fully down. Carillo and I didn't want to miss a thing. The string of thunderous bangs on Sixth Street was quickly followed by a dozen muffled bangs around the city. I heard three more faint bangs from nearby neighborhoods in Watsonville.

Sixth Street was one of twelve houses breached in one coordinated hit.

Every door splintered at 0600.

A thing of beauty.

Carillo and I had devoted our workings hours and most of our thoughts on our days off to this case for the last six months. Payday was grand. Almost one hundred and fifty personnel, all specializing in high-risk entries, breached twelve different homes with search and arrest warrants in hand.

I was done.

I'd worked the case.

Like a lot of us, I'd drunk more Red Bull than I wanted to stay awake for an operation pushing sixteen-hour days for weeks at a time. I'd spent multiple sleepless nights trying to calm Pequeño and assure him his paranoia about getting green-lit was unfounded—although deep down, I knew he could be clipped by CHW on suspicion alone. We'd typed endless mind-numbing reports, documenting every buy. I'd booked countless bindles of narcotics, guns, and dozens of 8mm videos of Pequeño's debrief for each buy.

I was burned out, spent, jazzed and anxious all at once.

Everybody was.

On Red Bull Day, we got our release.

Our role was to oversee as each team hit houses we tagged. The truth was, we finally got to sit back to enjoy what we'd slaved to build for months. Warrants were written, and case agents were standing by ready to collect evidence and write reports. Grand jury indictments were already prepared. There'd be no preliminary examinations in court.

Every profession has its emphatic way of making a powerful statement. A statement that sets the tone for future engagements. Serving these warrants when and how we did was our statement. We intended to make these gangsters suffer the same pain they inflicted on their victims.

Their doors were splintered and knocked down. Flashbangs made their homes shudder to the foundations. Loaded guns, cocked and safeties off, were leveled inches from their faces. Entire families, even young children, suffered the pain.

I felt zero remorse. I had nothing for them.

It was part of their punishment. An important part.

Eventually, they'd be sentenced and do time in prison. The sentencing day would be gravy compared to Red Bull Day. These gangsters would have plenty of time to anticipate their sentences. But Red Bull Day shook them to the core of their souls. All but the very hardest of them.

I grinned, picturing the terror in their eyes and the confusion on their faces.

These raids were designed to be as viscerally terrifying as they were vengeful.

• • •

I used to love Watsonville. One time many years before Red Bull Day, I'd driven down each city block praying for the families. Actually praying. I'd prayed for their lives to change, and for the liberation of young students from the all-pervasive influence of street gangs.

That compassion was gone and burned out of me. A cold dead memory now.

I wanted to see these gangsters jammed up in prison or dead, and I smiled whenever I thought about a dead drug dealer slouched in a puddle of his urine and excrement, the victim of his own wares.

On Red Bull Day, I would have loved to watch the evil part of Watsonville burn.

I would have gladly brought the gas and lit the fire.

PART TWO

———

*Whoever fights monsters should see
to it that in the process he does
not become a monster.*

- Friedrich Nietzsche

CHAPTER

3

Kalibo, Aklan, Philippines.
1987.

The mailman couldn't fully appreciate the gravity of the message he delivered.

It was life-changing for my dad and the rest of us.

Short and concise, it offered him the opportunity to pastor a church in California.

California?

So much to consider. The Philippines is incredibly vibrant, but America remains the ultimate destination for most Filipinos. The land of prosperity, we'd just hit the jackpot, so it seemed.

My parents quickly hashed out a simple plan: My dad would visit California alone. He'd scope out the pastoral opportunity, while the family remained behind. Then if the conditions were right, we'd follow.

Easy peasy.

Reality was otherwise. Men plan and God laughs. My dad ended up living in America for three years while my mom, my brothers, and I waited in the Philippines for the American and Philippine governments to process our paperwork. The extended wait was brutal for my mom. She became the interim pastor for two local churches my dad vacated. She kept her day job teaching English at a local high school while remaining the full-time mom for me and my two younger brothers. We were an overactive brood to say the least.

My brothers and I grew up sooner than usual. At ten I was driving my dad's motorcycle. By eleven, I was driving my brothers around town in my mom's Jeep.

Dad reminded me by letter that the motorcycle was only for outreach ministries, specifically, for outreach in Altavas. I observed his rules even from 7,000 miles away.

Mostly.

Altavas was a remote town about a two-hour motorcycle ride from Kalibo. The town itself was a small hub that blossomed out of a large open market, a bus stop, and an adjacent plaza. Altavanians were proud of their history and heritage, and the quaint, well-manicured town showed it.

In the early 1980s, my dad helped an American missionary conduct a series of evangelistic crusades in Altavas. After the American missionaries left, the small contingency of people that remained met at the local high school. The group grew steadily, and within a couple of years, the Altavas church had a building and a large congregation.

Altavas stands on top of a series of undulating hills, the edges of the town surrounded by steep mountain ranges lined with dirt roads leading to still smaller villages. In this terrain, the primary transportation is the motorcycle. Hondas and Suzukis were modified to extend the backseat, maximizing the passenger load. It was normal to see six to eight people squeezed together on one motorcycle.

Many of the church members lived in remote forest areas. Some traveled five hours just to attend the church service. To accommodate such arduous trips, services were held on Saturday afternoons. Worship services were incredible. Loud singing, exuberant dancing, prayers recited with deep sincerity and passion.

Despite working extremely hard for precious little, members of the Altavas church were always overjoyed. People who are happy to travel hours for church tend to truly love it. The Altavas church became my gold standard for genuine worship. An atmosphere I would yearn for the rest of my life but never find.

Finally, my parents reached the decision that we would all leave the Philippines and move to California. Being uprooted from everything you know—your entire way of life—is always painful. At the age of twelve, it was unforgiving. Like the town of Altavas, there were many things I missed. Friends, girlfriends, family, and childhood became memories overnight. Moving to such a completely strange distant land made me feel like my entire life before was a figment of my imagination.

At the airport in Kalibo, about fifty friends and family saw us off. Promises were made to write letters and to never forget each other. Promises to come back and visit as soon as possible. They were loving lies. Later I would remember a quote I'd read from the American journalist H. L. Mencken:

"Lying is not only excusable; it is not only innocent; it is, above all, necessary and unavoidable. Without the ameliorations that it offers, life would become a mere syllogism and hence too metallic to be borne."

I never liked the quote.
But Mencken was right.

CHAPTER

4

**San Francisco, California.
1990.**

We arrived at San Francisco International Airport on a late September evening. By contrast to the large crowd that saw us off, our welcoming party consisted of my dad and my cousin Rene. I'd heard a lot about Rene but never actually met him until that night. He was eight years older, and he owned a boom-car. The 1988 Toyota Supra was lowered, had alloy rims, a leather bra, a pronounced spoiler, black leather interior, and an incredibly powerful stereo system.

I'd never been inside such a luxurious vehicle. On the other hand, Rene never dove straight down a steep jungle trail at top speed on a Suzuki, his girlfriend squeezing his chest and her face buried in his back, the thick warm jungle air tearing at his eyes.

I had.

Much of what I knew about America was based on movies, most notably *Back to the Future*. To me, it was all blond, blue-eyed girls, suburban neighborhoods, beautiful town squares, skateboards, diners, and cool cars. Rene's Supra fit my American ideals. The futuristic orange dashboard lights glowed as soon as he turned on the ignition. Maybe in time, the Supra would fly. After all, this was America.

As we rolled out of the airport parking lot, my gaze was glued to the window, desperate for my first glimpse of America. At midnight I couldn't see much of San Francisco or anything else. The roadways were impressive. Mile after mile of smooth silk-like roadway, lined with reflectors, each exit marked and brightly lit. Every vehicle had working headlights and taillights. Traffic seemed to flow in some kind of massive organized dance everyone knew. Thousands of people were following traffic signs and specific rules as if it were instinct.

A completely novel experience for me.

Despite my excitement, I couldn't shake the lump in my chest. Everyone and everything back home was calling me. There it was—*back home.* The sense that home wasn't here and maybe never would be. I wanted to feel the warm thick humidity of island air, hear the chaotic horns of garishly colored tricycles bouncing and lurching across choked intersections, and the taste of *balon-balonan* from the weekend barbecue stands lining the streets of Kalibo. The family was finally together. But given the choice, I'd have hopped a plane, *any plane,* back to the Philippines.

In a heartbeat.

The parsonage was set back on the two-acre church property. It was a generous family home with three bedrooms and two bathrooms. I didn't remember much about the first night. The thirteen-hour flight combined with the debilitating effects of the time change suddenly numbed and overwhelmed my brain. My dad led me to my bed. I collapsed into a deep sleep without any choice, the lump still throbbing in my chest.

• • •

I woke up shivering. Even with a long-sleeve shirt on and under two sets of comforters, I'd never been that cold. My blood was thin. The product of a young lifetime spent in the ever-warm tropical air. The bedroom air slashed my bones like icy razors. The numbing chill was a completely new feeling. It hit me. I was in a strange world.

A new world.

America.

In the morning I surveyed our new home, room by room. My dad had worked relentlessly for years to prepare the family house. The carpets were dark brown, old and faded, but scrupulously clean. Each bedroom was sparsely furnished with a plain bed frame and fresh mattress. The outdated kitchen had a working refrigerator. The focal point of the living room was a vintage old television with turn-dial knobs inside a wooden frame. It sat next to a fireplace, which based on the thick cobwebs in it, hadn't been used in a while. There was a single old couch aimed directly at the television.

Like many teenagers, I suffered from a haughty superficiality, ill-manners, and no filter.

My mom and dad were huddled on the couch when I walked in. She had a blanket draped over her and was also suffering from the deep and sudden change of temperature.

"How'd you sleep?" Dad asked.

"Okay, I guess. But it was really cold!" I answered.

"You'll get used to that. It'll get colder."

"Colder? It gets colder?"

"Oh yes. Winter hasn't really hit yet. It'll be okay, we'll get some sweatshirts and jackets for everybody."

I wasn't fully awake and the cold strangled any excitement I could muster. Finally, I gave up, climbed on the couch, and huddled with my parents sullenly.

"Why is the couch so old and worn?" I asked.

My dad said nothing.

Being chilled to the bone couldn't stop me from complaining, so when he didn't answer I pushed.

"Why does the TV look so old . . . and the carpet? It looks all worn out too. I thought in America everyone had nice stuff."

My mom gave me the look. I knew the look well.

It meant I'd embarrassed her and myself. It meant I'd get it and not in a good way.

Later.

Despite my teen-shortcomings, my parents treated me like an adult. No sugarcoating. Discipline mixed with responsibility and privileges were administered in careful measured doses.

My dad stuttered slightly, something he rarely did, while trying to explain our living conditions.

"We're . . . we're going to have a tough life in America. You need to know. We won't have maids here like we did back home. We won't have much here at all for a while. Everything we do have, the car, TV, and the beds . . . they're all used. All second-hand items. We'll have to work really hard just to survive.

Your mom and I will be looking for good jobs. Things will get better. But you'll need to be patient."

He went on explaining that the church owned the large property and provided a house for the pastor's family, but couldn't provide a salary for the pastor. None of my parents' professional teaching credentials applied in California. They'd have to find another way to earn a living.

To meet living expenses, my dad took work at Ford's Department Store, for a few cents above minimum wage. Overnight he went from pastoring two thriving churches and teaching part-time at a local college to a minimum wage no-skill earner mopping floors and sorting clothes. It was the same for my mother.

I never heard either one of them complain.

All the furniture in our house came from the county landfill. In America, people threw away old furniture because it was old. Dad scoured the landfill and picked the very best items. It was amazing to see what Americans threw away. But it didn't make me feel one bit better knowing our household furniture came from the dump. He'd picked the very best pieces, vigorously cleaned them, and then he set the furniture out in the sun to bake out the musty smell. He'd done all he could do. The message was as clear as it was shocking. Life in America would be a struggle. In time I looked back on those early days and remembered a Mexican proverb I'd heard somewhere:

"That which cannot be remedied must be endured."

"We'll need to work hard. God will provide. Like when we pastored the church in Kajilo," Dad said.

We weren't going to endure the hard life we faced.

The family would remedy it.

Kajilo brought back warm memories for all of us.

"How are folks there?" Dad asked.

"You know how they are, they're the most faithful. They had a big going away party for us. Sister Nancy insisted we take some of her seafood harvest to America. I couldn't say no," Mom said.

Dad chuckled.

"What'd you do with it?"

"Gave it to your family."

• • •

My parents moved to the village of Kajilo in the province of Aklan to pastor a small church of about a dozen members when I was only a few months old. The village developed among the sloughs, estuaries, and fisheries bordering the Sibuyan Sea. Seawater seeped upstream into the terrain through scores of river channels, creating a vast mixed freshwater-saltwater slough system. Early villagers quickly discovered that the slough system was among the most diverse and fertile ecosystems on the planet. Raising fish and other edible crustaceans were easy and created a simple, nearly inexhaustible livelihood for many villagers.

Our house was a whopping 300 square feet. It featured three feet of cement knee-wall topped by a bamboo frame to the roofline. The roof was bundled coconut leaves, known to the locals as *nipa*. Our floor was clay dried and stamped rock hard by human feet.

I loved everything about Kajilo.

I crossed fishponds and sloughs on handmade bamboo rafts

with my friends. We made kites with coconut leaf stems for frames with cheap wax paper pasted over them when the wind howled across the low flat marshes as it often did. When the winds calmed, we fished and hunted birds with slingshots. It was a paradise for a boy my age.

My parents had humble beginnings, as is often the case in the Philippines. Although they both graduated from Bethel Bible School in Manila, they went back to college and got a second set of degrees in education. Throughout their life together, they steadily improved the breadth of their training, skills and livelihood.

Towards the end of my childhood in the Philippines, the family had a very comfortable life. My brothers and I went to private schools and we had two full-time helpers at home. My mom didn't have to cook. My brothers and I had no clue how to do laundry, wash dishes, or do any chores.

Then came America. We went back to square one. Not essentially back to square one, really back to square one. Our comfortable lifestyle vanished like a whisper in a Kajilo windstorm.

The parsonage had corroded old single-pane windows, no insulation, and no heat. We bought a portable electric space heater capable of adequately heating one room. In winter on cold nights all five of us huddled around it to sleep.

It wasn't long before I noticed a greenish-black substance emerging from the corners of the bedroom walls and around the window sills. It was mold, aggravated by the complete lack of insulation, poor ventilation, and the condensation created by five warm bodies.

No one knew mold was bad for you, but the entire family monitored the mold blooms, like a malevolent invader. Cleaning mold off windows and walls quickly became my least favorite weekend chore.

Our hut in Kajilo with the roof made of *nipa* was a palace by comparison.

We just didn't know it.

CHAPTER

5

A week after landing at SFO, I was strolling the hallways of Rolling Hills Middle School. An eighth-grade stranger in a strange world.

Two weeks before landing at SFO, I was in Science High School in Kalibo at the top of the class. I owned school, participating in every sport, intramurals, and Boy Scout events. I was surrounded by close, loyal friends, most of whom I'd known since kindergarten.

At Rolling Hills, I might as well have been a one-legged leper.

In 1990, pants were wide at the hips and pleated tight at the bottom. Girls' bangs were worn high and glued in place by an explosive amount of Aqua Net residue. Boys wore their hair in lines zig-zagging outrageously across the sides of their heads.

School before class resembled a controlled riot, with students screaming and running to classes. I'd never seen couples hugging and making out as teachers walked past. Public displays of affection like that were uncommon in the Philippines and much of Asia, especially in front of teachers. Teachers were typically shown great reverence in the Philippines. Students were expected to formally greet teachers, stand off to the side, brace, and bow slightly. This was also true in much of Asia and remains so to this day.

I missed it already.

The vast majority of the students had brown skin and dark hair like me. Rolling Hills wasn't Hill Valley High from *Back to the Future*. Not by a damn sight.

In the classroom, I was relieved. Some semblance of order existed. Teachers' instructions were clear, and their language was grammatically correct, just as I'd been taught. I had class down.

During lunchtime, I found the cafeteria and managed to get my food. The cafeteria was a big open space under a tin roof. There were several aluminum tables, the bench seats bolted to them, in an open area.

I spotted a handful of Filipinos occupying one of the tables. The truth is you actually can detect people like yourself at great distances without ever meeting them. The opposite is also true, and great misery and terror come from it. I was relieved to see them and instinctively headed their way. They were Filipinos, and somehow I knew they were: FROJJ. Fresh Off the Jumbo Jet.

Like me.

"How're you, *kababayan*?"

Just hearing a word of Tagalog provided a much-needed taste of home.

"I'm good," I replied.

One of the guys told the group to make room for me.

"Where are you from in *Pinas*?" he asked.

"Aklan, a true *Visayan*," I said, scurrying to sit down.

"Niiiiiiice. Sit, sit."

We connected then and there. Everybody ate lunch and talked about things we knew and loved. Most of it back home. There it was again. Home wasn't here. Not America.

Not even close.

• • •

After graduation, my class from Rolling Hills was bussed to the town of Aptos for high school. Aptos was a loose-knit community ten minutes from Watsonville. Not a city, not even an incorporated town, Aptos was a glorified village *that knew somebody*. The proximity of the two towns meant nothing. They might as well have been different countries.

The towns were fundamentally opposites. Watsonville was an incorporated city with a strong business-light industrial center and a large Hispanic community who lived mostly below the national median income level. Aptos was a predominantly white middle and upper-middle-class bedroom community with a village-like funky surfer attitude.

The steep hills that surrounded Aptos High on three sides served as a physical reminder of its isolation from the world around it. Buses from Watsonville strained their antiquated engines scaling Aptos High's heights. When the buses finally chugged up to the school, there were no welcome signs.

We weren't welcome. Watsonville students didn't want to be there. Aptos students didn't want us there. As we walked off the bus, everybody exchanged glares. The strain was unmistakable.

My class was one of the largest groups of students from

Watsonville bussed to Aptos High. Bussing meant that a relatively quiet and spacious school campus became seriously crowded. Classrooms were full, cafeteria lines were long, and student parking was complete chaos.

The buildings at Aptos High were scattered across steep hillsides. Goats would have been happy but students weren't. The campus almost seemed to have been designed to require basic climbing skills. Despite palpable tension, the first morning's classes were uneventful. Everyone needed to get their sea legs.

Lunchtime force-funneled the entire student body through an area dubbed The Quad. Aptos was a closed campus, so were no other places to go. There were no safety-valves to release the morning tension, and The Quad was so jammed with bodies, it was impossible to move without brushing against other students.

Fights broke out during the first lunch period and fairly regularly thereafter. The fights were always along ethnic lines—Hispanic students versus white students. Apparently, no one ever told Hispanic and "white" students that they were ethnically composed of largely the same race. Neither group believed it anyway.

My Filipino buddies were also bussed to Aptos High. We were immature, anxious to avoid the drama, and easily entertained by the commotion around the school. In the first two weeks, the words: "Fight! Fight! Fight!" rang out periodically. We'd all scamper over to get a glimpse of the action from a suitable distance. Fights became the most thrilling part of the day.

For a while.

CHAPTER

6

Violence is one of the original equal-opportunity experiences.

Christmas break of freshman year, Rene gave me a yellow sporty portable CD player, with the latest anti-skip technology. It was one of the best gifts I'd received since I got to America.

As I rode the bus I zoned out. None of my friends lived near me, so I typically kept to myself anyway. The headphones cut out everything and everyone. I ordered CDs in bulk from B.M.G., and promised to purchase one disc a month for the next two years.

One uneventful Thursday I trudged on the bus for home. The ancient behemoth sputtered and banged through the Aptos hills eventually limping into the outskirts of Watsonville. It had two stops before mine, leaving me and a handful of others aboard.

A tap on my shoulder interrupted U2's "Bullet the Blue Sky" pounding in my head.

"What?" I snapped. *Who dares interrupt my musical ride?*

Jeronimo "Bugsy" Ramos leaned in uncomfortably close from the seat behind me. He'd never said a word to me before which suited me fine. Everybody knew his reputation.

He was Varrio Green Valley, a gang member, in one of the more prominent Latino gangs. They called him Bugsy, I supposed, because of his big round bulging eyes. His brother was a jumped-in member, which meant nothing to me, but by context, I knew it had to be bad. Bottom line, Bugsy was someone to avoid.

I gave him a quick (but polite) nod, focused my attention on the front of the bus, and silently prayed he'd disappear. One of the few family members back in the Philippines who wasn't very religious once told me that God always answers every prayer. Then Uncle John Michael told me: "Often as not, His answer is No."

Bugsy tapped my shoulder again. I gave him another nod just as he lifted a headphone off my right ear.

"What?" I asked, trying not to sound upset yet firm enough to be cool.

"Nice CD player."

"Thanks."

Bugsy retreated as quickly as he'd appeared. I was relieved and nervous. It didn't feel right because the Little Voice in my head said it wasn't. My Little Voice never lied and never told me to do anything that would get me hurt. Now it was yelling.

I darted off the bus at my stop and started speed-walking home. Five Green Valley vatos waited at the bus stop for Bugsy to off-load. I sped past avoiding eye contact.

After a block of Olympic class speed-walking, I heard a group talking and laughing behind me. Praying to the Divine Sisters of the Perpetual Coincidence, I speed-walked even faster. Probably a personal best. But the voices got louder and closer.

Six blocks from home. God's answer was: No.

"Ay, let me see that player," Bugsy yelled.

I kept walking, feigning deafness.

"Hey, *puto*, let me see that player! Eh?"

My Little Voice told me what was gonna happen.

I'd seen it before, the same group. Seen them chase down kids, beat them up, and take whatever they wanted. Wherever and whenever they felt like it.

And nothing happened.

They were going to jump me and take my CD player.

I wanted to run. I was fairly fast and could probably outrun all of them all the way home. Then what? What about the next day, and the next? I'd see them again, and again. I had to ride the same bus and get out at the same stop, day after day.

The Little Voice told me that to have any chance I had to make a stand.

Summoned my courage, I turned to face Bugsy & Company.

"Nah, it's cool," I said.

"Awww hell no, ese', let me see the damn player!" Bugsy barked.

I zipped my backpack securing the CD player deep inside. Whatever happened, there was a better chance my CD player would stay with me if it was secured to me in my backpack.

"Nah, I don't think so," I muttered.

"Oh, I'm taking it you piece of . . . ."

I would like to think I put up a good fight, but I didn't. The last thing I clearly remember was throwing one terrific punch as Bugsy aggressively shuffled towards me. His face snapped away from me . . . then I was on the ground, drifting in and out of consciousness, with fists and feet bashing me. They gave me the classic thumping. I lay on the ground on my back, kicking when I could, but mostly covering my face. I wasn't going to lose the CD player.

The beating stopped.

Through blurry eyes, I saw Bugsy & Company running.

I had no clue why they stopped. The strap to my backpack was still in my hand. I pulled it close to my chest, patting the bag for the lump of the CD player. It was still there.

I got up and limped home.

Four more blocks.

Slowly.

On cue, all the adrenaline cooked off in my body as I stepped through the front door. My face was speckled with red marks and had begun to swell. My ribs hurt with every breath. I whimpered a little as pain started registering from all over my body.

My parents were furious and wanted to call the police.

I begged.

"I know how these gang members work. Don't call the cops please."

"The police will arrest them. They shouldn't get away with this!" my dad said.

"Please don't. You call the cops and it won't end there. It'll get worse. One guy may go to juvie, maybe not. But even if he's in jail, after he's gone, the others will look for me. They'll never forget who called the cops."

"If they touch you again, we'll call the police again."

"I'm begging you, please don't. I'm okay. I'll just avoid them."

Guys who called the cops were snitches.

Snitches got stitches.

My parents didn't understand what I was saying. They believed in the American justice system and thought their children would be protected by it.

But they deferred to my judgment. The police never heard a word.

CHAPTER

7

Violence persists.

Human history graphically shows that it only retreats when forcibly confronted. Yet the more forcefully you confront violence, the more you become the thing you confront. The true root of evil is that we as a species forget this, and in so doing, we cause untold human suffering.

Over and over again.

The Bible I read often talks of love and devotion, but in high school, I soon realized it just as often recounts tales of horrendous violence, fear, pain, and cruelty, often as not inflicted by good men and women out of necessity. Take Samson killing a thousand men with a donkey's jawbone. A thousand? Really? Did they all have it coming? Maybe it was best Samson's eyes were gouged and he never saw what he'd become.

As I grew up I realized most people, including me, remember evil done to them long after they've forgotten the good. In time it seemed pretty clear that I received something from the fights at Aptos High, something that stayed with me.

Always.

Bugsy & Company's attacks didn't stop. I got into more fights with random vatos on the bus and the walks home. Bugsy was behind it but I couldn't prove a thing. I didn't provoke them and couldn't avoid them. It was like a waking nightmare in which I couldn't move and couldn't wake up. Although I managed to get away relatively unscathed, I'd grown weary of fighting my way home from school.

My mom and dad's new strategy was to remove the bus from the equation.

It seemed like a great idea. School was relatively safe and there'd be no window of opportunity for *my fans*. But my parents had forgotten. Violence is insidious. I hung out in crowded places, with friends, and near school staff. I stayed busy. My grades were trending in the right direction, and I even got on the principal's list to end my freshman year.

On the weekends, I hung out with friends from church, but never in my neighborhood. For a time it worked. I managed to avoid all the places Bugsy haunted like a bad smell.

But violence persists. Bugsy and his homies never forgot me.

When I passed them in school, they stared me down, called me puto—and worse. It was constant. When they got the chance, I knew they'd finish the fight. It was just a matter of time.

It was inevitable.

• • •

I worked my way up through mountain goat country to the music lab, perched on the furthest, steepest hill of the campus. My legs were stiff. A directionless white mist rose from a patch of the frosted hill the sun beamed on. Bugsy was making his way down the same steep stairs alone. A handful of students scurried to their classes, peeling off the walkway. A silver pipe guard rail lined one side of the path and a line of lockers the other.

We were headed directly at each other with no place for me to go. I decided to ignore him no matter what.

That plan exploded.

"Still got the Walkman? Eh, *puto*?" Bugsy sneered.

I don't know what it was. His face, calling me puto, or maybe the fear of the confrontation I'd been avoiding for months. I was tired of being afraid. Many years later a friend told me he hated being afraid because it made him so angry he couldn't control himself. I'd never thought of it that way, but I think it's true for lots of people and it explains a lot of what happens in the world. Good and bad. Something inside blew, a fierce heat exploded in my brain. My face went bright red.

I punched Bugsy in the jaw and sent him stumbling to his knees. For a moment I thought he might stay there, but this wasn't his first rodeo. He got up slowly, while I threw a flurry of punches, hoping one might magically finish it. Actually, he'd fully recovered. Bugsy had been fighting since young childhood. He'd taken and given many beatings. For him, it was like breathing, and now he was breathing *just fine*.

We brawled mostly on the ground, for a full minute, an eternity in a real fight. A minute and ten seconds in, we were spent. A teacher rushed up, ceremoniously breaking up a fight already at its end.

My parents were summoned to the principal's office.

Again.

I hadn't instigated the fight. Not really. But that was irrelevant to the principal. That day I realized why violence persists. It wouldn't make sense to anyone at Aptos High or even my parents. Bugsy's words weren't sufficient provocation. It was everything that came before, and all that would surely come after that mattered.

When I first came to America I noticed some Americans said things that didn't make sense, at least on the surface. Grammatically they were all wrong in the classic sense in which I'd been taught English. But underneath they did. After a while, you could feel what they really meant.

"Always retaliate first." I'd heard a man say that once in Ford's Department Store. Logically and grammatically it made no sense to me. The thing was Americans said stuff like that on purpose, and it made complete sense once I realized what it really meant.

It meant I had to attack Bugsy suddenly violently as cruelly. I had to, and I had to do it first, without any warning before he and his vatos did it to me. I had to hit him hard, make him feel pain . . . maybe a little fear he didn't expect. I had to strike first, fast and hard, not wait to attack and respond. It meant Dad, Jesus, and God were all wrong, at least as far as Bugsy was concerned.

So I retaliated . . . first.

Bugsy wouldn't get to gloat. He and his thug friends weren't going to throw me another beating at the time and place they chose. I'd gladly take my licks and whatever punishment rather than let him assert that kind of dominance. I'd punched him, hard, suddenly, many times, taking him utterly by surprise. In our future bout, if there was one, he'd have to fight what he couldn't see. He couldn't see what I had inside or know for sure what I might do.

The principal was adamant that I had to be punished, of course. I was suspended and placed on disciplinary probation. One more incident and I would be kicked out of school.

I said nothing on the drive home. In the living room, I let 'er rip as I threw myself on the old sofa.

"I just want to go to school!"

"I know," Dad muttered.

"I don't wanna fight, but these guys won't stop. Not ever!"

"Avoid them . . . their comments . . . tell the teachers."

"It doesn't work that way. It'll never work that way!"

It was strange trying to tell my dad the facts of my life. Trying to explain how thugs operated. At some level, I knew he didn't know and couldn't know.

"There's a bunch of them. On the bus, in the classrooms, in the streets. Everywhere! They're not gonna stop. They're not!"

"I know . . . I . . . ."

I was right. Maybe my dad knew it too, maybe not. But we didn't have many options either way.

My parents decided then and there to send me to Monte Vista Christian High School, despite not being in any financial position to do so. It was an expensive, college-prep private school, and an incredibly costly sacrifice for parents whose home was furnished courtesy of the county landfill. So was born their master plan to get Bugsy & Company out of my life.

But man plans and God laughs.

CHAPTER

8

Monte Vista Christian High School lay at the end of an idyllic winding country backroad flanked by large, well-established ranches, their boundaries marked by white horizontal wood fences. The school nestled in the foothills of Mount Madonna, surrounded by lush green rolling hills. Apple orchards and strawberry fields dotted the landscape as far as you could see. The campus occupied nearly a hundred acres, much of it covered by green, meticulously manicured lawn. Palm trees dotted the borders between greenery and paved walkways. The school boasted some of the best sports facilities in the county, a spacious pool, and a spectacular football field next to a golf course.

Their brochure said as much.

The entrance to the campus was framed by an ornate black iron gate with a metal arch, prominently displaying the Monte Vista emblem. The gate kept gangsters out.

Soon I forgot the young gangsters who tried to rule my world. I even forgot what Bugsy looked like. Occasionally I heard about shootings and stabbings in the city, most of them within a couple of miles of my home. But they might as well have been on another continent.

The lack of random violence combined with a highly supportive religious atmosphere seemed too good to be true. The school was a haven and a shelter from the outside world. Grit and strength aren't built behind the gates of safe cozy places. The real world where Bugsy lived was an afterthought, hidden, but not gone.

• • •

One of my first professors at Cabrillo Junior College ranted against Christians and Christianity at every possible juncture. He questioned and ridiculed the historical accuracy of the Bible and the validity of the Genesis creation account ad nauseam. He was an academic who loved to hate anything he didn't personally understand or believe.

Welcome to junior college.

The challenges my professor posed struck a chord. At times I felt like the professor knew this and was talking to me directly. I had to address them. Not for him, as my argument wasn't with him. I needed to plumb the basis for my faith.

I read voraciously from both the theists and atheists, in the process discovering the writings of C.S. Lewis among others. I spent hours digging through books, talking to other professors, asking and arguing with my parents, and challenging my youth pastors.

What followed was months of confusion and uncertainty.

I spoke to my mom and dad about my struggle. I asked them

whether in their private moments, away from the pulpit, they doubted God's existence. It was the kind of question that only has one clear answer one way or the other. Without equivocation, they both smiled whispering almost in unison:

"No."

When I asked them to explain their reasons for unwavering faith, they skipped any long-winded explanation or arguments. Both were more than up to the task, but they simply said the same thing over and over:

They knew. They just knew.

Their journey with God through their lives assured them of His existence. I might as well have asked them how they knew they were alive. How they could be sure their hearts were beating. Incomprehensible to my professor, but to them, completely, organically certain. It infuriated me somehow. I wanted that kind of conviction, one way or another, no matter where I came down on God's existence.

And I didn't have it.

A year at Cabrillo jolted my faith in God to its foundations. Jesus intrigued me as a figure about whom much was known historically that could not be easily disputed. Hardly anyone else in history was so unifying and polarizing. His words, assuming they were accurately recorded, were compelling. I had to dive deeper into the Gospels and the cultural climate from which all the accounts of Jesus sprung. If there was viable solid ground to plant my spiritual flag in, I suspected they might be found in the life and teachings of *this man*.

After a year at Cabrillo, I transferred to Bethany University, a campus tucked in the middle of the redwoods in the small town of Scotts Valley. By the end of my first week, I knew I was at the right pace: sitting in a macroeconomics class, dabbling in business law and church history at the same time. College helped me synthesize my religious path and forge lifelong relationships, including the one with the woman who'd become my wife.

. . .

Hope was one of the attractive girls I'd seen around since junior high at Rolling Hills. She'd also gone to Aptos High, although she admitted later she didn't know my name back then. I'd had a massive crush on her at Aptos but never saw her after I moved to Monte Vista.

Hope began attending my church during our first year of college. Raised as a Roman Catholic, she too was cultivating her faith. She even convinced her mom to host Bible studies at their home so she and her friends could scour the scriptures.

On the day of my nineteenth birthday, I arranged to show up for a home Bible study at Hope's house. Hope was amazed that I faithfully attended a Bible study even on my birthday. There was, in retrospect, more to it than that.

In truth, my birthday fell on a weekday. I didn't have any birthday plans. More importantly, I heard rumors that she was on a temporary break from her then-boyfriend.

God helps those who help themselves.

Nevertheless, she seemed so suitably impressed by my outward piety that she offered to take me out for birthday brunch.

Game, set, match.

PART TWO / 47

The next day, Hope and I met at Cadillac Café, a small, adobe-style cafe at the corner of Freedom Boulevard and Corralitos Road that had been a classic rural fixture in the county for years.

The cafe buzzed with morning crowd voices and the air was filled with the pungent smell of strong coffee, pancakes and old wood.

What started as a simple meal would be the first date of hundreds. Although it was easily my most memorable meal, no matter how hard I strain, I still can't remember what she or I had for breakfast.

PART THREE

Once more unto the breach,
dear friends, once more.

Shakespeare Henry V, Act III, Scene I

CHAPTER

9

College. Graduate school. That was the natural progression. While I had no desire to be a lawyer, I'd read enough John Grisham books to believe the fiction of an exciting life as an attorney. Law school seemed like it might be a perfect fit.

I happened upon an ad in the Register Pajaronian the summer before graduate school. The Watsonville Police Department needed a crime analyst intern. Not sure what crime analysis was, I decided it sounded more appealing than all the summer jobs listed in the want-ads. And it paid good money. Hardly a noble or cerebral move, I applied because it just *sounded better*.

• • •

Lisa DeVasio greeted me with a cup of coffee in her hand. It was her trademark. It was almost impossible to catch her without a cup of coffee. She was in her late forties and seemed genuinely eager to welcome me. She walked me through the records department, introducing me as the new intern.

DeVasio was a Seminole from Florida State University. She was an elementary school teacher turned criminalist who married a Navy sailor, which brought her to Monterey Bay. She exuded excitement about the world of crime statistics and analysis. As she led me to my work station, the very last one in a long dark room, DeVasio gave me the ten cent tour.

"That's your desk at the end. These are for the DART team," DeVasio said, almost as a precaution that I needed to stay away from the other four desks.

"The DART team?"

"Yeah. They're the gang and gun team for the department. You gotta excuse 'em. They're rowdy and loud now and again. You'll get used to it. They're okay guys, just loud."

"Did you say dart? Like D-A-R-T?"

"Yep. It stands for direct action response team. Cops love acronyms! They're easier to pronounce over the radio. It's a bit fancy if you ask me, but it's not the worst." DeVasio rolled her eyes.

I knew little about the world police inhabit. I went on one ride-along with Watsonville PD while in high school. The patrol officer drove me around the city for two hours, all the while exhibiting zero enthusiasm for police work. I couldn't decide if he hated his job or me or both. By the end of the ride-along, I was just as disinterested in him and what he did as he was.

All I knew about cops came from episodes of *Law and Order*. I knew there were patrol officers and detectives, but a team like the DART team was new to me. I'd never been exposed to even the idea of special units like LAPD's S.I.S or NYPD's Plainclothes Anti-Crime Unit. Both units stopped or prevented massive amounts of street crime in the cities where they operated. But very few knew what they did.

Guns and gangs . . . . Hmmmmm.

DeVasio eventually revealed that the department's old database couldn't accurately glean statistics to report to the FBI.

"Your job is to go through every report and manually count criminal numbers in the city for the past two years."

"Sounds easy enough."

"It's not tough, but it is tedious. Honestly, you'll get bored after a day or two."

"No problem. I'm on it."

"I promise that once you're done with these reports, I'll have you working on interesting crime analyst stuff."

DeVasio's enthusiasm about crime statistics almost had me going for a while.

Almost.

As she walked away I began manually counting crime statistics one page after another. She was right. It got old. Quickly. Alone in a big dark office, the silence numbed my senses.

After a few hours of totaling numbers from the weekly columns of burglaries, robberies, assaults, and the like, my gaze wandered onto the forbidden DART desks.

The desktops featured the obligatory framed photos of extremely attractive women, presumably wives or girlfriends, and sometimes both. Some of the photos left little to the imagination. Back then cops did that pretty regularly. Nowadays at the very least, you'd get a reprimand or days off. Depending on *how little you left to the imagination*, cops get fired for it now.

The wall next to the desks featured a mixed fruit pudding of photos ranging from Polaroids to poster-size prints. These photos featured the team's swag: rifles, shotguns, handguns, drugs, needles, shivs, clubs, the whole Maryann.

The largest photo was a team photo.

Taken in a dark alley, the flash overexposed their faces. All four team members looked to be in their late twenties. They looked menacing, muscular, and ready to throw down at the drop of a hat. They were all grinning in their dark blue BDU(s). Every man had facial hair, a mustache, a goatee, or a beard.

The big man on the team wore a shotgun slung across his chest. The weapon looked like a broomstick strapped to a mountain of meat. Another guy puffing on a cigar wedged between his index and middle fingers blew a bright white smoke ball into the darkness just as the flash went off.

I stared at the photo so hard the cigar smoke seemed to move a little.

DART had me. The unit looked open for business. Their business was the daily delivery of fresh whoop-ass to street criminals. Desperados like that had to have war stories—vehicle chases, gun battles, drug busts, five minute all-out punch-fest ground fights down below in the mud and the blood.

Every day for weeks, I strolled past their desks, stopping to stare at the photos a bit longer each time. I worked mornings and they worked nights. I never saw them and everything I knew came from the photos.

Who are they really? More urgently, I felt a strong need to figure out how to join that team or one like it.

Or one better.

CHAPTER

10

DeVasio decided one day it would be great for me to go on a ride-along.

"That way you'll see the numbers you're compiling *come to life*," she said one morning as I was about to chow into a pile of crime stats.

Jeremy Dunn met me at the back lot of the police station at exactly 1000 hours. A lot of cops are fastidiously punctual that way. Dunn was a regular beat cop on day-shift patrol who'd agreed to chauffeur me around his beat for a couple of hours.

"Good to meet you. Dan is it?"

"Yeah, Dan. Thanks for letting me tag along."

"Nah, no problem. We gonna have us some fun."

Dunn shook my hand with a firm grip as he moved his bag from the passenger seat. I sat down and kept going. My line of sight scarcely cleared the dashboard when my descent finally stopped. The passenger seat was much lower than Dunn's. Given he was easily over six feet, that meant that he talked down to me the entire day.

Dunn was physically intimidating, in his mid-twenties, with

a strong build, blond hair, and green eyes. Overall he looked like the prototypical Nordic Blond Beast. In ancient times he could have been Beowulf's kid brother. Cruising down Main, he drew beaucoup stares from Hispanic ladies young and old. Dunn loved it and reciprocated with a nod, wink, or a smile everywhere he drove.

"How long you been a cop?"

"About two years."

"How do you like it?"

"I love it. But then I'm a badass and I'm really good at it." Dunn burst out laughing.

Dunn was the funny, down-to-earth cop who broke the ice minutes into the ride-along once he felt comfortable. If I'd been a different kind of guest, that would never have happened.

He loved being a cop. A lot of the best ones do. Often cops reach a point where they can't imagine doing anything else. The art is making that feeling last an entire career. For those who always love it, the job is as satisfying as any job ever can be. For those cops who fall out of love, there is seldom much good that comes from it for them or their departments.

Dunn made neck-wrenching hard turns into alleys that I didn't know existed. His head on a swivel, he constantly checked cars and people everywhere, all the time. He didn't miss much. The lovely ladies and the nasty street criminals got his full attention. Pleasant to all, subservient to nobody, Dunn took zero crap and gave none, unless and until it was go-time.

He was a college graduate who before being a Watsonville cop had a distinguished career working for Oakland Athletics Security.

"Wait, you worked for the A's?"

"Yeah. Started out as a security agent, basically a guard, and moved up pretty fast. I was there for four years and became the assistant director of the stadium's security."

"You hung out with all the players?"

"Oh yeah. I still stay in contact with some of 'em. Timmy Hudson. Eric Chavez. Tejada. Great guys. It was the best job ever."

"Whoa!"

I knew just enough about the Oakland A's to recognize names. The guys Dunn named were rock stars.

"That must have been a dream job! Why'd you quit? Why'd you become a cop?"

"I grew up here. I pretty much always knew I wanted to be a cop here. Working the A's Stadium was great, but it wasn't my dream, you know? I'm a white boy from Watsonville. I'll always be from Watsonville, and I always wanted to get back here."

"Really? Man, I don't get it . . . ." I didn't believe Dunn. Maybe he got fired and being a cop was the only job he could land after. *Who gives up a job with the Oakland A's?*

"I'm telling you right now, there's nothing like being a cop. Nothing more thrilling than chasing bad guys, running 'em to the ground. Stadium security was great but it became routine day after day. Wait'll we get you in the action. You get in it, you'll know."

Dunn-the-Badass was 100% serious.

"You see those guys right there?" he said, nodding towards two young men walking on Rodriguez Street near Second.

"Yeah."

"They're Poor Siders. That's a sureño gang."

"Okay . . . okay?" I had no clue what he was talking about. I asked, "Are you going to stop them?"

"Let's do it!"

As we got closer, the two saw us. Their heads were also on swivels. Dunn's intent was obvious. He drove across two lanes of traffic and beelined for them.

"What'd we do? What's the problem, Dunn?" one of the teenagers asked as Dunn stepped out of the car. He moved fast for a big guy, faster than the two sureños expected. At about seventeen years old, the first sureño to speak was the younger of the two. "We legit today, and none of us, ain't on probation."

"It's all good. No problem. Just wanted to say hey," Dunn said.

I wasn't sure if I should stand up, sit down, shoot, or salute. It was an odd feeling, so I decided to get out of the patrol car and stand a few feet behind Dunn. I figured if Dunn went hands-on full-contact with the sureños, they'd have to go through him before they could get me, and I'd have at least a few seconds to take off running like a spotted-ass ape. Standing behind Dunn's large frame with all the hardware hung off his Sam-Browne somehow made me feel stronger than I was. *Cop by association* is probably the best description.

"You guys got anything on you I need to worry about it?" Dunn asked.

"Nope," the teenager answered. The other said nothing.

"Can I check?"

"I know you can't, but you'll check anyway."

The older sureño in his mid-twenties didn't speak or move. Dunn patted the teenager's waistband and then moved to the older gangster. The older sureño automatically placed his hands behind his back. This wasn't his first fiesta. Dunn searched his waistband in one smooth quick motion.

Out of nowhere, Dunn directed their attention to me.

I froze, every muscle in my body registering Force-9 on the *Sphincter Meter.*

"He works for the P.D. I'm just showin' him around," Dunn said.

Ever since Dunn flew out of the patrol car I'd been off guard. Now it was worse. I didn't know if I should wave, shake hands, pee, or go blind.

"You want to be a police officer, too, eh?" the teenager jeered.

"Be a part of the biggest gang of them all, W-P-D." The older sureño finally spoke.

"Since you guys are cool, can I show this guy your tattoos?" Dunn asked.

The teenager agreed instantly. I couldn't believe it and started to wonder if Dunn would eventually sweet-talk the duo of gangsters into dropping trow so he could check their bums for a hidden machine gun. Nothing seemed impossible.

Dunn the Tour Guide walked me through the teenager's tattoos.

Some were obvious ones: the three dots below his left eye, "Watson" on his right forearm, the large letter "P" on the right shoulder and "S" on the left shoulder, the words "Puro Pobre" across his chest.

Dunn eyed the older gangster. He wasn't having any. While the teenager babbled nonstop, the older sureño's gaze continuously swept the streets.

"Can we go now or what?" the teen asked.

"Yeah . . . you coulda' left any time."

"Oh, I ain't dumb, homie. That ain't ever true."

"What do you mean?" Dunn quipped. "You're not on probation anymore, right?"

"Be real, ese. If you wanna stop us, you'll find a reason, probation or no. *Tu siempre tienes razon.*"

"Okay, you got me." Dunn smiled broadly.

On the street, Dunn was always right.

Dunn shook their hands and thanked them.

The sureños moved down the street keeping a loose eye on us. They reminded me of wolves watching a passing freight train. I scrambled back into the safety of the patrol car.

As we drove, Dunn explained what had just happened.

"There are two big gangs in Watsonville. There's the norteños and there's the sureños. Those two are sureños. They're usually pretty cool with me."

"Are they dangerous?"

"Oh hell yeah they are, all of 'em," Dunn said. He couldn't help himself. He laughed. My question was just dumb. "The older vato is Miguel Sandoval. They call him Droopy. He runs Poor Side Watson."

"Is that another gang?" Another dumb question, but I could tell Dunn was willing to tolerate it at least for the time being.

"Poor Side Watson is a sureño gang. Remember, again, there are two big gangs, north and south. But under each gang are a bunch of smaller gangs. They call them subsets. Poor Side Watson, for example, is a subset of the sureños."

It felt like Dunn was speaking Urdu.

"The sureños claim the number thirteen and the color blue. That's why Dasher had three dots below his eye," Dunn continued.

"Dasher was the young one?"

"Oh yeah, if Dasher has a warrant on him, you'll never catch 'em. Hence the name. I've made that mistake once, trying to chase 'em down. Never got close. Last time I ever tried. He's greased lighting!

"Remember they're *always dangerous*. They don't look like much, but Droopy and Dasher are suspects in at least two shootings this year. That's the stuff we know about. Never underestimate 'em and never let your guard down. They're cool with me until they're not. If it comes down to it, they'll kill you. Sure as can be . . . if you're in their way."

The patrol car felt like an M-1 Abrams tank. I snuggled in and resolved to stay put if at all possible.

"This is Grant Street." Dunn continued as we motored down the boulevard. The homes looked like they were built in the 60s and haven't been touched since. "This area is controlled by City Hall."

"Are they norteños or sureños?"

"City Hallers are weird ducks. They're norteños but they're sorta independent. They don't really answer to La Nuestra Familia. They're almost a mix . . . like a confused bunch. Do you know why they're called City Hall Watson?"

"I'm clueless."

"Ol' city hall, right there!" Dunn said as the front steps of the city's old city hall appeared dead ahead on Grant. "These guys used to literally hang out on the steps of city hall, and that's where the name came from."

I knew gangs appeared early in history and were well established in Ancient Rome. Dunn made it fascinating. Except for my brush with Bugsy & Company, the gang world was totally alien.

Gangs controlled neighborhoods? How?

Three adult males stood on the sidewalk at the end of Grant looking in our direction. They were posted-up as though guarding the intersection. All three glared at us. Dunn appeared unfazed, but if they were trying to intimidate me, it was working. Given I had Dunn alongside me, I found myself eager to see him brace the trio and put them in check.

A faint voice crackled on the radio followed by a tone.

An instant later we were flying down the street faster than I had ever driven on a city street in my life.

Dunn had turned on his lights and the siren before I realized it. He held the radio mic in his right hand and drove with his left. We blasted through traffic like we'd been shot from a cannon. I squeezed my seat to keep from flying around the squad car.

All the cars began pulling to the right as we roared by. Finally, the street was too congested and Dunn drove into oncoming traffic. Cars began darting off the roadway just in time. We raced up the wrong side of the street, hurdling through intersections. Telephone poles seemed to go by like pickets in a huge fence.

After two blocks, Dunn made a hard right, the tires screeching, then a quick left down a narrow alley. I'd lost my grip, slamming against the passenger door like a loose grocery bag.

Clearing each turn, Dunn accelerated to full speed through the straight-aways. Cars obliged as he navigated the traffic maze, seemingly in control despite the breakneck speed. After a couple of long minutes, we roared into the parking lot of a small strip mall.

Another patrol car was parked in front of Taqueria Mundial. Dunn pulled so close to the building's front door I braced for impact. We screeched to a halt as the siren died.

Through the windows of the taqueria I saw a uniformed officer trying to push a big shirtless male against the back wall. The officer shoved the guy with no effect. Shirtless easily over-powered him, slammed the officer against the opposite wall, and pinned him there.

I'd never seen real full contact, hands-on, go-time between grown men.

Dunn casually strolled up on Shirtless's blindside like he was ordering a chile relleno. Grabbing Shirtless's thick arm, Dunn pivoted away, his back almost completely turned, and violently pulled the man's arm across his body. Shirtless whipped around, toppling tables and chairs as he flopped on the tile floor.

Both officers mounted Shirtless like runners tagging home base, turning him on his belly. Shirtless kicked wildly trying to stand as Dunn worked his way up to the man's torso and began viciously and rapidly punching him in the jaw.

Shirtless became dazed and confused in seconds. He tried pushing Dunn and the other officer off him, but the fight was over.

Shirtless was done.

As two more patrol cars flew into the parking lot, Dunn and the other officer handcuffed Shirtless. Later the backup officers took him to jail.

Dunn walked to the car, his face flushed, and both his arms peppered with red marks and scratches. His jaw was clenched and the sinews stood out from the skin in both arms like steel cable. The top two buttons of his uniform were gone, his duty belt was disheveled, and his pants were filthy.

I stood alongside the patrol car and decided not to speak or move until he did. Finally, he looked at me and asked if I was okay in a sharp, forceful tone, far from the cordial, silly, *Easygoing Dunn* I'd met previously.

He was still *bowed up*, his body loaded with adrenaline.

Eventually, I forced out an "Okay."

Something told me not to engage Dunn even with idle chit-chat while his blood was up.

I'd just met Feral Dunn, the wolf who fed on other wolves. Other than that, *it was all good.*

• • •

As I drove home three hours after Dunn's taqueria thump-fest, my heart was still racing. Like, *I'd been in the fight.*

It felt great. Had to admit it, it did.

I couldn't believe what I'd seen. I'd watched the application of controlled skillful violence. Dunn later called his takedown the *Hands to the Pocket Technique.* I wanted to perfect that takedown and a lot of others. I had no clue what it would take to be a cop like Dunn, but at that moment, I was hooked.

No doubt. No hiding from it.

A month before, being a police officer was not even a thought. One ride-along later, it was everything. The ride-along triggered a primal desire to perfect the skills to exert controlled force and join a fight that has gone on since we became human.

There is always a palpable explosive tension between rival Watsonville street gangs. Police officers form the only line and physical barrier between innocent bystanders and the full fury of gang violence. Everywhere that line waiver or fails, innocent people suffer and die. Those who remain retreat and surrender some or all of their lives to the corrosive effects of the gang life that plagues the city.

I had no real grasp of the conflict, but now, I knew it was real.

And I would enter that fray.

CHAPTER
11

I moved to San Jose to start the first year of law school at Santa Clara University when my summer internship ended. Sitting in orientation, I couldn't shake the idea of becoming a cop. Here I was, facing the certainty of incurring a massive loan to get a law degree, followed by the uncertainty of even wanting to practice law. My law school gambit was doomed before I launched it.

I knew law school wasn't for me, at least not then. The prospect of sitting behind a desk (any desk) for life was a non-starter. Reading and litigating cases was sterile and detached.

On the third week of classes, I broke the news to my family.

I was going to work my way into a patrol vehicle. I wanted back where Dunn was. I called DeVasio to see if she was still looking for a crime analyst.

She was.

I moved back to Watsonville and took up life as a crime analyst. DeVasio embedded me with the investigations unit, making my job infinitely more interesting. In short order, I was working cases alongside detectives, *real ones*, doing analytical work that none of them had the time or wanted to do. But the urge to get into the streets never let up.

• • •

In the early winter of 2000, the city of Watsonville was seized by a series of violent takeover robberies. The suspect, armed with an assault rifle and a bandana partially covering his face, stormed Mom and Pop stores one after another all over town. The robberies were potentially extremely deadly precisely because the robber attempted to own all the bystanders at the scene and compel them all to obey.

The more innocents in a takeover robbery, the greater the chance someone zigs when they should zag, runs when they should freeze, or runs their mouth when they should zip it. Sooner or later somebody doesn't do what *Simon Sez* and the result is death or critical injury. Worse still if the robber has to shoot one person, likely as not, others will panic and get shot as well. This guy loved to own all the clerks and unlucky customers at gunpoint until he'd cleaned out the registers. Takeover robberies work great.

Until they don't.

Armed robberies happened regularly in the city, but this series was unique. Twice, the suspect put a burst of shots through the ceiling to get everybody's attention and let them all know he was open for business. This showed he wasn't afraid to use his weapon and might be looking forward to it. Might even like it. In time, he got brazen. He was hitting the neighborhood mercados, gas stations, mini-marts, two to three times a week.

I worked the case hard, mostly temporal analysis, to figure out when he might hit again based on the take he'd collected at the last place he hit. The violence he flaunted convinced police administrators to focus extensive resources on him before the inevitable occurred. Bulletin boards were choked with overtime sign-up sheets and advisories to keep an eye on certain stores likely to get hit next.

Despite the effort, there weren't nearly enough surveillance teams to cover every store, and he managed to avoid getting braced. Surveillance units were always one step behind—off by a day, a few hours, or they were up on the wrong store while he hit somewhere else.

Scott McMahon was the primary detective on the case. McMahon was a clean-head, his head intentionally shaved shiny-bald. Tall, wiry, and blue-eyed, he was energetic, bordering on manic, around police work. Bandana Man was wearing him ragged.

McMahon coordinated surveillance units on the streets 24-7, seldom getting four hours of sleep in twenty-four. It got so bad he took to catching power naps when he could in one of the department's dark rooms. He knew what would eventually happen if Bandana Man wasn't taken soon.

McMahon walked to my desk thumbing through a bundle of reports. They all came from Salinas PD, a neighboring city thirty minutes south of Watsonville. The reports tended to indicate Bandana Man had taken up hitting stores in Salinas in his free time.

"Here." He tossed a pile of reports on my desk. McMahon was never the cordial type. With this case looming over his head, he was even less friendly. The guy talked at me avoiding eye contact. "I don't see anything good, but I'm tired of reading this crap over and over. See if you can find anything we can use."

As he dragged his exhausted body back to his desk I sensed he'd thrown me a challenge with a dash of desperation on top.

I scoured each report.

A witness to one of the Salinas robberies caught partial plate letters "BT" from the getaway vehicle, described as a gray 1990 Honda Civic. Using our department's report system I found ten possible vehicle plates with the letters "BT." Out of the ten, three were Hondas. Of the three Hondas, only one registered owner had a criminal history.

Police work.

A long shot, but we weren't up on anything else at that point.

I walked up to McMahon, not knowing if I was gonna give him a viable lead or a migraine.

McMahon in his chair, fully reclined, eyes closed, either grabbing another power nap or deep in thought, and I couldn't tell which. I tossed the reports back on his desk with a photo of our one possible suspect, including the latest address, and the full Honda plate number.

"This guy has a pretty long criminal history. No robberies, but plenty of dope arrests. We stopped him in a Civic matching the two letters from the Salinas case. Could be our guy . . . could be nothing." I hedged my bets.

McMahon snapped awake. He gawked at the booking photo of the suspect and bounced out of his chair.

"Whoa! Whoa! This guy looks a lot like the surveillance photos."

"I know! He could be a good one." Pretending like I knew it along.

McMahon immediately hailed the other detectives out of their cubicles into a large conference table in the middle of the room.

"Get your vests and cover coats. We've got a lead and we're going to set up on the house." McMahon roared with revitalized zeal, deliberately making eye contact with everyone in the room.

The teams proceeded to hash the plan: who would be at which street, what they'd do if the Bandana-Man left the residence, and how they'd handle a vehicle pursuit if one developed.

The room vibrated with energy of men hunting men.

The detectives geared up, briefed the final details, and dashed out.

Leaving me in the office.

They arrested Bandana Man within the hour, leaving home in the car bearing the plate number I found. They recovered cash, a police scanner, an assault rifle, and meth in the car. He was probably on his way to another robbery when they rolled him up.

The detectives all thanked me for breaking the case and even the chief shook my hand. Still, I felt like four pounds of fertilizer in a two-pound bag. The gratitude didn't even start to counter the bitterness I felt for being left in the office like a lap dog while they hunted *my suspect* down. I sat in my cubicle, looking out the window, listening to the radio, imagining the takedown. I felt empty. It wasn't near enough.

It wasn't gonna happen again.

Next time I'd be hunting suspects as a cop.

PART FOUR

———

But many who are first will be last,
and the last first.

Matthew 19:30

12

Watsonville sits in the heart of the Pajaro Valley, surrounded by farms growing strawberries, apples, lettuce, and a host of other vegetables. Because most of Pajaro Valley is farmland, a large portion of Watsonville's population were and are migrant workers. Many were transient farmworkers moving from one farming community to another in California, Oregon, and Arizona, as they followed the agricultural growing seasons.

The nomadic nature of farm workers made it difficult for workers and their children to establish themselves in any community. Most of these families weren't even accounted for in the official census data. Many lived in converted garages, basements, attics, storage sheds, and containers. They were truly disenfranchised at every level.

Watsonville City jurisdiction covers eight square miles. WPD had over seventy sworn officers patrolling well over 70,000 people, as opposed to the 50,000 "official" residents. Over five hundred documented active official gang members belonging to at least a dozen gangs. These numbers didn't account for the hundreds of hang-arounds, prospects, and wannabes.

In 2000, the city had less than a dozen murders. However, during the summer of that same year, there were twenty-seven non-fatal stabbings and shootings. These jarring violent acts shook the community no matter how often they happened. The residents of Watsonville never got used to it.

Parents were terrified to let their kids out to play in the evenings. There were repeated rallies at the town's plaza urging the local government to find answers to the seemingly never-ending violent cycle.

A heroin epidemic had swept California and claimed an entire generation of young people in the city. Methamphetamine was poised and on track to harvest another.

The church my dad pastored was relatively small, with just over sixty regular parishioners. In 2000, there was no youth pastor. The opportunity seemed like a natural fit. I had turned a blind eye to what was happening in Watsonville for a decade but I couldn't look away any longer.

Like Dunn had said, it was *my city* too, and I was eager to make a difference.

The distinction between juvenile and adult crimes was blurred. In most parts of the county, juvenile crimes were still juvenile: petty theft, vandalism, minor possession of alcohol, and so forth. But in Watsonville, juveniles were committing horrendously violent crimes, just like their adult counterparts and often at their direction.

This was the segment of the population Christ would want to reach. Given He wasn't available to pastor, they'd have to make do with me. I decided to crusade even though I wasn't sure what would come of it. But I did know there was a tangible, glaring need, and I was ready to answer it.

The plan was simple: introduce students to the gospel of Christ, and let the Gospel's transformative power fundamentally change the trajectory of the students' lives. Sounded simple enough.

I ran the ministry idea past Hope, whom I'd been dating for a couple of years by then. I knew she was the woman I wanted to marry but when we'd started, I was headed to grad school and intent on becoming an attorney. I'd abandoned that plan and was actively applying to become a cop. This idea wasn't high on her list of worthy pursuits. Now, I was proposing we start a youth ministry to jointly pastor at-risk teenagers. These many dramatic changes could've scared her off. Actually, they could've scared anybody off. But they didn't. Hope was immediately onboard and our youth pastor journey took off.

• • •

At the first youth service, four students showed up, two of which were my younger brothers. It was a less than a stellar start. I was determined Hope and I weren't going to be out-of-touch glorified babysitters for students from our own church. If we were going to reach the students in our community, we had to leave the church grounds and go out into the community for real.

I rallied a handful of college students and young adults from our church for our first outreach. Many of the homes in Watson-ville's neighborhoods were in a state of disrepair. The streets were littered with garbage, and the front yards were dominated by overgrown plants, dead lawns soaked with motor oil and abandoned cars.

We were going to walk the neighborhoods offering to clean people's yards for free. It was a simple and inexpensive outreach that required minimal coordination. We walked the blocks surrounding the church with brooms, rakes, garbage bags, and lawnmowers.

"Hi! We're from the church right around the corner. We're here to clean your front lawn, for free!" we repeated at each door.

At best, we were greeted with skepticism.

"Is it really free?" residents asked.

"Yes, it really is."

"What do you want after you clean our yard? C'mon, what's the catch?"

"Nothing. Not a thing."

The first Saturday, we cleaned three yards, spending about an hour on each yard. Then we offered to pray for the families.

The catch.

Almost all of the homes welcomed our prayers. We handed out flyers for our church services and invited students to our youth service on Friday nights.

Another catch.

At the end of our first outreach, we were drenched in sweat and exhausted. We hauled back to church six large bags full of garbage and yard waste. For eight consecutive Saturdays, the same group of volunteers met early in the morning, walked another block of the surrounding neighborhood, and cleaned yards. The families were extremely grateful but we had no idea if our efforts would result in anything. It didn't matter. The whole point of the outreach was contact and service.

• • •

Within a month of the outreach, two new young students walked into Friday night youth night service. Camelia Solorzano and Victoria Diaz were both in junior high and were first cousins. They were both just slightly over five feet tall. Camelia had a round friendly face. Victoria was skinny, with a narrow face that matched her physique.

"I live right there on Airport Road. You can actually see my house from here," Camelia said rapidly. I wasn't sure if that was her normal speech pattern or she was just eager to meet everyone.

"Cool," I said. "How about you? Victoria, right? Where do you live?"

"Not there," she allowed reluctantly.

Camelia jumped in immediately. It was a pattern we saw many times. There were lots of young people who didn't want anyone to know where they lived or how they had to live.

"No. Victoria lives somewhere else," Camelia said. "She's always at my house, mostly every day. Do you know where Landis is?"

"Yeah, I do," I answered. Landis Street was a well-known norteño stronghold.

"She lives in the ghetto on Landis." Camelia chuckled. "So what's this place all about? What kind of church? Is it Catholic? Cuz we're Catholic."

"It's a church for young students just like you," Hope said. "It's a Christian church, not Catholic, but the same Bible, the same God." Technically, it was a Pentecostal church, but it was pointless to demarcate one tradition from the other. Camelia and

Victoria could've cared less.

"Oh, okay. Cool. Yeah . . . it's something different but we gonna try it."

Camelia was all smiles, eager to be there and easy to talk with. She and Hope instantly hit it off. Victoria was quiet and cautious, listening closely to everything said. She analyzed every word and was reflexively skeptical. Like a lot of young people we'd meet it was a habit that kept her alive and relatively safe.

The girls sat together through the entire youth service and lingered afterwards. It was clear neither wanted to leave.

"My mom lives with us but my dad lives somewhere else." Camelia confided in Hope like they were childhood friends. "My dad's in big trouble right now. That's why I've been praying a lot and came to church tonight. And not just my dad, my brother too . . . they're both in trouble."

"We'll pray for them. You're in the right place," Hope assured.

"My dad and brother are good guys. They said my dad had drugs in his car. I know my dad . . . he didn't . . . it wasn't his. He was just helping someone out. He's too nice and people take advantage of 'em.

"My brother . . . I don't . . . he's different. He's on probation but he still keeps on messing up. He carries a gun, but only for protection. It's not like he's out there shooting people. This town is crazy. He's just protecting his wife and baby son."

"No, I get that." I didn't.

•   •   •

Hope and I instantly liked Camelia. She promised she'd be back for the next youth service and she showed up the following Friday. Two weeks after attending her first youth service, Camelia managed to bring three more friends to youth night. Two months later, Camelia had convinced five of her friends to attend.

Two of the friends that Camelia brought to youth service were brothers Joaquin and Santiago Quintero. Joaquin was twelve years old and Santiago was fourteen. After the service ended, Joaquin and Santiago lingered and helped me and Hope clean the multipurpose room where we held services. Since they lived closed by, I decided to walk the brothers home.

"We live in a yellow house with the black '69 Impala," Santiago said pointing down Airport Road.

"I know exactly which house that is. There's a big muscular guy always working on that car," I said.

"That's my dad," Joaquin proudly announced.

The brothers' house was easy to remember not just because of the black Impala but also because of the serious crew of seasoned gang members that hung out in front.

Santiago Sr. would be an imposing figure anywhere, but on Airport Road, there was little doubt he was the shot caller.

Bulky and muscular, he was shirtless on hot days, displaying prison tattoos that covered his upper body. The most prominent tatt was a Huelga bird spanning his entire upper back. The Huelga bird is a stylized ancient Aztec black eagle. The image resembled the logo of the Mexican American labor movement. In Watsonville, the tatt meant one thing—Santiago Sr. was a norteño and an important one. He also had the tattoo of a sombrero pierced with a machete, marking him as a Nuestra Familia (NF) gang member. The gang members who hung out at his house were in their thirties and forties, not the young teenage gangbangers common around town.

They were the real deal *representing* for all to see.

Joaquin and Santiago were exactly the kind of students we wanted to reach and intercept. Without some sort of intervention, they'd inevitably follow in their father's footsteps, which meant death or prison, one way or another, sooner or later. If we could disrupt the cycle, they had a chance.

The Quintero brothers were full of energy. They invariably attended the youth services, showing up an hour before the service started to arrange seats and volunteer for anything else needed. They were always the last to leave.

Joaquin quickly became one of my favorite students. He sat dead still when I spoke of the Gospels, focusing on every word, soaking up everything. When I discussed the redemptive love of Christ and how it could free anyone from the oppressive weight of their past sins, Joaquin internalized the message, receiving it like it was the first time he'd ever heard of such a thing. The idea of a second chance, of forgiveness and redemption, mesmerized him.

After services, Hope and I often walked some students home if they lived nearby. Joaquin always insisted on being the last one taken home. When we were alone, Joaquin seized those moments to ask deep, thought-provoking questions:

What if someone raped a girl, could God still forgive them? What sort of sin would God never forgive? How many times do I have to pray to be forgiven?

At twelve years old, I wasn't certain why Joaquin was so taken with the concept of redemption. His questions always had a sense of urgency, as though the question he was asking would keep him up until it was resolved.

Joaquin and Camelia's fervor was infectious. In six months, youth service attendance grew from six people to over twenty students. Almost all were directly invited by either Joaquin or Camelia.

They both had strong personalities. They were both charismatic and students followed their lead.

We were making a difference. Their lives were different. They had a decidedly different outlook on life than when we met them. Camelia talked about going to college. Joaquin dreamed about owning his own business. They were far from reaching their goals, but they were thousands of mental miles along the way to their dreams.

Hope and I took Joaquin and Camelia to every youth activity for two years. We saw every one of their school performances. We spent holidays with their families, and their families attended our family gatherings.

They were family.

CHAPTER
13

"You're attending a task force meeting this afternoon," DeVasio said.

"Sounds good," I said.

I tried to sound nonchalant, seated at my desk as I put a spatial analysis map together with new software. DeVasio peered over my shoulder with her signature cup of coffee in hand.

"The map looks colorful."

"I know, but it's missing data I've been trying to add. It's alright," I said, snapping my gaze away from the monitor. "I'll work on it later. I'll noodle it."

Another moment of processing what she's said and I blurted out:

"Wait, what task force meeting?"

"Get this . . . ." She paused for effect. "The FBI has a task force targeting some of our higher-ranking gang members. I don't know much about it but looks like they need your help. Not my call. You'll get to do some analysis for them. Hope you like it."

Like it? I was elated but determined not to show it. *The FBI.*

A task force. High-ranking gang members? Lions and tigers and bears, oh my! I'd never met an FBI agent and now I'd be working in an FBI task force. They couldn't call the meeting quick enough.

• • •

As I got out of my car and walked to the brown boxy two-story building, I realized it was half a mile from my house. Next to a gym in a modest business center on Aspen Way, I couldn't believe I'd grown up walking distance from an FBI Resident Agency and had no clue it was there.

Climbing to the second-floor landing, (there was no elevator) I looked for suite 210, per DeVasio's instructions. The one *tell* with FBI Field Offices and Resident Agencies that does tend to give you a hint is that every entry door is way above average in weight, thickness, number of locks and surveillance. In fact, the overall security exceeds anything most people ever see. The offices and reception areas are designed and built to repel all but the most forceful entries by heavily armed personnel. This office was no exception.

I pressed a button that was wedged between a camera shielded by a thick glass cover and a small speaker.

"Yeah?" a disembodied voice called out.

"Yeah . . . uhhh . . . Dan Bautista. Analyst from Watsonville PD. Here for a meeting."

The door buzzed, throwing two heavy bolts out of their seats in the reinforced steel jam.

I pushed the heavy door open and stepped into a confined

room. An FBI seal the diameter of a garbage can lid dominated the wall next to a thick glass window and another thick heavy door. A fortyish Latino man, wearing a white long-sleeve shirt and a bright beige tie, stood at the window.

"Sorry, never met you before. I'm Doug. Do you mind showing me your ID?"

As I pressed my police ID against the two-inch-thick bullet-resistant glass, Doug glanced at my ID, disappeared, and in a moment the final entry door buzzed open.

"Welcome aboard," Doug said. We shook hands.

Doug was a classic FBI. Right off of a recruiting poster. Polite, well dressed, intelligent, deliberate, and of course temperate in speech. He would most certainly use the words *Ascertain, Individual,* and *Academy* in the first few minutes.

He led me to a large open area from which half a dozen smaller offices branched off. A large conference table dominated the open area. Doug introduced me to three colleagues who'd peeled out of their offices for the meeting.

Within minutes, two more Watsonville Police investigators, a Salinas Police Department detective, and an ATF agent all settled into their seats. The last one to arrive was Tony Reyes, a Santa Cruz County Sheriff's Office investigator. Reyes was *the* seasoned investigator of the bunch. He grew up in Watsonville and once considered all the major players his own homies—his childhood friends, family members, neighbors.

An oversized chart covered the wall next to the conference table. Two dozen photos of menacing gang members were pinned to the board. The photos came from the local jails, the DMV, and the California Department of Corrections. I was looking at the beginnings of what would later become Operation Northern Exposure (ONE).

At first, I didn't recognize anybody. Then one face jumped off the wall.

Jeronimo "Bugsy" Ramos.

I hadn't seen Bugsy since our high school social punch festival on the stairs above the main admin building. Almost a decade ago, his face was etched in my memory.

Like yesterday . . . .

As the FNG at the meeting, Doug regaled me with a history of the investigation as we waited for two investigative stragglers.

"The FBI has been monitoring the activities of the Nuestra Familia in Watsonville," Doug said. "You know much about Nuestra Familia?"

All eyes shifted to me, as though I'd be providing a definitive monograph on the subject. As my sphincter ratcheted upwards, I decided it was better to declare that I didn't know what I didn't know, than to pretend like I did with *this crowd*.

"No, not much at all," I said.

Doug gave me the Reader's Digest version of the organization's history.

The Nuestra Familia, which translates as *our family* in English, was the overarching head of the norteño criminal organization. Its roots trace back to the 1960s in California's prison system. It is organized in a military-like hierarchy. The Nuestra Familia's upper-tier leadership, composed of generals, were confined in the SHU (security housing unit) of one of the country's most violent and notorious prisons, Pelican Bay.

Although the generals of the Nuestra Familia were severely

isolated behind bars, they imposed their collective will on vast regions throughout Northern California and controlled the streets through paroled Regiment Commanders or "RCs."

The RCs are required to teach norteños the ways of the Nuestra Familia, control the illicit drug industry in their region which is central to the organization's functions, handle disciplinary matters for the organization, and sanction or "green light" major activities such as murders.

Enter Bugsy Ramos.

Bugsy's older brother, Mauricio "Toro" Ramos, spent five years in California's state prison system for shooting a rival gang member. The day Toro stepped out of prison seven months ago, he was a made-man and a Regiment Commander.

Toro was hell-bent on establishing a Nuestra Familia stronghold in Watsonville.

"I think Toro has more control than we know," Doug continued. "We can't prove it yet, but he may be running things in Gilroy, Hollister, and for sure, Castroville."

"Why is that?" I asked.

"Since he's been out, all the typical violent red-on-red crimes across these towns stopped. I mean, no shootings, no stabbings. All the norteño subsets are on the same page, like they're on strict orders. They're all behaving. It was never like that before. We think he's controlling everything. He doesn't tolerate any unsanctioned violence."

"Unsanctioned violence? We've had several shootings just this year alone."

"Yeah, there are murders alright, but if you look closer you'll notice some things. They're strategic, executed with precision.

No red-on-red. Not norteños against norteños. Not random. No innocent victims. I bet you every one went unsolved."

He was right. Of the seven homicides that year, we hadn't cleared one.

"Under Toro," Doug continued, "all murders are greenlit for disciplinary measures against drop-outs or against rival gang leaders."

Toro made his mark on the streets of Watsonville by clearly and ruthlessly imposing brutal Nuestra Familia military-style discipline on every single gang member. The penalty for violating his rules was death.

Bugsy stumbled into a windfall of status and power as a result of Toro's rise to the rank of RC. He became Toro's right hand, running the affairs of the Nuestra Familia in the Central Coast. Bugsy rocketed from street thug to the majordomo of a top RC. Overnight he achieved instant notoriety, his photo now gracing the wall of an FBI bullpen.

The low-level wanna-be gangster who'd tried to steal my CD player was now effectively second-in-command, running the underworld gang network throughout Watsonville.

CHAPTER
14

Two days later, I was in church when two large stretch white vans emblazoned with the words "Teen Challenge" parked in front. Half an hour before Sunday Service I walked in and noted the four back pews on the right side filled with two dozen *teens* from a local faith-based rehabilitation program Teen Challenge. My dad was one of the biggest supporters of the program and taught classes at their campus.

It was ludicrous to call them teens.

The youngest men were in their early twenties, most were in their thirties and forties. All of them looked like they could handle themselves in a fight. Their handshakes were friendly but firm. Most had tattoos, not the typical stuff like tribal bands around the bicep. Their tatts were forged in the depths of randomly dark, unpredictable lives. They were parolees, probationers, divorced fathers, convicted felons, recovering alcoholics, and straight dope fiends.

As the singing started, their deep voices boomed out dominating the room. During the sermon, their thunderous "amens" garnered everyone's attention. Their presence at the service was a highlight for the entire congregation.

One of the most boisterous was Albert Gates.

In his late forties, Albert was fiercely proud of his Irish-His-panic heritage. Like most men from Teen Challenge, his entire upper body was speckled with tattoos. The cobwebs on his elbows, the teardrop below his right eye, and *norteño* across his chest stood out even now. All the tattoos were old, faded, and almost blended into his dark-brown, wrinkled skin. The luster had long since gone out of his once baby-blue eyes. Any remaining radiance now buried, deep, under facial creases from age severely aggravated by a rough life, mostly spent behind bars.

I didn't know it then, but Albert was a piece of living history. His people descended from Saint Patrick's Battalion (Batallón de San Patricio reorganized as the Foreign Legion of Patricios). Albert's ancestors volunteered for a unit of immigrants who became part of the Mexican Army against the United States in the Mexican-American War of 1848. The unit included many deserters and defectors from the United States Army, a good many of Irish descent who had been horrifically treated by the US. The San Patricios deliberately fought in the toughest battles with the United States.

The unit was composed mainly of Irish Catholics to whom the Mexican government offered incentives for those willing to enlist including citizenship, higher pay than the US Army, and huge land grants. Many of the San Patricios later settled in rural Mexico and took Mexican wives. Albert and his family descended from this group of Irish fighters who to this day are remembered in Mexico and Ireland.

Albert had slipped far below the traditions of his ancestors.

But the spark of pride remained. When service ended, he stood by the door waiting for me as the room emptied.

"I'm Dan." I extended my hand.

"Albert." We shook hands. "If you got a minute or two, I'd like to talk."

"Yeah . . . sure. Let's step out. For privacy."

I was pensive, having never talked to him before and with no idea what he might say.

"I've been talking to your dad about helping the church out," Albert said. "I've been with Teen Challenge for a couple of years now and I'm at the point where I can go to any church I want. I can help in ministries. It's part of the program. Your dad was thinking I could help in the youth ministry. What do you think?"

I felt dry-gulched.

Just days ago, I was at an FBI office plotting to take down norteños. It was already uncomfortable for me to be in a worship service with a norteño. Now, one wanted to join our youth ministry.

"I gotta think about it."

Sensing my hesitation:

"I know it'd be hard for you . . . to, like, say yes. I mean . . . look . . . I'm . . . I promise you though: I'm not active. I'm not with 'em . . . any of 'em. The gang stuff? I'm out. That's the past . . . for me? Now . . . not who I am. Give me a chance. I could like really help, you know? In the youth ministry? No pressure. Think about it. K?"

"Okay, man. I'd like to kinda need to get to know you. Sound fair?"

"Yeah. Yeah . . . I get it. You don't know me. Yeah . . . let's do . . . we can go fishing or something?"

I took the offer.

• • •

Albert and I fished the local wharves and lakes. Albert bragged about epic catches in the Sacramento Delta. The white sturgeon and striped bass he caught in the Delta started at three feet long and grew every time he told the story.

He'd been born and raised in Oak Park, a neighborhood in Sacramento, the fourth child of seven raised by a single mom in one of the poorest and most dangerous neighborhoods. Albert's teenage years were typically turbulent, in and out of juvenile hall from the age of twelve. By his eighteenth birthday, he'd been convicted of armed robbery after pointing a stolen Snub Nose .38 revolver at a store clerk during what turned out to be a botched robbery.

Each time he got out of custody, he invariably committed another crime and earned a longer sentence with incarceration becoming a way of life.

All of the guys in Teen Challenge had looming issues they battled daily. Albert, along with everything else, had a brutal heroin habit. For most of his adult life, he'd shot heroin into whatever veins he could find, occasionally inhaling the golden-bluish acrid smoke from heated foil.

Albert and I spent most of our time at church, fishing, or watching football, and rooting for mediocre Bay Area teams. Albert faithfully followed the Oakland Raiders with little reward.

I followed the San Francisco 49ers with little better to show for it.

An afternoon after church, we finally got wise and skipped the lackluster Sunday football card and went fishing. We sat slouched in folding chairs facing the boardwalk, lines in the water on the Santa Cruz Wharf. We were both hoping for a nibble when Albert let the shoe drop:

"I was twenty . . . when it happened."

"What? When what happened?" I asked.

"The shooting. The one you's always on me about."

Once, Albert allowed how he'd *had* to shoot someone. The moment I asked him for details, he clammed-up. I'd always wanted to know more but didn't want to press it. Now it was coming on its own.

"Oh . . . yeah . . . listen . . . you don't have to tell me a thing you don't want to. I was just curious that time, man. You know? When you first said it. I didn't mean to . . . ."

"Yeah, you did." Albert cut me off.

"Yeah . . . okay . . . true. I'm curious. I work at a police department. It's my job to be curious."

"So, you wanna know?"

"C'mon, don't keep me in suspense. Think about what you wanna say to me and how. Tell me the damn story any way you want . . . or not. But make up your mind."

"We're not gonna catch nothin' anyway, might as well burn the time. So . . . K . . . here goes . . . ." Albert took a long deep breath like he was about to blurt out the entire story in one run-on sentence.

"Back in the day? I used to move kilos of coke and heroin from LA to Sacramento. I'd take the San Joaquin train when

I moved dope. It's a great way to move dope. Somehow cops got on me every time I drove. The train was my thing. My LA contact dropped me in Bakersfield, so the train could take me through the Central Valley, all the way to Sacramento."

"Who were you moving dope for?"

"I had a few big-time connects in LA. Big dope dealers, man. I've seen these guys handle pallets full of kilo bricks. These guys were the real deal. They're backed by the cartels. You don't wanna owe them money. You don't wanna owe them nothin'. They only deal with people they knew . . . real tight crew . . . and I'd been working with 'em for years.

"They broke me off some kilos and I brought dope in for me and my crew to sling on the side. I made . . . we all made good money. I mean *really good money*." Even after all this time, he couldn't hide it. He was proud.

"Damn . . . ." I stammered, not sure if I was supposed to be impressed or not.

"So . . . this one time, I had two keys of coke in a duffel bag. I'd just picked up the bricks from my connect in LA and I'm making my way home. When I made these runs, I always brought my go-to weapon: a 12-gauge Remington 870 Wingmaster. I'd sawed off the barrel and buttstock so it was nice and short. It fit under my jacket no problemo. In a jam I could even tuck the thing in my waistband."

Crooks and their shotguns.

"I had the shotgun in the duffel bag with the coke. Everything's going fine. No hitches, no problems . . . until we hit Lodi."

Albert paused to check his pole for movement even though there was none. I think back now and know he needed that moment to gather himself.

"So . . . we're stopped at Lodi and this deputy with his K-9 board my cabin. My cabin . . . directly . . . first thing . . . my heart's banging then feels like it stopped. They're moving towards me and that dog is sniffing everything. *Everything.* I know I'm done. The coke is shrink wrapped under two layers of plastic and pasted up with fabric softener. But them *pinche pero* . . . hell . . . I knew they can sniff through anything . . . and I panicked.

"I stand up and walk away from the deputy towards the closest exit. I tried, man . . . I really tried to play it cool, but it was impossible. I tried walking really slow, so I didn't draw his attention. I didn't look back. Should have just left the duffel bag . . . but I'd have lost all the dope. *Pinche 'pero*!

"I made it off the train and kept walking. But . . . you know? You know how you can feel it? When someone's following you? I could feel 'em behind me. I wanted to turn around real bad, but I knew if I did, I was done.

"Hell . . . I was done *anyway*."

"Sounds crazy . . . like a movie . . . a bad one," I said. "You better not be lyin' man." I stared into the distance as screams drifted up from the roller coasters on the Boardwalk.

"Nawww . . . I swear . . . it's all good, it's true. I kept walkin' but then I hear the deputy telling me to stop. I'm hopin' I'm dreamin'. But I know I'm not. So I keep on walkin' and I know it's gonna be a bad day . . .

"I'm on parole . . . I got two keys of coke and a sawed-off shotgun. I'll be doing federal time for sure. So, I ignore the voice and keep walkin'. Now he's yellin':

'Sheriff's Office! You! In the black jacket! Stop!'

"I hear 'em closin' in, so I sprint towards the end of the train and cut to the right between two carts and hide. But I know he's not goin' away."

Albert paused again. He was visibly gathering himself, trying to decide whether to tell me the rest.

"Listen, man, I don't tell people this story," Albert whispered.

"Look . . . it's cool, I don't care . . . really. You can tell me or not. It doesn't matter. I mean . . . like, I'm curious sure, but it won't change things. I pretty much assumed you're a monster," I said. It was bungled attempt to lighten the mood.

Albert ignored me. The story had to come out and he didn't want to linger longer than needed to *get it out*.

"I knew that cop wouldn't stop. If I ran, he'd send the dog and I'd be done for. I didn't want to, but I wasn't thinkin' clearly . . . you know, man? I was smokin' H real heavy. I couldn't go back inside . . . I had to do what I had to do. At least that's what I thought then.

"So I yank the shotgun out of the duffel and dropped the bag with the dope. I got on the other side of the train and waited for 'um to round the corner.

"I can still see it . . . fresh in my mind . . . in my eyes . . . like it was yesterday.

"Didn't rack the shotgun cuz I always carried it ready to go with a round chambered. Just for times like that. If I'd've shucked a round in the pipe, he'd've known what was comin'.

"I pushed the safety off and raised the shotgun . . . and waited.

"The dog came around first, but still on the leash. I knew the deputy had to be right behind it. He came around . . . and man . . . he had no chance. I had him."

I tried to keep an open mind. Figuring I'd hear the story eventually. I assumed I was ready to hear it. I wasn't.

"I shot him," Albert muttered. "I shot him."

Albert paused a few moments, allowing the words to hang in the air. My mind raced, trying to figure out if Albert was remorseful, and even if he was, so what?

"He dropped to the ground kinda falling sideways," he continued. "I racked in another round for the dog. But, I didn't have to . . . it got scared, or somethin' . . . I don't know . . . maybe just protective. It kept barking and growling at me, but didn't leave the guy. It stayed right by 'em . . . by his side. I'm glad. I remember thinking that I'd have felt real bad for a long time . . . shooting that dog too."

"What? You? You just shot a man . . . and you? You felt bad about maybe shooting a dog?" I objected.

"Hey, listen man, I wasn't right in the head . . . no way. That's how my mind was workin' back in the day . . . back then. He was trying to catch me . . . the cop . . . but the dog was just there, doing his little doggie job. I hated cops. Straight up . . . no doubt. That's how I thought . . . back then.

"So I grab the duffel bag and start runnin'. Thought for sure I'd made it out. But while I'm runnin' I look back quick and see two more deputies chasin' me.

"Just my luck! They musta been searchin' another train car and heard the shot. Lucky they didn't see me shoot that deputy. I'd have died right there. They only saw me runnin' past the train they were searchin'.

"I knew I couldn't shoot my way out, so I dumped duffel, with the gun, and the dope.

"Them deputies weren't nice guys. I knew what they'd have done. I'd have been dead for sure. This way without the shotgun, I had a chance. Plus, I needed to get light.

"I got off the train tracks and beat cheeks into a backyard right off the rail siding. I didn't know Lodi, and I figured if I kept going, I get lost. So I hid in a backyard shed, but they'd be right on me.

"I heard 'em run past the yard and for a second, I thought I was clean.

"But then I hear one of 'em say: *'He's gotta be here somewhere. He didn't make it far.'* I heard more voices. By then they must have got a lot more help. I was surrounded. I was done.

"The longer I waited, the more likely I'd get shot. My best chance was to give up quick . . . then and there . . . uh . . . I mean . . . if they found me and found out what I did, I'd be dead. Cop killers don't ever make it out. Not from places like that. It's not what happens . . . it's how they write it up . . . .

"So, I walked out with my hands up high as I could, man. I come out yelling: I give up! I give up! And I'm waitin' for bullets to rip me up. I really thought I was dead. If they knew what I'd done, I would have been. No question. They roughed me up a little and took me in. I was more than happy with *that deal*."

I sat stunned, fumbling with my fishing line.

Reeling my line up to check if my bait was still on the hook, I was glad to see it wasn't. I needed to prepare another piece of shrimp and think real hard about the next words out of my mouth. Even in the open sea air, I needed more fresh air, something to give me a quick mental break. Re-baiting my hook was a perfect time out.

I always figured Albert had a dark past, but not this. A cop killer.

I didn't know if I could ever get past it. We sat there, both realizing what he'd done, no matter how long ago, would change our friendship. It was all up in the air. So we sat waiting to see how it would fall.

"That was twenty years ago," Albert croaked and broke the silence.

I sat back in my chair and said nothing.

"I'm a different man now. I don't know if it makes a difference, but the deputy? The guy I shot? He made it. What I heard was he made a full recovery. Whatever that means . . . I copped to the case, and they sent me to prison double-quick."

I sat motionless, thinking about the verbal exchanges in life where the next man who speaks, loses. I let another long silence hang.

"I'm just telling you, man, that was the old me. It was. That guy died," Albert muttered.

Albert and I didn't say much for the rest of the fishing trip. The day started with Albert Gates as a dope fiend with a dark mysterious criminal past. It ended with Albert Gates the convict who'd smoked a cop and lived to regret it for the rest of his life.

Now I worried that my association with Albert would ding my background check. If he'd told me what he'd done when we met, it would have been easy for me to walk away from any association, let alone friendship, with the guy. But Albert and I had been close friends for months. We'd eaten countless meals together and prayed for each other, our families and friends.

We'd gone on trips together. Once when he had enough drama at the Teen Challenge, he'd spent the night at our house.

Albert and I were friends. Faults, wounds, cuts, scars, tattoos, and all.

CHAPTER

15

The youth ministry grew rapidly. We'd started with four teenagers. A year later we had over thirty students regularly attending the youth service. Another year and we had fifty students.

Albert was a key part of the leadership team. Almost all of the students who attended the service weren't churchgoers. To say that they weren't from traditional Christian families would be an understatement.

Albert was popular with the students precisely because he'd gone through a complete full life cycle of a gang member and lived to tell about it. All the students, and especially the boys, gravitated to him. It was probably inevitable given there was comfort and a sense of familiarity with the tattoos sleeving his arms. His life was a retelling of their lives or one of their family member's lives. It could be Tio's, primo's, their dad's, or their brother's. Albert made the Gospels' message real.

No doubt.

An hour before our Friday night youth service, I walked through the neighborhoods around the church with the adult leaders to gather the regular students and invite new ones. They were always a group of Varrio Green Valley gang members posted up by the retracted metal gates of the Green Valley apartments. They watched us gather students with the same intense gaze birds of prey give mice caught in an open field.

Bugsy, whose mugshot now graced the FBI's Watsonville Resident Agency, was a regular among the Green Valley gate-watchers. He stood with the others trying to haunt the youth ministry students the same way he'd haunted me in high school. A big man in a small pond, Bugsy who sported a chopped and lowered Chevy Silverado with sixteen-inch chrome rims, was always flanked by two or three younger gang members. They'd circle the block like bull sharks while we gathered students.

Gangsters use continuous, oppressive stalking as a terrifyingly effective recruiting tool. By making sure their targets are always aware of their presence, gangs reinforce the fear and certainty that there is nowhere to run and nowhere to hide. Bugsy & Company were omnipresent, reminding all in the neighborhood that they were the real power and that they and they alone controlled the streets. This psychological pressure and the fear it caused was seductive to many young minds.

Students talked about Bugsy and gang members generally with a sense of admiration borne of awe. I just couldn't *get* the attraction. Nothing about Bugsy's thug lifestyle seemed glamorous. But long ago my parents had gone to superhuman lengths to make sure Bugsy never touched my life again. I'd never spent one second living on their streets, walking in their shoes, unable to escape, within the gang's easy reach.

Anytime.

. . .

I wanted to destroy any and every attraction gangs created. I was convinced that our students' admiration for the gang lifestyle was caused mainly by their limited view of the world and what it had to offer them.

Most of the students had never been as far north as San Francisco or as far south as San Luis Obispo, both only a couple of hours from their doors. A worldview developed inside eight square miles of the City of Watsonville was no worldview at all. I wanted them to see serving God and others as infinitely more satisfying and important than a life of endless drug addiction and violence. I wanted them to dream of beautiful places to visit and adventures to be had and then achieve those dreams. Sometimes just knowing there are grand alternatives to what you're born into is all it takes.

That summer, we drove a dozen students to the Eastern Sierra Mountains for a backpacking trip, packing them all in the sixteen-seater white van. Three hours into the drive, everyone was in their own private worlds, listening to music streaming through their headphones.

Camelia glanced out the window, and then looked back in her lap. I moved two rows up to see what had her attention.

"A journal?"

"Yeah, it's not a diary." She giggled.

"Cool. I don't see many people writing anything anymore."

"I love writing, really. I write whenever I can."

My conversations with the students were often full of awkward pauses and painful silence. I could never be sure if

my questions were just enough to bring them out of their shells
or I was being a pest . . . or worse.

"Can you tell me what you're writing about?" I said, pushing
the envelope.

"Uhm . . . I'm . . . it's . . . ."

"You know, it's okay. You don't have to tell me unless you
want . . . ."

"No . . . I just . . . I don't want to forget anything about this . . .
the trip. So, I've been writing about the places we've driven by.
I've never been to any of these places."

"You've never been to Sacramento?" I couldn't believe it.
We were only three hours away from Watsonville. "But you've
driven by it a few times I'm sure . . . right?"

"No, all's I've ever seen is Salinas and San Jose."

"You've never been to LA? San Francisco?"

"No . . . this . . . all of it . . . ." Waving her hand in a circle
above her head. "It's all new . . . ."

It was worse than I imagined. I was stunned.

At sixteen, Camelia was one of the sweetest and most mature
students in our youth group. Every night she slept in a cramped
single bedroom with her mom and two younger siblings. Despite
her devotion to her dad, he cut ties with Camelia and the family
long ago. Camelia's mom held down two jobs that required her
to be away most of the day, often six days a week. Camelia was
the mother for her younger brother and sister.

Days off, vacations, and road trips were unheard of and about
as realistic as an all-expense-paid trip to Tahiti.

The van went dead silent as we entered the Yosemite Valley.
None of the students had ever seen anything like the marvels in

the valley. They gasped as we passed Yosemite Falls and broke into a chorus of "OOOO's" as the enormous Half Dome granite mountain reared up in their view. None of the students had ever seen a national park.

Not ever.

Camelia stopped writing in her journal and sat soaking in the pristine rivers and snow-capped granite mountains. The journal would have to wait. There was so much. Almost too much. Camelia had to experience it as deeply as possible to have any chance of ever writing about it. Writing would have to wait.

Our students weren't church kids, and I cringed when cuss words flew out of their mouths during group competitions with other churches. If our students felt like someone cheated, their first reaction was a resort to violence. It was all they'd ever known and it had worked reasonably well in their world. Our students wouldn't readily raise their hands when a worship song started, and while they respectfully bowed their heads during prayers, they never closed their eyes. These were hard-learned lessons from unpredictable lives punctuated with fear and random violence.

Our students didn't fit the young, teenage Christian mold, because Christian behavior was a novel idea that played zero part in their daily lives at home. They were unconventional youth ministry students, and we wouldn't have had it any other way. We loved being youth pastors for a group of young up and coming Christian misfits.

PART FIVE

Praise be to the Lord my Rock,
who trains my hands for war,
my fingers for battle.

Psalms 144:1 (NIV)

CHAPTER
16

Police department locker rooms are often cold in winter and brutally hot in summer. It seems to be a point of pride not to waste law enforcement resources on something as trivial as climate control in a cop's dressing area. My first day of field training, the locker room felt like a sauna in the dead of winter.

Vest, okay. Yeah. Double mags, yep.

Cuffs, notepad, FI cards . . . got 'em.

Despite arriving an hour before the shift, I was rushing and bumbling as I desperately tried to get my gear together. Putting my Sam Browne belt together was like force-fitting a jigsaw puzzle with five extra pieces.

My academy duty belt fitted comfortably around a twenty-nine-inch waist. That area now hosted an extra set of cuffs, an audio recorder, and a bulky radio wedged in what was now vanishing real estate.

It was Sunday, the first day of the work week for the gold team. I was on my way to the squad room as veteran officers rushed the locker room fifteen minutes before the 1500 briefing.

As an FNG I knew better than to try to sit in the back. That gets you nailed for sure. If the watch commander didn't notice you hiding, one of the veterans was sure to *feed you* to him for giggles. Although the squad room could easily fit at least thirty people and had open seats everywhere, I sat in the front row just left of the watch commander. If he intended to hack on me, he wouldn't have to look far.

My field training officer (FTO), Corporal Anthony Guzman, was the only other Filipino on the force. I don't know if it was a coincidence, a joke, or by design, but I figured having the only Filipino cop as my first FTO couldn't possibly be all bad.

My vest was uncomfortably tight and my utility belt seemed like it was getting tighter every minute. I could hear and feel the air conditioning, yet I was sweating. I hadn't hit the street yet and I was about to faint. It was beyond nerves. Something had to give. I wondered for a second if childbirth was anything like this and decided *no way*.

This was way worse. Maybe.

During academy inspections, WPD training officers reminded me that three of the last four trainees in the field training program didn't make it. Watsonville Police Department's training program was notoriously tough. It was a point of pride for the program to fail trainees, who then often went on to work for other departments.

The watch commander suddenly stood and started the roll call. Everyone was adjusting equipment, tearing Velcro, ripping pages from notepads, counting rounds in mags, and cycling their cuffs to zero. I was seated, ramrod straight as I could get, with one job: Listen to the watch commander.

Yep . . . I'm the quintessential pain-in-the-butt FNG.

"Tony, you and the trainee have One beat tonight," the watch commander barked.

I didn't even get to have a name.

"Copy that," Guzman grumbled.

"Is your trainee driving or is he a ride-along?"

"He's drivin'. Might as well get his first crash over and out of the way."

A few giggles from the entire shift at my expense. My first official roll call was on.

"Make sure he gets *the really good calls*." The watch commander nodded to Guzman.

"Oh yeah, you betcha. He gets every shooting, stabbing, rape, robbery and every man-bites-dog. Anything good, we'll take it, and he'll get it."

There was more to their little convo than I knew at the time. Training officers routinely line up police trainees for fight calls and domestic disturbances where the trainee can get *blooded*. Many believe it's essential to determine quickly who will last and who will not and that there never has been a better way.

The truth is that there are certain things you cannot know about yourself, despite unlimited amounts of training, until you do them. Officers who haven't been tried and tested in this fashion are routinely distrusted and actively disliked by veteran cops. A cop in the field untested in a fight is like having a student pilot on his first solo trip flying an airline full of seasoned troops.

Nobody wants to be on *that plane*.

I'd watched a few roll calls as a crime analyst, but this was my first as a trainee-officer. It was incredible how safe and unchallenged I'd felt before and how vulnerable I felt now. I had a badge and a gun, but I didn't feel like a cop. I wasn't one of them and I might never be. I was the FNG and they all knew it. They weren't rooting for me or against me. They damn well intended to test my mettle in "the forge" for my sake and theirs. If my mettle tested out, I'd be welcomed. But that *real welcome* wasn't now. It had to be earned.

My time would come quickly.

Watsonville is broken into five beats for patrol with one officer assigned to each beat. There are seven officers on swing shift and a sergeant acting as a watch commander. The two extra officers are a cover officer and a K-9 officer. These two officers are rovers who wander around the city supplementing the beat officers.

The guys on swing shift were giants. I stood 5'4" tall and maybe a pinch with my boots. Everyone else on the shift was over 6 feet, except Guzman. At 5'10" he *was* the shortest officer in the shift but still half a foot taller than me. With me on the shift, Guzman was no longer the shift shrimp.

What Guzman lacked in height, he made up in pure bulk. His biceps were the diameter of my thighs. His dark-blue wool uniform had been carefully tailored to accommodate his musculature. I pitied anyone he put in a headlock. Rumor had it that Guzman was a state wrestler in high school. I didn't doubt it. Guzman could clearly handle himself in a fight. They all could. The average person has no concept of what it is like to be in a physical ground fight with another human being who is intent on injuring or killing them outright. They have no clue how critical physical strength, speed and stamina can be. The news media is even worse.

A three-minute ground fight takes at least one hundred thousand mental years. Typically one or both combatants are utterly exhausted. But if the suspect is drugged up, mentally unstable, or both, the usual fight-laws-of-physics don't apply. Drugged crazy people will fight on with hellish strength long after being tased or shot multiple times. For the cop in that fight by the roadside in the gravel at 3 AM, it means he or (she) is in Hell with a madman at their throat for an eternity.

Alone . . . in the dark.

They're called ground fights because usually, but not always, both fighters end up on the ground when it goes full contact. Skinned knees, cuts, scrapes, bloody broken noses, dislocated fingers, chipped teeth, and torn uniforms are always on the menu. The aches and pains in the two–three days following an all-out ground fight are difficult to describe to anyone who has not experienced one first hand.

In the best of cases, your FTO watches you fight with other cops nearby in the wings. They let the recruit fight it out with a safety net close at hand. In the worst of cases, a recruit makes it through the probationary period and the test comes later when they're typically completely alone and help may or may not arrive.

Ground fights are incredibly dangerous for cops, even though they typically prevail. Often the officer is physically out of gas by the end and barely able to stand up afterwards. In the worst case, if they don't win, they're severely injured or killed. No matter what, the stakes for a cop in every ground fight are incredibly high.

Every single officer in the room was a made-man. They'd been fight-tested. You either passed or you didn't. They had all passed a test where there was no middle ground.

I wondered if my envy was showing.

Every officer in the room had that stature and swagger seasoned cops often display. I felt like Shrinking Violet at the high school dance with the cool kids. I'd have to fight to make the club. How hard I'd have to fight wasn't in my control. There was no way around it. I'd asked for it and now I was gonna get it.

Ten minutes into roll call, a triple tone hissed over the radio. They made us master lots of useless subjects at the police academy, but radio tones weren't among them. Triple tones were urgent calls. I keyed on the tone and listened carefully to dispatch.

Armed 211 with a handgun . . . levee . . . suspect was last seen running eastbound.

The female dispatcher's voice was level, loud and crystal clear. She spoke for at least thirty seconds, reciting the critical details, but perhaps because my heart was pounding or my hearing wasn't attuned to dispatchers yet, I missed most of them.

Guzman gave me the go-time look as he moved towards the door.

I walked out, knowing we were going somewhere on the levee that keeps the Pajaro River from flowing through hundreds of living rooms in Watsonville. I figured if I kept myself glued to Guzman's hip, I'd be at least close to the right place.

As I drove out of the PD's parking lot and cruised down Main Street to the intersection of Riverside Drive, both of us realized I didn't know where to go. If I kept going on Main, I'd cross the Pajaro Bridge and leave the city.

"Turn left on Riverside. Pretend like you're in a hurry!" Guzman snapped.

"Go code-three?"

"It's a robbery with a gun. What do *you think?*"

I hit the lights and sirens with surprising ease, and made a left turn on Riverside, only to come upon another four-way intersection.

I had no clue where to go next.

We were headed to the levee but a half-dozen streets all led there. I gambled and turned right on Union Street, the closest one leading to the levee. It turned out to be the right choice.

"Keep going straight into the park," Guzman said, jabbing his index finger in the direction.

River Park is a small, two-acre park nestled between East Front and the levee. The park's lone bathroom featured walls marked by the gang that controlled the neighborhood known as Loco Park Watson.

We flew into the park's loose gravel lot a bit too fast, bottoming out the patrol car on the slight ramp leading into the lot. Before I could stop, Guzman was out and running.

"Stay attached to Guzman's hip," I muttered.

It was my mantra for the day.

I sprinted after Guzman like my life depended on it because it might.

The Pajaro levee spans several miles from east to west. It's also the landmark that defines the southern city limits. The Army Corps of Engineers built it in the 1940s to keep swollen winter floodwater from flooding Watsonville and the tiny town of Pajaro. In the summer, you can easily run across dry patches of the river at many points.

Cresting the levee, we saw groups of men hanging out in

knots spread across several hundred yards. One group caught Guzman's attention instantly. Even I noticed them.

Unlike most of the groups of older men hanging out, who appeared to be field workers, these three men were in their twenties and looked cleaner. They were. They were only about twenty yards east of our location.

As soon as they saw us, all three young men walked eastbound, away from us.

"STOP!" Guzman roared.

The instant Guzman yelled, one man exploded into a full sprint like a runner hearing the starter pistol. We darted after him, ignoring the two who stood frozen in place.

RULE 1: Guilty men run.

RULE 2: People remember a running man.

RULE 3: Smart guilty men stand still or walk away slowly.

The trio of mantras rushed into my head from the academy.

"Watsonville 2-1 we are in foot pursuit!" Guzman huffed over the radio.

I was the smaller guy, but I was way quicker than Guzman and had been running sprints for this scenario. I was confident I could chase anyone down.

The kid was a rabbit. I needed to catch him. Easy peasy.

I blew past Guzman at the thirty-yard mark. My initial confidence deflated the moment I realized running past my FTO meant I'd be making all the critical decisions. Now I was committed and couldn't slow down.

Catch the bad guy and everything will be okay . . .

Or maybe not.

Closing on the one-hundred-yard mark, Sprinter slowed.

Tackle him . . . prone him out . . . shoot him?

I had no clue what to do when the luxury of indecision ended.

The suspect slowed, and then suddenly stopped, reaching into his waistband . . . .

This was a scenario they threw at us in the academy. The suspect, usually played by some frumpy retired police officer, reached for something in their waistband. Out came a gun. Or a cell phone. The poor trainee had to make a split-second decision to shoot or salute.

The academy was gone and it was happening.

I'd stopped ten feet from a real suspect. I knew there was no chance pudding, a puppy, or tickets to the Ice Capades were coming out of his waistband. Sprinter had a gun, a knife, or contraband. He'd either use what he was pulling out or toss it.

I'd come to a full stop from full speed in two steps. But I was far too close to the suspect. Tueller's Law says at least twenty-one feet and many departments prefer thirty. If Sprinter moved on me, he would reach me no matter what I did to him. My pistol was out, up, and on Sprinter in an instant. Much faster than I'd ever done, muscle memory allowed me to move faster without thinking than if I did think about it.

It wasn't logical but it was true.

Sprinter hurled a black revolver as far as he could into the river before I could get a word out.

"DON'T MOVE!"

Is that all I say? I wondered.

"Don't you move!"

I repeated myself with less enthusiasm.

"Get on your knees," Guzman barked. Materializing suddenly

on my right, his voice was a massive relief.

The booming tone enabled me to add:

"Damn right . . . get on your knees."

Sprinter sagged to his knees, hands up.

"Go hands-on . . . I'll cover." Guzman took control.

My gun back in the holster, I grabbed the cuffs and warily approached Sprinter. I tried to cuff him as quickly as I could, but couldn't pull off the fancy smooth cuffing technique I'd been practicing for weeks.

Scenario over, I was ready for a break, a bite to eat, maybe hot cocoa, and a debrief like we did at the academy.

But that never happened.

CHAPTER

17

On the way to the patrol car, I noticed everything in my duty belt had shifted out of place. Now it felt like the belt was inside-out and upside-down. We'd intended to head back to the office and complete the paperwork while another officer took our "in-custody" to the county jail.

Thirty seconds after we got in the car, three more beeps screeched over the radio.

Another one.

This time, my brain harvested all the details:

Group of males fighting with weapons . . . parking garage . . . 35 West Beach St. Five to six subjects . . . one armed with a bat.

I hit the lights and siren, confident that I knew exactly where the parking garage was. We were a few blocks away and arrived within a minute of the call. The parking garage was a five-story structure with a narrow entrance and an equally cramped exit.

A unit coming in the opposite direction on the street roared into the garage ahead of us and I tailed-gated it.

The first unit suddenly stopped in the middle of the lot on the second floor. The officer sprang out of the unit, drawing his pistol. I followed, stopping our unit and racing after him.

The first officer leveled his pistol at a knot of four young men in a full-blown brawl a car length away. There was an off-white Honda parked hastily in the middle of the lot, its passenger side windows all shattered. Broken glass and spattered blood littered the cement floor where the men were fighting. In the fading light, the blood looked surprisingly black. Not at all like TV or the movies.

The primal sounds of the fight echoed off the garage's cement walls. Only scattered weak sunlight streamed through gaps between the buildings surrounding the garage. We were encircled by dark corners and nooks adding a sense of foreboding to the savage fight.

The "brawl" was one-sided. The guy in the middle of the fight was taking a savage beating, despite easily being the biggest guy there. The rest of the pack rained punches and kicks to his head shoulders and abdomen while the Big Guy was on his knees, turtled-up, with his arms over his head.

When another unit arrived, we all advanced slowly towards the brawl.

The guys hosting the slug-fest paused, and two suspects rabbited to the third floor. Big Guy, thinking he might be in the clear, lowered his arms, exposing his head. The beat-down specialist who remained saw the opening and took it. Big Guy's optimism cost him. The lone attacker viciously stomped Big Guy's exposed head, knocking him unconscious.

Stomper looked up, glanced at us, and leering with delight, casually jogged to the third floor like it was grade school recess.

"Get the car!" Guzman yelled.

I jumped in the car, drove towards the victim, halting long enough for Guzman to hop in the passenger seat.

With Guzman aboard, we drove to the third floor pursuing the suspects. I noticed my seat must have shifted because now I had to sit forwards just to reach the gas pedal and brakes, which made handling the Crown Vic dicey.

I'm off to a great start. I don't even know how to lock my seat in place.

Fortunately, adrenaline flooded my body, canceling any discomfort. We topped the next floor, found nothing, and roared up the ramp to the next floor. There we found Stomper, who hadn't traveled far. Tall with a large frame and a huge gut, he was breathing hard, and almost out of gas. It wasn't that he was jogging casually when he took his leave a floor below, Stomper was utterly out of shape and doing all he could just to make a half-hearted attempt to flee. We parked a few feet away while Stomper stumbled weakly along.

When Guzman ordered him to stop, Stomper shot us a glance with all the interest of a cow watching a passing train, and stopped. He wanted to stop. Stomper was pooped. After all, kicking guys in the head who aren't fighting back was hard work.

Guzman warily approached Stomper, pistol leveled pointed at his broad back, which was an easy target, considering. I slowly approached from the driver's side with Guzman slightly in the lead.

Stomper started to turn his head to get a better look at us.

"LOOK AWAY!" Guzman roared. "You move, I'll shoot you. Cuff him, Bautista."

I'd never heard a cop tell someone not to look before but in our situation, it was clear why. Guzman knew Stomper needed to get a clear physical bead on us both to do anything unpleasant and that wasn't gonna happen.

I cuffed Stomper as fast as I could and moved him to the back of our patrol car. He went easily. It was time for him to rest now that he'd spent all his gas on Big Guy and walking slowly up two flights in a parking garage. It was a big day for him; besides he was getting hungry and said so. The other two suspects vanished. We cleared paramedics to enter the garage and to see on Big Guy two floors below.

Another marked unit roared up the ramp to meet us.

It was "Blackjack" Houston.

Houston, also an FTO, was a classic. Jack Houston was the Big Cop With Bad Temper poorly portrayed in hundreds of movies and TV shows. Most decent-sized departments have at least one, sometimes many. Well supervised, guys like Blackjack are excellent, solid, long-serving deterrents to violent street crimes. Poorly supervised, they easily become stupid, vicious bullies that produce large civil verdicts when the department inevitably gets sued.

Houston's well-groomed mustache framed his perpetual frown. I'd seen him verbally rip a female trainee from chin to groin while I was on a ride-along. The female trainee fought back tears during his five-minute tirade. Blackjack didn't discriminate. He was flat out cruel to everyone everywhere, using just enough restraint to avoid getting fired.

I'd made up my mind to steer clear of him.

I noticed Houston slowly walking towards me with his jaws clenched and realized my plan failed. His gaze made me feel like frost under a blowtorch. As he closed on me, his massive stature dwarfed mine.

For a moment, I felt it.

He's enjoying this. He likes it. Whatever it is he's gonna do . . . .

My faint hope that he might have roared up on us to make sure we were okay, evaporated. He hadn't come to congratulate us for catching Stomper or see to our safety. I knew it. This was Blackjack. Every conversation with him ends badly just as it did with any citizen he'd ever interacted within his career.

"What the hell are you doing?"

I had no idea what he meant and my laundry list of mistakes for the day was too long to easily guess what he was on about.

"Sorry, T.O. I don't understand."

I'd deployed my *Polite Bautista* go-to defensive mechanism, hoping it would lighten his mood.

That failed too.

"You don't even know? Wow. You really don't know. That's great. That's just great!"

His reflex sarcasm, anger, and profanity were building like a storm wave. I couldn't help wondering if there was a Mrs. Blackjack (or ever had been one). Worse yet, I imagined little Blackjacks running around. Seemed like even the idea of this guy having family and loved ones, might be a Penal Code violation, or perhaps animal cruelty.

I still had no clue what Houston was working himself up about but I knew he'd let me in on it soon.

"Sir, sorry, what did I . . . ?"

"Look at the car. The one you're driving, Einstein."

Houston cut me off stabbing a mottled scabby index finger

at the car with Stomper aboard.

Now I figured the answer must be obvious, but not to me. The events leading us to the top floor of the parking garage were a blur.

"YOU TOOK MY CAR!" Houston shouted.

I couldn't believe it. I walked closer to the unit. It wasn't the right one. We were driving vehicle 40. I'd jumped into vehicle 21 two floors below.

No wonder I had a hard time reaching the pedals. Blackjack probably needed a pinch bar to get in our patrol car with my seat all the way forwards and raised. He'd looked like a huge dark circus clown prying himself out of our unit when he showed up. Now I knew why.

Houston shook his head disgustedly as he pulled Stomper out of *his* car. Shoving Stomper at me like a sack of potatoes, Blackjack piled into unit 21 and slammed the door extra hard for effect. He dolloped a cherry on the cake of his displeasure by roaring off, tires screeching.

Big loud-mouthed, foul-tempered bullies can be right. My dad often said even a broken wall clock is right twice a day. Blackjack was happy, as happy as guys like him ever get. He'd dominated and humiliated me, which meant he was batting a thousand that evening. Nothing could be better. Maybe he'd find a puppy to kick or mice to torture, but he'd scored big early on, so the rest of the evening was a gimme. With luck, he'd stop someone in town and verbally savage them because he was still annoyed with me. His evening was looking up. Then when I thought about the helpless trainee he might have that night I felt like a dog who peed on an exquisite white carpet that no one found yet. That trainee, whoever he or she was, would be *getting it* . . .

Out of the blue.

Like the Sphinx, Guzman was silent and expressionless. I couldn't tell if he was being gracious, felt sorry for me, or disliked Blackjack intensely but wasn't gonna let me know it.

With Stomper snoozing in the back, dreaming about the baloney they serve in jail, we made the long drive to the county lockup.

18

After tucking Stomper in bed at county, Guzman and I drove back towards the station for a long night of report writing. I was eager to get at it. figuring it would be pretty hard for me to screw *that* up, plus I might find ways to make myself look slightly or perhaps significantly better than I felt.

Then another triple radio tone sang out immediately fixing my attention:

Stabbing just occurred . . . alley behind 600 block of Davis Ave . . . suspects last seen running across Freedom Boulevard. Multiple callers.

Multiple callers meant it was credible.

We're on the line with reporting party . . . will try to get a suspect description . . .

The 600 block of Davis Avenue was in Four beat and not our call. As a trainee, I knew better than to avoid hot calls no matter where. The veterans on shift and elsewhere would likely be taking bets on whether I'd duck and dash or dive in. A few sidestepped hot calls would automatically fail any trainee. Under the right circumstances, even one ditched hot call could wash you out of Watsonville PD.

We were back on Sudden Street and Freedom Boulevard when the triple tone went out. I hit the lights and siren *again* and flew down Freedom for a little over a mile in what felt like ten seconds. I knew the gang members who controlled the 600 block of Davis Avenue.

The Zendejas.

Six Zendejas brothers were ranging from fifteen to thirty. A crime family in the purest sense, the family committed crimes and had done so for decades. As a crime analyst, I'd copied and plastered their mugshot photos into officer safety bulletins close to a regular basis. Most counties in California have similar families. Most were nothing fancy, but they kept law enforcement and the California Department of Corrections busy and fully employed year after year.

Our red and blue strobing lights painted the fences of the alley behind the 600 block of Davis Avenue. A thick ground fog had rolled up off the dunes causing our wig-wag lights to illuminate the grey mist with blinding effect.

Guzman pointed a white spotlight down the alley silhouetting two guys hunched in the gravel. The thick mist wildly diffused the spotlight as it tried to cut through the gloom to illuminate the men.

As we exited the unit, we both drew our weapons and pointed them at the pair. There was no way to know what we had at first, but a few seconds later it was obvious and I holstered my pistol.

"Help him! He got stabbed! Get an ambulance! NOW!"

The guy screaming at us was on the verge of tears as he crouched next to the young man prone in the gravel bleeding out.

"GET AN AMBULANCE!" he screamed again, spittle spraying from his mouth.

The guy bleeding out on the ground was Joshua Zendejas. I'd never met him in person, but I knew his face. Tattooed right below his right was the word "kill," and below his left eye "scrap," a not-so-endearing term for sureño gang members. Anyone who looked Joshua Zendejas in the face read "Kill Scrap" every time they looked. So if those words offended the viewer, he literally couldn't avoid it.

Every time.

Seeing his chest soaked with blood, I scrambled for the rubber gloves in my back pocket.

If it's bleeding, plug it.

A mnemonic from the academy bubbled up.

"Where were you stabbed?" I asked

"Ahh . . . I . . . it . . . uh . . . ."

He shifted to his right side pulling his shirt up. There were two small puncture openings on the left side of his chest.

I followed the gushing trail of blood spewing from the wound and positioned both my hands to cover the holes, hoping to slow down the bleeding, but no dice. Men can easily survive dozens, even hundreds of slashing wounds all over their body, but puncture wounds as shallow as 1.25 inches are frequently fatal and very difficult to treat.

The Romans discovered this and perfected the signature killing sword carried by Roman legions everywhere. They experimented systematically by stabbing thousands of captured prisoners and slaves, then carefully noting the time it took the man to die. The result was the Roman Gladius, whose overall length including the grip varied from twenty-four to thirty inches. Compared to medieval swords, it was pathetically short and small. But it was supposed to be. The sword was designed to deliver puncture wounds using the tip of the weapon. The design was pure genius in the hands to legionnaires trained to use, and it efficiently killed hundreds of thousands of men.

That same concept was killing Joshua Zendejas before our eyes. Blood pulsed through the puncture wounds despite all the pressure I could apply, dripping on the gravel where he lay.

"Who stabbed you, Josh?" Guzman asked Zendejas like they were old buddies.

"C'mon, Guzman, you know I ain't going to say nothing. Just help me . . . please."

Josh remained defiant even as he writhed in agony. All he wanted was medical help. Hunting down the guys that stabbed him was his job.

Any cooperation with the police, especially giving up any description of the person or people who stabbed you, made you a snitch. Bonafide gang members never snitched. They'd die first and often did.

La placa (cops) are the enemy.

Always.

His stabbing would go unsolved, at least by us.

I kept up the pressure on the wounds, even though I had a feeling I was missing other wounds somewhere else. In the dark, with Joshua's entire midsection drenched in blood, I didn't look for more wounds. I only had two hands.

Guzman didn't speak or help so I figured must be doing okay.

Finally, I heard ambulance sirens closing. Their sirens are

distinct, slightly higher pitched than police sirens. I figured officers were on their way but Josh needed medics.

Eventually, at least four officers arrived on scene before the ambulance. All four walked up, looked at Zendejas bleeding out, walked back to their units, and left. Not one gave me a hand.

I figured it was rookie treatment.

When the medics arrived, I gladly gave Joshua to them.

As I stood and peeled my gloves off, I noticed his blood had somehow found its way through. My hands were covered in sticky slick goo that appeared almost black. I might as well have not been wearing gloves at all.

Blood finds a way.

Another mnemonic bubbled up in my brain from the academy.

We drove from the crime scene straight to the satellite office, where I rushed to wash my hands with copious soap and water. I tried to keep my hands still but they trembled uncontrollably.

What kind of disease did I just get exposed to?

As I walked back in the car and plopped into the driver's seat, I flexed my fingers and balled my fists hoping to slow the incessant shaking.

Nothing worked.

"Where to, T.O.?"

I figured he'd tell me to head to the barn to start writing our reports. Wrong again.

"Let's just cruise around our beat. Familiarize yourself with the streets."

"Shouldn't I start working on my reports?"

"It's your first night, you get a pass. No reports for you. I'll write everything from tonight, but I'll do it tomorrow. Like I said, just drive around. Let grave units handle all the calls. Don't respond unless you really need to."

It was midnight, with one more hour to go on swing shift. Clearly, Guzman's work night was over.

I returned to the One beat, cruising up and down its streets. As I drove through its many alleys, I found myself hoping nothing would happen right in front of me and realizing it might.

The last hour of swing went down like a lamb, giving my hands time to stop shaking. I drove as smoothly as possible while Guzman snoozed. I did such a great job I had to tap his shoulder to wake him when we pulled into the office driveway.

"T.O., we're back."

Guzman sat up, alert like he'd been awake the whole time.

"Copy that. Park the car and clean it. We'll go at it again tomorrow."

At that point, I knew I'd accomplished something. He could have flat washed me out that night and it wouldn't have been the first time. Far from perfect but I was in the mix.

"Thanks, T.O."

"Good job today!"

I wasn't sure if that was true, but I took his word for it because he didn't have to say anything. Telling me I did good when I didn't made zero sense. I'd need every positive bit of feedback to build my confidence going through training.

Day one of the field training program was finally over.

CHAPTER
19

Mitigated speech is the linguistic term that describes deferential speech designed to demonstrate manners and to show reverence to authority. These patterns of speech are extremely widespread throughout all of Asia and are an integral part of the Filipino language and culture.

For me to survive and pass training I had to utterly destroy a cultural pattern of speech I'd spent a lifetime learning and used every day. Most trainees who had issues with hesitancy or had a tendency to deferential speech and action quickly made the adjustments to *reflect assertive conduct.*

I battled the essential need to employ direct assertive speech and action as though it challenged my life because, from a cultural perspective, it did. During my first six weeks in the field training program, every training officer noted that I:

"Lacked command presence. Needs to be more assertive. Unable to convey authority."

Mitigated speech isn't just about conversations. In regions of the world where it is the way of life, it determines how you relate to other people and is mastered at an early age, like walking.

It was an integral part of my personality, enriched by my childhood, and reinforced by Filipino culture.

• • •

My dad was born and raised in Nalook, a small village five kilometers from Kalibo, in the province of Aklan, Philippines. The roads to Nalook were flanked by large rice fields on both sides. An irrigation ditch, about five feet wide, ran alongside the roadway and was an indispensable feature of the landscape. The ditch had generous amounts of water flowing through it. If it didn't, the region would be unoccupied in a matter of months. One of the best ways to gauge the economic and social prosperity in large parts of Asia is to examine the expanse and health of their irrigation networks. The larger, more robust, and extensive it is, the healthier and more stable the society becomes. Entire dynasties in China can be charted from rise to fall by the state of their irrigation infrastructure.

My dad grew up in a cluster of homes in the middle of vast well-watered rice fields. Everyone knew everyone in Nalook. Villagers greeted each other by their first names. Dad had an anecdotal story about every person in the village. This fundamental face-to-face networking system forged an interdependence among all the people of Nalook.

As a kid, I remembered several typhoons blasting through the village. Before each typhoon hit, everyone scrambled to fortify their homes and the preparations never ended. Neighbors held nothing back in helping each other. Ropes, batteries, food and water were all shared freely. Strong able kids from larger families were loaned out to help families with young children. Families quickly secured their own homes so they could move on to help their neighbors.

In Nalook, mitigated speech and action was a way of life. My grandparents used to offer passersby meals out of the blue with the interaction invariably following a set pattern:

The sincere offer to stop by for lunch was made.

The reply would always be a polite, "No, thank you," even if you were on the brink of starvation.

The offeror would insist you should come into the house and partake in a meal. The offeror would persist even if the offeror may not actually have enough food for the passerby.

The passerby would decline again.

Only after the third or fourth insistence should the passerby accept, if they were truly hungry.

Even then, the acceptance would still be softened with qualifying deferential language:

"Okay, but only if you insist."

This dance seemed senseless but wasn't. It was considered a mandatory courtesy, and the formalities, although cumbersome, were required gestures of respect.

• • •

In law enforcement, mitigated speech and action is a death sentence. Suspects have no idea how serious you are. Meanwhile, your speech and action tend to embolden them to find out. One way or another it will get you or them killed or seriously injured. Worst still perhaps was the inevitable death or serious injury such speech and action brings to innocent third parties.

Or other cops.

It was the heart of my struggle in the field training program. In some agencies where most contacts were with cooperative and supportive members of the community, a smile and a respectful tone could work most of the time.

But not in Watsonville and not at 2 AM with a car full of gangbangers.

In Watsonville, I had to order subjects to do exactly what I needed them to do, without negotiation or arbitration. One clear command, if met by resistance, REQUIRED a resolute order with robust colorful profanity for emphasis. In law enforcement, the "F" word carefully applied and colorfully expressed can and does save lives. It wasn't chess. It was checkers. Every escalation takes you to the next level to see who blinks first. Equivocation is a sign of weakness that gets people killed or worse.

Because there are worse things than death.

The academy taught us that command presence and verbal judo resolves almost all your conflicts in the streets. The training was based on the premise that if I engaged people through empathy, it would allow me to successfully communicate my point of view and control the conflict. It sounded great and certainly, the nice person who came up with the idea probably had an impressive PhD in some such.

But after weeks of the academy way, I was losing ground and I knew it. My struggles with contentious street criminals were so devastating that they overwhelmed every other aspect of my training.

I became hesitation incarnate. The confidence I garnered in

the academy by working out longer, practicing more scenarios, listening to radio traffic on days off, and navigating the city streets in my spare time, had withered away.

On the first day of my seventh week of field training, I got called to the office of the training sergeant before day shift. I knew I was struggling. I had zero ideas if I was progressing, and even if I was, whether my progress would be fast enough.

The training sergeant threw the gauntlet.

"You gotta turn it around. Soon . . . really soon. Like yesterday soon. Or we gotta let you go. It's better you should hear it now . . . from me."

I was on the brink of failing.

Week seven started almost as badly as it could. They hadn't washed me out but the writing was on the wall.

I left the FTO sergeant's office ready to accept that my career as a police officer was probably over. I'd have to find another job and turn in my gun and badge. Not because I found a better opportunity.

Because I failed.

My new field training officer for the next phase was a welcome sight. Dunn had always been accommodating during ride-alongs, so especially that day, it was great to finally see a *friendly* face.

Wrong again.

"Let's hit the streets!" he yelped.

I'd been working the graveyard shift for the last month, so hitting the streets during the day sounded great. Daytime law enforcement is an entirely different world from the dark of night. Not nearly as many hot calls and far less action occurred.

"Will do, T.O. Anything you want me to focus on?"

"We need to work on your contacts. Find people you *need* to get up on. No stopping grannies, grampies, soccer moms, or paleteros. I want you to stop people we need to talk to."

Dunn's intent was unmistakable. He was gonna put me in the meat grinder. No doubt and no way out. I'd have to either lay down or get down.

As a ride-along, I was a guest, and he'd treated me cordially. Now I was a trainee officer, and Dunn meant to test me in the fire. It wasn't long before I realized he'd wash me out right then and there if he felt the department and all its officers were best served by doing so. Memories of his tussle with Shirtless bubbled up.

After ten minutes of driving, I spotted a vehicle with an expired registration pulling into a driveway on Madison Street and East Lake Avenue. The driveway led to a house that had been converted into offices. I slipped behind the car and hit my lights.

The driver stepped out and started walking away, utterly ignoring me and the blaring police lights.

"Sir, I need to talk to you."

The man was clearly in a hurry and anxious to show me that he was.

"About what?"

"Your registration is expired."

"Are you serious?" Indignant now.

"Yes sir, I am. I need you to get back in your car."

"Look, I'm in a hurry. I'm not going anywhere. Here's my driver's license. My registration is current. I just forgot to put the sticker on."

"Sir, I need you to stop moving around. Just stand by your car."

I was trying to hang on to some illusion of control.

He didn't move. Instead, he stood motionless, defiant, and daring me to take it to the next level.

"I work here. I'm a counselor here at the rehab center. You're wasting my time. I have an important job to do and I need to go. I'm late. Okay?"

As he said that, dispatch confirmed that the registration was in fact, current. I ran his driver's license and it came back current, valid, no priors. He had a clean record.

Was I really harassing a pillar of the community? Is he the type that would complain to the chief?

"Alright, sir, looks like everything is good to go. You're free to go."

"You really gotta find something better to do . . . figure out what real police work is." He snatched his license and registration from my hand.

Back in the car with Dunn, anxiously expecting either an affirmation or criticism. I had no idea if that was a good contact or not. It didn't feel great, but nothing has felt right in weeks. I was hoping that I was just second-guessing myself. I was hopeful that maybe I would get some credit for discretion—essentially showing favor to a good citizen.

Dunn's silence was deafening. He was writing notes on a small notepad. A lot of notes for a small pad.

After several minutes of driving aimlessly, Dunn calmly told me to pull into the parking lot of Edward A. Hall Middle School.

Is this it? Am I going to get fired and told to head back to the office?

"Did you have a valid reason to stop that guy?" Dunn asked.

"Yeah. His registration tab was expired."

"Is there a reason why you wanted him to be in the vehicle?"

"For my safety. We don't want people walking around because they could fight us. He was also unsearched, and he could have been armed," I answered, regurgitating phrases hammered into me in the academy.

"Can you legally keep people from getting out of their cars during a traffic stop?" Dunn continued.

I knew where this was going and it wasn't good for me.

"Yes, T.O. You can keep both the drivers and the passengers in the car because they're detained."

"So you knew you could legally stop him and keep him in the car?"

"Yeah."

"Then tell me this . . . why did you let that guy walk all over the place? Why did you let him walk all over you?"

"I don't know," I whispered in defeat.

The answer was clear. Painfully clear.

"Here's the deal . . . ." Dunn snapped, cutting the long silence.

I'd seen his blood get up in a fight, but even then, he didn't seem nearly as bowed up as he was now.

"I don't give a damn if you put yourself in danger. You wanna get hurt? Fine, your business. You wanna let people walk all over you, that's on you. But you're not workin' with me and you're not workin' here."

Dunn let his words hang in the stale air of the patrol car.

"This is what pisses me off. When you let someone like that

to talk back to you, do whatever he wants, you're putting me and every other cop in danger. You've emboldened that guy and anyone who saw him or hears about what he did. That makes it MUCH harder for me or any other cop to deal with him.

"Next time one of us stops him, he's going to think that he can put his arm up our asses so far that we're his hand-puppet. I'm gonna have a built-in uphill battle with that guy because you didn't do your job! I may have to fight him bigtime for real because you were afraid. That's a coward. In my book and every other cop who patrols here. You can't be a coward and be a cop. Not here. Some other department maybe . . . but there's no room for fear and hesitation in this town on this job."

Dunn's face was flushed. He was righteously pissed. Even more devastating, he seemed resigned to the idea that I wasn't gonna get it or ever learn how to puff up. He reminded me of a guy who finds a mangled deer by the side of the road and has to decide to shoot it ending its misery.

Dunn was ready to end my misery. He wouldn't like it but he was up for doing it.

Then and there.

"I'm sorry, T.O."

"Fuck that! I don't want apologies! You either act like a cop or call it a day. You need to be okay with being an asshole. A BIG ONE! If you're not, you need to go do something else."

That said, Dunn visibly relaxed, letting silence engulfed the car.

I couldn't stay still. He'd amped me up somehow. For the first time since I charged Bugsy Ramos on the staircase at Aptos High, it was REALLY go-time. I was ready to go. I wasn't sure if it was anger, fear, or frustration. Maybe all three. Mostly I was tired of feeling afraid, screwing up and apologizing.

I had to change.

"Let's roll," Dunn said.

Inching down several alleys, I felt a sense of relief flowing over me. I was as good as fired mentally and pretty much done in every other way. I'd heard of trainees spiraling into the dirt on duty and figured that was what was happening in my head. But it was strangely liberating.

My career as a cop was about to be over and I had nothing to lose.

I was either going to be the cop that Dunn wanted me to be, the badass who never let anyone get over on me, no matter what, or I'd go down like a submarine in the nastiest fight of my life, swinging, kicking, and gouging the next person who got in my way, whether I had to or not.

No more.

If I got hurt, then I got hurt. In that moment I realized the trick was getting to the mental place where you don't mind losing everything. I wanted a confrontation. I wanted someone to jam me. I had to unlearn everything I'd learned in my entire life and turn against my natural and cultural inclination to be polite.

I was out of time.

If this was my last day as a cop, I was going down swingin'. Throughout my training, I had restrained myself, ever worried about making a mistake. In so doing, I ensured I made the biggest mistake there is in law enforcement.

No more.

I drove through alleys looking for contact . . . hunting assholes . . . looking for a fight.

Five minutes after Dunn's parking lot smackdown, I spot Jimmy "Downer" Melgoza riding down Hill Ave. I'd never talked to Downer before but was familiar with him from prior shift briefings.

The 200 block of Hill Avenue was a target-rich area for gang-bangers, specifically North Side Watson Chicos. Downer was a Chico. His right eye drooped but never fully closed or opened, giving him that half-asleep look twenty-four hours a day. Hence the moniker: Downer. He should have been called Droopy, but that was already taken by another Chico and a sureño. No recycling good gang monikers for Downer.

Downer was definitely on the menu for good contact. He was violating a clear city muni code by riding his bike on the sidewalk, and he was a gang member with a long, well-deserved rep for violence.

I whipped in behind Downer and chirped my siren to say: "Hi." He glanced back but didn't stop or even slow.

This was it! The test.

I couldn't have cared less about redemption. I'd failed. The next two or three days we'd go through the motions so Dunn could thoroughly document my failures, before the big *adios*.

I would end training on my terms.

We shot past Downer and I aggressively cut him off, jumping the sidewalk to block his path. As I got out of the car, Downer hopped off his bike and angrily threw it in the gutter. The clunk of the bike hitting the asphalt jarred my senses like a starter pistol.

Go-time. Ready to fight.

"What the hell you want?" Downer barked.

He took a few calculated steps towards me and squared off.

"Stop. Turn around."

Somewhere in my mind, all the legal criteria for a cursory search fluttered around, but I wasn't gonna be reciting any of them.

"The hell . . . what for? I bet you want me to turn around, *pinche maricon*."

"I stopped you for riding your bike on the sidewalk. You can't do that here. Now I'm going to search you for weapons."

My adrenals were kicking up to full throttle.

I was excited, nervous, and angry all at once.

"No, you ain't touching me! You got no reason to search me. No probation. Owwww." He threw his arms up in the air, like a referee signaling a touchdown, then snapped them towards me. I flinched. He saw it. *Downer up one–nil.*

It was a defining moment.

Downer had drawn a line I was determined to stampede right over. No gangster was gonna tell me what I could and couldn't do. Not ever. I was ready to pay the price.

Any price.

It was primordial; a scene that had played out millions of times in pre-history; as old as our species. I knew what I had to do.

"Turn around RIGHT NOW!" I yelled.

I tucked my arms against my body, bladed my stance, and shuffled towards him. I felt awkward but it didn't matter. I was ready to go. My vision went black everywhere outside his body. I didn't know where Dunn was, how long the contact had taken or would last. I didn't care.

Then Downer turned slowly away.

He blinked.

Compliance.

"Move your feet apart . . . more . . . MORE!"

I made Downer spread his feet so far, it nearly brought him down to my height and nearly ripped the crotch in his chones. Now I could comfortably search him.

"Hands behind your back. Interlace your fingers . . . DON'T MOVE!"

Pat-searching him was easy now that he was half-a-head shorter.

"Turn around and sit on the curb."

"Nah. I'm good stand . . . ."

"SIT DOWN!" I snapped cutting him off.

I hoped he'd push it. I wanted to release all my pent-up frustration. If Downer would only oblige, I'd gladly let it loose on him.

He hesitated for effect but we both knew the struggle was over.

I won.

He knew I would do whatever it took to get him to sit.

So Downer sat while I wrote his name and date of birth on a field interview card. I kept pushing the limit. After completing the field interview card, I photographed his tattoos. Externally stoic and terse, I was grinning from ear to ear inside because it felt great.

He was mine, I owned him. Hands folded in defeat, Downer sat on the curb while I took a victory lap.

It was primitive, juvenile, and the only way. I cited him for riding his bike on the sidewalk. It was a petty ticket but it wasn't the point. He'd relive this day when he paid for the citation and a long time after that. It would define his relations with me in the future and shape his approach to every other officer in Watsonville PD.

A ticket for riding his bike on a sidewalk. Makes me grin every time.

Dunn and I got back on patrol. As I turned left on East Lake Avenue, he whipped out his notepad out and furiously scribbled more notes. I had no clue how he viewed the contact.

Had I gone too far? Was there any such place? Did I violate Downer's rights? Am I going to get fired for that or for something else no matter what?

Dunn gave me nothing but silence. Again.

Finally, he folded the notepad and tucked it away in his shirt pocket. I kept driving towards Mount Madonna, wishing the day could just be over. The whole field training could end.

"THAT'S WHAT I'M TALKIN' ABOUT!" Dunn screamed, half laughing. "That's exactly how you do it. Every. Single. Time. You controlled the guy. You owned him start to finish! No backin' down! No backin' off! No lettin' up. Not ever. I want ALL your contacts to go like that from here on out. GOT IT?"

"Yes, T.O."

• • •

The day after Downer, I spotted a gang member slowly riding his bike behind parked vehicles, clearly trying to avoid eye contact with us. I jumped out of the car to talk to him. He dumped his bike and rabbited across an industrial parking lot.

The chase was on.

"Watsonville 1-2, foot pursuit," I radioed.

A tone sounded across the city.

"1-2 on a foot pursuit. Go ahead 1-2." Dispatch clueing in all the officers on patrol.

"We're crossing over a parking lot from Beach and Walker. HMA, blue shirt, black jeans."

"Copy 1-2. Units responding code 3 to your location."

I chased after the former cyclist for two blocks and tackled him in a parking lot flanked by big rigs on both sides.

He struggled to get up, but I slammed his head into the oily cement as hard as I could, stunning him. At that point, he stopped and followed my instructions from there on out.

I was cuffing the suspect when Dunn drove up and slowly exited the unit. He casually approached me with that same calm swagger he'd displayed when he approached Shirtless rampaging in that Taqueria.

Dunn was grinning ear to ear. He'd gotten through to me and knew it.

He knew I got it.

Reluctant, passive Bautista was dead.

After two short days with Dunn, I was determined to fix my frame of mind throughout my training. Every time I went out, I would hunt and fight. I was smaller than all the rest, but as a hunter, what I lacked in size, I made up with heart, courage and determination.

I would think like Dunn. What he said, I did.

It transformed me from a trainee on the verge of washout to a surprising rising star in the program.

The next three weeks with Dunn were some of the most exciting times of my early law enforcement career. I wallowed in confrontations, fights, and foot pursuits and regained my confidence. All my practice and preparations finally jelled.

I cruised through the next phase of the field training program and was released from training a week ahead of schedule.

Thanks, Dunn.

Thank you, Downer.

CHAPTER

20

During the two years I was navigating the academy and field training, Hope took over the youth ministry. Enrollment grew numerically and in spiritual maturity with Hope as the youth pastor. We saw clear tangible changes in the students' lives.

I found myself wishing I could be the same person I had been once I got back to the youth ministry. But it was impossible. The police academy was one thing, but field training transformed me as a cop and a person. There was no way back.

I wasn't the same and I never would be.

I'd heard of defining moments in life but had never really thought about them and what they did to those who experienced them. My outlook and worldview had drastically shifted. I couldn't put *that genie* back in the bottle after what I'd learned and seen. With barely a year under my belt, the whole world and everything in it had permanently changed. I wondered if I had defining moments before and perhaps never noted their effect on me.

Where I used to be excited to meet new students in youth ministry, they now seemed potentially menacing. Gang tattoos, the contentious attitude, and strange bulges in their clothing all put me on guard now. I'd always been excited to meet every student, to know them, and speak life into them. In a sense, I was still excited, but my optimism was guarded and jaded.

Norteños and sureños rival gang members regularly attended the youth ministry services. There was an unwritten mutual understanding between the groups such that differences were put aside momentarily for church.

I used to welcome everyone with open arms. I'd had no reason to doubt or question their intentions. They came because they were curious, spiritually hungry, bored at home, or maybe had a crush on a girl or a boy who attended.

Now every time I saw a new guest with gang signs, hyper-vigilance kicked in. I was on guard reflexively. I assumed they carried some kind of weapon. It hadn't mattered before, but now I couldn't help imagining a worst-case scenario every time.

Would some twisted gang leader send a few young ones to shiv or shoot the "Youth Ministry Cop"?

Gangs often dispatched little ones to mule drugs, deadly weapons, and even to assassinate gang enemies because kids stood a better chance of avoiding adult prison sentences. I could never know for sure if one of the smiling faces I met would break off a rusty shank in my neck.

Week after week, I poured over my sermons at youth service. I wanted to deliver a life-changing message in a forty-five-minute, high-energy blast. That had never changed. My love for God and the students never changed. The more I worked the streets, the more passionate I became about the power of the Gospels.

But my job as a police officer was to neutralize the impact

of violent people on their communities. Getting arrested was a powerful wake-up call for some folks but simply a required rite of passage for others. It was far-fetched and outright stupid to think that booking everyone into the county jail would change the course of their life. For many, it was as essential to their career as their next breath.

More than ever, I believed that a sustained change in life came from a spiritual awakening. More than ever, I believed that a relationship with God was the impetus and sustaining force for that change.

I still wanted to inspire, to speak life, to compel change. With all the creativity and energy I could muster, I did. Every youth night, I preached with a greater sense of urgency. I preached believing the timeless message of a resurrected Savior had the same life-changing influence on each student as it did in the time Christ was alive to speak the words.

Now I preached with a Sig Sauer P239 nestled in my front waistband.

The youth ministry hadn't changed a bit.

I had.

CHAPTER
21

"Watsonville 2-5, foot pursuit. Clifford and Main."

The voice was Chuck Stanley.

He was the only WPD officer in the academy with me. We'd bonded over the mind-numbing academy and field training hell. That shared experience produced a solid friendship.

I tromped on the accelerator pushing the unit to its limit along with my driving skills. The Crown Vic lurched hard, gearing down into the low ascending tonal roar thrilling to many beat cops who've felt it and heard it.

If the unit had wings I'd have been airborne.

"2-5 Watsonville, update your location." Dispatch's prompting tone was level.

"We're on . . ."

A flurry of mic clicks on the radio meant Stanley was fighting.

I drove past his unit at the busy intersection of Clifford and Main. It was pointing up Clifford towards Terry Loop.

He's gotta be somewhere past Terry Loop.

A guess. As good as any.

I blew past Terry Loop and caught a glimpse of two men fighting in a driveway. I slammed the brake pedal to the floor and threw the unit in park. I dove out and ran towards Stanley, leaving the engine running.

He was on his back, a Hispanic male astride him throwing wild punches at his head and chest. I torpedoed into the suspect headfirst at full gallop, knocking him off Stanley. Anger and adrenaline flooded my body. I threw punches at the most vulnerable easy target. My personal favorite: the temporomandibular joint connects one's jaw to their skull. Hit just right, it's a knockout ON-OFF switch.

Three well-placed strikes to the TMJ stunned the suspect and the fight went out of him. I'd expected more, but he was spent from the vigorous unskilled flurry of punches he'd thrown. Ground fights and ground fighters have built-in timers. When the timer dings, one or both fighters are done. He was done. I was batting cleanup.

Stanley popped back into the fray to help cuff the suspect. A good look at the kid made my heart freeze.

Santiago Quintero's swelling face looked up at me. A favorite youth ministry student, and one of the first ten in our ministry. He'd asked me to pray for him the week before. He'd been struggling with alcohol and drugs, served up at home as a daily part of an all-American healthy meal, and the conflict was ripping him apart.

I'd laid my hands over him, earnestly asking God for spiritual guidance on Santiago's life. Now mere days later, I used the same hands laid on Santiago's head for healing, as weapons to punch him senseless.

He attended youth services even after the fight. We were polite. But our relationship was never what it had been, and would never be what it could have been.

I didn't tell Hope or the youth staff what happened. Santiago did the same. It was our secret and we kept it. He never again asked me to lay hands over him in prayer. Deep inside I hoped the fight would be the first and the last, or at least, the worst.

But it wasn't.

The collision of two opposing worlds continued, more painful each time.

CHAPTER

22

I loved being a cop despite the conflict between police work and work with the youth group. Driving down a busy street in a marked patrol car on a beautiful day is impossible to describe unless you've done it. Those who have and thrived, often say they can't imagine not doing it for a living.

Everyone's watchin' all the time. It's intoxicating. Moreover, I loved dangerous calls. The more precarious the call, the higher the excitement level. I didn't want to avoid getting in harm's way. Chasing down the bad guy, getting into a fight, or squeezing the trigger in a life-and-death conflict—I'd concluded few were better suited for the task.

My patrol routine was to hit the streets as soon as roll call finished. I wanted to be first on a hot call and never miss a violent, wanted suspect. I haunted every street and alley.

Looking for it.

I thrived on adrenaline, tension, and conflict, like a lot of cops at WPD. If you were a REMF or a pogue who waited to be assigned radio calls, you were in the minority. Most beat cops were haters. They hated street criminals and relentlessly prowled the city looking to mess with them. Someone had to put them in check.

My shifts were full of hunters.

As much as I loved patrol, it was natural to seek out a new challenge. Besides, over time worthy opponents were hard to find. Patrol cases were gratifying and thrilling, but they were mostly simple. I needed a different kind of challenge.

Narcotics was all-that. On the cutting edge of police work, you're privy to the secret operations, undercover buys, surveillance, and drafting complex search warrants. It was appealing all the way around. The allure of undercover dope work dovetailed with my work with Albert, and all the future Alberts in my city.

• • •

"He's in the room, to your left, down the hall."

The security guard for Teen Challenge motioned me past. He was an overweight middle-aged guy without a uniform, but clearly in charge of who walked in and out of the facility.

"How's he doing?" I asked.

"Not good. Keep it short."

The Teen Challenge center was an old church converted into a halfway house and rehab center. The hallways were cold and carpets had that tell-tale musky-dank smell of mold. Yellowed linoleum flooring led to a heavy wood plank door. Behind the door, the large bare room held a dozen bunk beds empty except for pillows and tidily piles of folded blankets.

The far end of the room was dark. Albert rolled off a bunk and sat on the edge, his eyes sunk deep in dark sockets.

He scanned the room slowly from one corner like an animal expecting an attack. Keeping his blanket over his back, he shook uncontrollably, avoiding eye contact.

"You good?" I asked.

"Nah . . . uhhh-uh . . . not yet . . . I will be."

"What happened?"

Right or wrong, I figured I deserved answers. Albert had gone missing for three weeks. Nobody knew where. He'd missed all his scheduled appointments, causing Teen Challenge staff to send a search group to his home in Sacramento. He'd been in Watsonville the whole time, drunk, stoned, couch-surfing from one house to another.

Heroin took him. After two years clean, he'd gone full choke on a three-week heroin bender. Teen Challenge staff found him in their parking lot, slumped over the wheel, asleep, an empty syringe on the floorboard. He'd gone on one last tear, shooting up one last time before kicking.

"Hey, man, do you want another blanket?"

"Nah . . . I'm good. Just going through it . . . *las malias*."

He stared at the floor, still shaking.

"The what . . . ?"

"Malias dude. It's when you're really sick . . . withdrawing from heroína . . . it's what happens when you stop using all of a sudden. I'm going through it . . . ."

"You get sick?"

"Yeah, it'd be like . . . like, like you have the flu and someone is taking a pipe to your back. You come down man, you know? Like a hammer hitting an anvil? The pain, it's unreal. I'd do anything to feel good, even a little better."

He lay back down and instantly began writhing uncontrollably.

"Alright man. Get some rest . . . I mean try. You know how to reach me. I'll come by in a couple of days."

I'd do anything to feel better. Words I'd never forget after watching a man go through *las malias* for the first time.

I thought his heroin addiction was buried.

It wasn't and ever would be.

As I walked back to the guard's station I wondered:

Could I ever trust Albert again? Should a guy like that be around students? Could a cop be close friends with a righteous dope fiend?

"Okay, brother. Thanks."

The guard nodded his head slightly but said nothing as I walked past his post. He kept a watchful eye on me until I left, as though somehow I posed a threat to his facility.

CHAPTER

23

"I'll take the Big Mac," Miguel said.

"Just the burger or the meal?" I asked.

"I think just the burger. No, wait . . . a'ight . . . maybe the meal."

"Whatever you want. It's on me."

"The meal."

"What'd you want to drink?"

"Mountin' Dew. The big size. Mountin' Dew."

Dopers and Mountain Dew. They love it. They can't get enough of it. Veteran cops told me it was because of the high caffeine level.

Miguel sank lower in the cage of my patrol car, making me nervous. I'd moved his cuffs to the front, a major party foul, but the rules and policies always got bent around snitches.

"You alright back there?" I asked.

"Yeah . . . I'm good. Just laying low. This is no good 'ey."

I really hoped he wasn't grabbing a revolver he'd keester-stashed that I'd missed during his body search. Turned out he was worried about being spotted in a patrol car getting food with a cop. That could cost him his life.

We parked behind the East Lake Shopping Center after we got our food. I stood by the back passenger door while Miguel inhaled the Big Mac. He took a massive gulp of the extra-large Mountain Dew.

He was visibly nervous for good reason.

I stopped him an hour before on one of my favorite muni code violations. Municipal code 4-5.903 required pedestrians to cross the street at right angles or by the shortest route to the opposite curb. No diagonal crossing or willy-nilly wandering across the street was allowed. It was a dream petty violation and one of few available for pedestrians.

Imagine someone coming up with a wonderful local law that one can't lollygag while crossing the street. There are hundreds of vehicle codes to use to stop anyone driving a car, but when someone is walking, your choices rapidly peter out.

The lolly-gag violation was a perfect pretext for stopping Miguel. He consented to search without any fuss. I suspected the stop would yield bupkis, because those who allow you to search are either nervous and cave into the pressure of an officer's presence, or they're clean. I conducted my obligatory search of Miguel's waistband and pockets, knowing full well I wasn't going to find much and he'd soon be on his way.

When I asked him his birthdate the second time, he gave a different date than initially. Miguel had a strong accent but the second birthdate wasn't even close to the first one.

No one forgets their birthdate. The ref was throwing red flags all over the field. He was hiding something.

We played cat-and-mouse question games until I threatened to take him to jail to get his fingerprints because I knew he was lying. He caved. Miguel had a small warrant under his real name and birthdate. He'd need to take a room without a view at county for at least a couple of days. Not a big deal except Miguel was a heroin addict, and two days in a cell meant he'd be waist-deep in *las malias* before he could say "Jimmy crack corn."

Heroin addicts will do anything to avoid cold turkey withdrawal.

Two hours after I stopped Miguel, he was still languishing in my patrol car as the game clock ticked down to the *real sudden death*. It wouldn't be long before he'd be wishing his mother and father never met.

"What's this guy's name again? Can't remember . . . something about a horse . . . right?" I asked.

Miguel worked his fries like a PhD thesis, deliberately slow-gulping the Mountain Dew, before answering.

"Caballo . . . it means horse . . . ." Miguel said, slow-walking the response.

"You think he's gonna be on time?"

"I think so. Sometime he is, sometimes he not. You want me to call again?"

Miguel wasn't convincing. The watch commander had given me some leeway to work him. He'd ordered half an ounce of heroin from Caballo in a deal that was supposed to happen an hour before our trip to McDonald's. Caballo was either running late or flat running. Service calls in my beat didn't stop, which meant my beat partners would resent this unless I came up looking good. Nobody likes answering other cop's calls and doing *their* reports without a damn good reason.

"Yeah, shoot him another call. Tell him it's gotta happen in the next thirty minutes," I said.

"K. But if he can't make it 'til later, what do I say?"

"What can you say? The deal is off. You're headed north."

Miguel paused letting my words sink in. He was getting sick. If the deal was off he'd be singing "Here comes the pain" toot sweet.

Watsonville heroin addicts worked on a strict schedule. Early morning, they scuffled around the city putting money together. They rummaged through garbage bins for aluminum cans to muster eight to ten dollars from the recycling centers. From there, they funneled off to a handful of drop-locations—which vary daily, depending on where the cops were thickest. The drops went off like clockwork with a morning group and an afternoon drop.

Caballo was Miguel's dealer. To make a little money for himself occasionally, Miguel bought a piece (un pedazo) or half-piece from Caballo for another street-level dealer. A piece is a term dealers use to describe an ounce of Mexican black tar heroin. It weighs 25 grams, unlike an actual ounce, which is 28.5 grams.

Miguel missed his morning drop and his morning fix; his lips were chapped. He was growing restless. Burgers and Mountain Dew would only hold off the horrors for an hour or so. Eventually, his body would demand the dose of heroin it was used to getting twice a day.

We both needed Caballo to show up, but Miguel needed it more. I could wait for another time. Miguel couldn't stand to think about that concept. He said, "I need more damn coins. I'll call him again!"

He was getting angry. If Caballo didn't come, he was going

to jail and living hell would follow him there. I took his cuffs off so he could make the phone call.

"Okay, okay, he comin'. He close. He's here any minute he says. You gotta hide me . . . NOW!" Miguel jumped into the back of my car. He was worried. Rightfully so. He'd jumped in and out of the back of the patrol car to make the phone calls. It was amateur police hour and he knew it.

Caballo drove into the East Lake Shopping Center in a white Bronco resembling O.J. Simpson's getaway ride. Unlike O.J., he seemed in no particular hurry.

"That's him . . . THAT'S HIM!" Miguel said stabbing his index finger at the Bronco.

Miguel slumped behind me in the cage, his eyes peering through the crisscrossed divider in the patrol car. I drove him to a corner of the shopping center and he reached through the window to open the back door from the inside. Hopping out, he sprinted out of sight in seconds. Later, Caballo would have difficult legal challenges to face but figuring out who set him up wouldn't be one of them.

I darted through the parking lot blocking in the Bronco as it pulled to a stall. The stop was a cinch. The Bronco had enough mechanical defects to justify the stop and probably enough for an impound.

Caballo was clean cut, wearing a white-collared shirt. In his thirties, he looked like Mr. Goodcitizen on his way to the office. He spoke no English, at least not with me. I understood and spoke enough Spanish to determine he didn't have a driver's license. That's all I needed. This Bronco was mine.

When a backup unit arrived, I searched the Bronco, finding

four ounces of black tar heroin tucked under the driver's seat in minutes. I'd never seen so much heroin.

Satisfied with a solid arrest, I took Caballo back to the police department for booking. Curious officers rallied there meeting me in the grubby holding area to ogle my prize.

Jeremy Dunn, the acting watch commander for the oncoming swing shift, had his ideas about what to do with my loot.

"Where's he live?"

"Best I can tell, he lives off Springfield Road in Moss Landing," I said.

"He have a set of keys?"

"Yeah, I got 'em. I think there's a house key on the ring . . . somewhere . . . on here." I fumbled through the keys.

"You see where I'm goin' with this?"

I wished he'd just tell me. The games cops play.

"Should we go to his house?" It wasn't my best answer but all I had.

"We figure out where he lives, we freeze the house, and you can write a search warrant for it. I guarantee he's got a bigger stash of drugs there."

Freezing the house and a search warrant? I wouldn't even know where to start.

"Look, I'll have someone take him to county," Dunn continued. "We'll check and see if he lives on Springfield. If we find the address and one of the keys work on the door, we will go into the house and freeze it. Yellow tape and the works. That way no one can leave or enter the house while you write the warrant. But here's the thing, we gotta get there now before someone cleans it up."

"Let's go, then." I was overwhelmed processing his info dump. "You know I've never written a search warrant before, right?"

"Yeah, no worries. I'll walk you through it."

I was in. To a young, impressionable officer, Dunn was the super cop. I'd follow him into hell and put out the fire.

• • •

Moss Landing is a small community five miles south of Watsonville. It is easily recognizable by the two massive smokestacks towering above the power plant at the mouth of Elkhorn Slough. Your nose tells you that you've reached Moss Landing even if your eyes are deceived. The musky smell of the sea and all things maritime is in everything there.

Once a whaling station, Moss Landing still had a robust harbor filled with yachts, private and commercial boats. Nestled around the fertile slough, farmlands, and beaches, were pockets of residential neighborhoods including a house on Springfield Road.

Dunn and I, along with two recalcitrant day shift cops, who didn't like working past their shift, knocked on the door at 125 Springfield. The house was little more than a small, unkempt rickety box crudely built.

No answer.

I tried Caballo's keys. The third key slipped in easily. We cleared the house guns drawn, checking every corner, then taped off the premises with the official "don't mess with this place or we'll prosecute you" tape and notices.

125 Springfield Road was officially frozen pending a search warrant.

0813 hours the next morning, almost twenty-four hours after I'd stopped Miguel, I hadn't had a minute of sleep, and now had over thirty items of evidence to book including three handguns, $21,000 in cash, dozens of *pedazos* of heroin, and two large kilo-size chunks of black tar. The search warrant for Caballo's house was patrol's equivalent of boxcars in a casino.

We'd hit it big.

Exhausted and overwhelmed, I had all of the evidence on a table in the report writing room while I processed each item. Word got out and everybody from day shift stopped to envy my plunder and congratulate me.

Southern California cops seize multikilos all the time. But Northern California was different. Over three kilos of narcotics was a significant seizure that didn't go unnoticed.

Guzman, my first training officer, popped in the report writing room to peek at my plunder. Like a boy anxious for Dad's notice and approval, I quietly desperate to know what he'd say. His words always had weight. Guzman slowly browsed the evidence pile like a lion sniffing a fresh kill:

"Son, you hit the motherlode. Goddamn! Ask for whatever assignment you want and you'll get it."

If I could cobble together a search warrant without sleep, I was just getting started. Caballo built my confidence. I wrote more search warrants in the next month and fumbled through more narcotics cases until it became second nature.

• • •

The more I worked in narcotics, the more my goal came into focus. I desperately wanted to join CNET. The CNET crew was an intimidating group of guys. You couldn't spot them, as they exhibited a random variety of looks from heavy facial hair to scruffy beards, goatees, long hair, mohawks, each guy exploiting the best undercover look he had. All wore plain clothes unless they were doing a takedown, even then, only throwing ballistic vests over their dirty shirts and stained hoodies. They looked more menacing than most hoods I'd seen.

Nobody knew what they did or where they did it. Most of the employees at the police department didn't even know where the CNET office was. It was designed that way to eliminate any chance of anyone finding CNET's lair.

The agents rolled into the PD parking lot with an eclectic collection of cars: lowered black Mercedes E350, nasty beat-up trucks, SUVs, and soccer mom's vans. We patrol cops watched them put their gear on and disappear for hours. Their polite name was Task Force Agents. Drug users and dealers knew them as Pigs in a Blanket, Down-Lo 5-0, Low Pro-Po, Undercover Bacon, and my favorite: Reservoir Dogs. They used their secret radio channels. They had their own report writing system and intelligence network.

The Santa Cruz County Narcotic Enforcement Team (CNET) was a program created and funded by California's Department of Justice's Bureau of Narcotics. Each law enforcement agency in the county sent a representative to the task force, along with a few feds from the ATF, DEA, and FBI.

CNET Task Force Agents were the legendary local spooks whose every move was shrouded in secrecy. I couldn't imagine a more exciting gig. Rumor had it that the WPD special agent in CNET was due to rotate out after being in the unit for five years. That rumor quickly became an official opening.

I handcrafted my interest memo to maximize what I had going after only a tad over a year of actual law enforcement experience. I owned that fact in one paragraph. I figured it would be a long shot, but I had nothing to lose. Small things sometimes contain great power and in law enforcement, the less said can often be more. As I timidly handed the memo to my sergeant, I hoped Guzman was right.

• • •

Three weeks after I submitted my memo, the Chief's office called me in.

"C'mon in, Bautista." Chief Romero opened the door stepping aside for me to enter.

"Thank you, sir."

I liked Chief Romero. Most cops did.

"Have a seat." He pointed to the loveseat in the spacious office. I'd been around the department almost four years as an analyst and as an officer, but this was my first time in his office. Probably a good thing. Romero was always approachable and most officers genuinely believed that he had their backs when it counted. Even though I'd never been in his office, his demeanor put me at ease from the get-go.

"So you want narcotics?"

"Yes, sir!"

"You've come a long way, Bautista. And quickly . . . an

analyst then patrol . . . and now? Now you wanna be a narc?"

Romero had a smirk on his face as he said it. I feared the worst. He looked down at my interest memo like it was a curiosity in a museum.

"You really wanna do this?"

"Yes, Chief. I do."

"Okay. It's yours. One condition: Talk to your wife first. Your whole life will change. Big time. The narc life can destroy you and your family. A lot of guys do this when they're single, and the ones who don't, often end up single. Do you know what I mean? I wanna make sure your wife knows what she's getting into. No shame in passing this up if she's not ready."

"Chief, thank you! Okay . . . I'll . . . ."

"No . . . no. I'm serious. Talk to Hope *then* get back to me. If she's okay with it, the job is yours."

The rank and file loved Romero because he paid attention to details and made it his business to know his officers. He'd met Hope on two fleeting occasions but that was enough to remember her name.

I was so excited I couldn't sit still.

"I'll talk to her, sir, and get back to you . . . today . . . ."

Hope had no say in the matter. In retrospect, my approach and attitude could have cost me everything I love. The chief was right. Undercover narcotics work eats cops alive, along with their spouses and their kids.

I waited on pins and needles two full hours before calling the chief's secretary to accept. I'd made CNET.

I broke the news to Hope later that evening.

PART SIX

---

*And a great and mighty wind tore
into the mountains and shattered the rocks
. . . but the LORD was not in the wind.
After the wind, there was an earthquake,
but the LORD was not in the earthquake.
After the earthquake there was a fire,
but the LORD was not in the fire.
And after the fire
Came a still, small voice.*

I Kings 19:11b–12

CHAPTER

24

I woke up late, tired and groggy from surveillance that lasted past midnight. Nobody cared if I came in late. That was a great thing about CNET: start times were never fixed. That also meant nothing ended when it should. There was no *should* when it came to off-duty time. The general expectation was that you were at work sometime before noon, and you knew there was no chance you were going home on time. If you were doing your job right that meant you went on as long as you had to go.

I walked out of the house in dark sunglasses, squinting painfully in the harsh Capitola sunlight. The CNET-issued vehicle was a white, soccer mom Dodge Caravan. Nobody in the criminal world cared about a soccer mom van. I'd been a narc for three months, which ensured I got the crappiest car in the UC fleet, but I didn't care. The van made me invisible to criminals. I could sneak up on anybody in my mommy van.

What the . . . ?

An oil dipstick was jammed into the van's ignition. I struggled to shift focus and make sense of what I was seeing.

Is this a joke? A CNET initiation? Somebody gonna put a

bucket of warm chicken gizzards above the door before I walk in?

My heart pounding as it dawned that my van may have been burglarized, I rushed to the back and opened the trunk. The equipment box was gone. All my gear, gone.

A flash of panic turned to anger, then hypervigilance.

I check-pressed my waistband with my forearm, a habit cops and anyone carrying a weapon uses to ensure that their weapon is where it should be.

I had my pistol.

The gun in my waistband brought much-needed relief. Losing all my equipment—vests, magazines, ammunition, helmets, goggles, tasers—was bad. But my gun was with me, not in some gangbanger's hand about to be used in a murder.

I had no idea if my vehicle had been targeted because of my job. In some ways that would be much worse. I wasn't sure if the thief was still around, maybe even close by. Maybe in my house. Hundreds of scenarios raced through my head. I wasn't sure what was happening, but my odds were way better with my handgun in my belt.

Running back to the house, I searched every room, gun drawn, expecting someone to pop up any moment. Clearing the interior, I searched the entire backyard.

I called Eddie Parra. He was my go-to guy whenever I was in a pinch. He was *that guy*—never panics, always comes up with a solution. He was on his way to the office but diverted to my house after the call.

"So what's happenin', doggie?" Parra slipped out of a brand new pewter GMC Silverado. Rookie narcs drove mommy vans. Veteran narcs like Parra drove spanking new trucks.

I led him to the trunk of the van.

"Bro . . . DAMN! They broke in the van. Got everything," I said.

"Son of a . . . . What is *this* about?" Parra said pulling the dipstick out of the ignition.

"I got no clue. I don't even know where they got that."

"Pop the hood."

I popped the hood and we scanned the engine compartment.

"Yup. They used your own dipstick. Old school, amateur hour. Tried to use the damn thing to start the van," Parra said.

"What do we do, Eddie?"

Parra was my designated training officer for the narcotics task force, but unlike the TO-Trainee status at WPD, he treated me as a peer from the get-go. Eddie was a former boxer, a tad shy of six feet, and in fantastic shape. He attracted women everywhere we went and had more pricey clothes and shoe ensembles than anyone I'd ever known. He had game. Parra's flash persona made most mistake him for a drug trafficker.

He'd been in DART several years before making CNET. Parra knew the underworld better than most gangsters and drug dealers. When things went sideways, I called Parra before I called anybody. Very early on I learned that you told your supervisors what you had to report, but only after you got your story straight with your partner.

Cops don't report everything that happens. They reach out to trusted peers first to mentally noodle through messes. Mostly, it's not an attempt to conceal anything. Over time, cops come to understand that when their supervisor gets involved, the officer's statements set up like fast-drying concrete: final and irrevocable.

If they're able to, street cops need to talk things out with peers to make sure they've considered all the aspects of a given problem.

I trusted Parra. Like a lot of good cops, he'd lived in the law's gray areas where many fear to go. His experience assured me that he could work through the toughest problems.

"Call dispatch and have Capitola PD take a report. Call the lieutenant right after. Tell her what happened."

"Okay. Damn, I feel like a dumbass."

"Dan, we'll get whoever did this, I promise you that."

I never doubted Parra. I wasn't sure how, but Parra was relentless. We'd get the mopes who broke in my van.

• • •

Although I was a fresh narc officer, I developed five informants in the first few months. Most were crap, untrustworthy flakes, but two were rock stars. They came through, answered my calls, and were plugged into the underworld.

These two were the first to know when a new up-and-coming drug dealer hits town. When major crimes occurred, they tapped into huge information nets and always got me going in the right direction.

Informants are the eyes and ears of law enforcement. Both revered and reviled, they're routinely privy to case-breaking info citizens and law enforcement never get any other way. They're ironically disposable and indispensable in the war on real crime.

We made calls, Eddie to his informants and me to mine. Somebody boosted good stuff from a cop's car. It didn't matter if it was petty theft or a grisly multiple torture-murder; if you tapped the right person they'd come around and tell you all about it. It's always been like that.

• • •

Valentina was a charming grandmotherly type. Full of life, she rarely frowned. She'd lived in Watsonville all her life and knew everyone in town worth knowing. Her silver Dodge Caravan, just like my UC ride but newer, darted back and forth across town, carrying *her nietos*.

She had that throaty, deep cough and raspy voice common to heavy smokers. But Valentina didn't smoke cigarettes. She'd been a heavy meth user for a long time. She puffed the glass pipe in the morning to get started and hit it several more times to keep her day going. She'd started using meth to deal with chronic back pain, but inevitably her meth use escalated to the point where she was utterly dependent on methamphetamine to function.

To support her $100 a day habit, Valentina did what most heavy meth users did. She sold some on the side. What started as a little side-action to fund her addiction quickly became a highly profitable business. Valentina learned the narcotics game from the ground up and became a high-level meth dealer disguised as a charming grandma.

Valentina was my first target at CNET. I felt embarrassed when I posted her photo on the operation plan as *the target*. We served the warrant for Valentina at Zero-Dark-Thirty before the sun and Valentina got up. She'd just stumbled out of her bedroom in a frumpy nightgown when the team burst through the door. She was so frightened she fell over backwards. We all felt like a sack of dirt scaring grandma.

No one was looking to send Valentina to prison. It was always about flipping her. My deal with her was the standard *three and free*. She'd give us three high-level cases, and we'd request probation instead of prison.

She agreed.

Parra walked me through the informant packet. The informant's contract specified the informant's agreements. To wit: Not act like a cop, not carry a gun, not sell or use drugs, *unless at our direction*. Everyone knew the last promise on the contract would be broken, daily. Informants had to stay connected. We just didn't want to know.

It was the classic narc's wink and a smile deal.

Valentina treated Parra and me like her kids . . . or grandkids. Every time we met, she brought food. She liked me, but she was in love with Parra and didn't hide it. She often said that if she were younger, she'd have already hooked up with him. If it weren't for her infectious sense of humor and boisterous throaty laughter, it would have been awkward to work with her.

"Here she comes." Parra was the first to spot the Dodge Caravan screeching through the back parking lot of the old hospital on Holohan and Green Valley. Valentina got out and limped to Parra's truck, carrying her oversized purse and the customary grocery bag with gifts for us.

"Hey, Dan and Eddie, I brought you guys some oranges. You work hard and you gotta eat healthy."

There was no doubt who Valentina liked best. She pronounced Parra's name with that unmistakable doting tone. I got mentioned pleasantly.

"So what's up? Why the urgent meeting?" she asked.

"Dan's car got broken into," Parra said.

"Which one? The van?"

"The white—"

"Oooh, I love the truck, Eddie." Valentina interrupted. "Smooth and clean, just like you. You should take me for a ride sometime."

Parra blushed. After the life he'd lived, he didn't blush easily.

"Yeah . . . the white van," I said, interrupting the awkward love fest.

"Oh dear God, somebody broke into that piece of crap?" Valentina burst into her distinctive zesty laughter. We joined in. "What was taken?"

"Dan's vest, his taser, helmet . . . but not his gun. I'm sure you're going to know who did it," Parra said.

"Damn right, I will! But you know . . . you know . . . I'd do this for you boys for free, but do you think this . . . ? Does it . . . ?"

Valentina didn't need to finish her question. We knew what she wanted.

"Yeah, yeah. Absolutely. This counts towards your three. Big time! This is a big one. You give us who did this, or who's holding, and you're done," Parra said.

"This is gonna be easy. Oh, I love you boys!" she said.

She was clearly gearing her attention to Parra. I thought about pinching myself to make sure I was still there.

"Give me a few. I'll get back quick and let you know who's got it, Dan."

"God . . . I really appreciate it," I said.

"I got a little favor to ask," she said.

"What is it?" Parra bit.

"Can I keep the handcuffs?" she asked.

Everyone busted up laughing.

As quickly as she appeared, Valentina popped out of our truck. Limping double-time back to her van, she zoomed out of the parking lot.

Two hours after our meeting, Valentina called.

"I know who broke into your car. His name is Fernando Avila. He's driving a stolen white truck."

Before I could interrupt Valentina to ask for more specifics, she blurted:

"Don't worry, I'll find out where he's at. I'm on it . . . just wanted to get you boys movin'."

One quick convo with Valentina and we had a ton of solid leads. We pulled booking photos, probation terms, and turned up Avila's old address. He didn't seem like a stone gangster, more like soft-shoe stuff. That gave me some relief, but I wasn't sure if he was alone or if I'd been targeted by an organized crew who sent him.

A random street rip was bad enough, but if it was more than that, I'd been made. I might have problems nobody could fix.

CHAPTER

25

Threats were immediate and recognizable on patrol: A car full of gangsters with handguns, domestic violence suspects who fight the minute they realize they're getting cuffed, burglary suspects nabbed in the middle of a three-day out-of-their-gourd meth rager.

Narcs, by contrast, are spooks. Never in the limelight, their cases don't make the news. They're the utility infielders of law enforcement. They do the dirty deeds dirt cheap, leaving no trace. Working the law's fringes, they build cases from involuntary statements and other evidence inadmissible in court.

Narcs specialize in walling-off cases. We do this by gathering intelligence, triggering police actions based on that intelligence, and intentionally leaving the information out of any reports. Walling-off cases is an art form and we're artists.

We drop a dime to local patrol units based on intelligence we didn't want to disclose IE:

"There's a black Mercedes parked at . . . . It'll move around 3 PM. Pay attention to it."

Marked units look for the Mercedes, stake it, and use the Vehicle Code to find an independent probable cause to stop and search the vehicle. Surprise surprise, patrol finds a large pile of drugs. The official report will read: Officer utilized solid police work to nab the suspect . . . .

Not a peep about us anywhere. It's not what happened, but it's what gets written down.

Clandestine units are gold. If there's a murderer loose, who do you call with specialized plainclothes surveillance capacity and a vast criminal intelligence network to dime him out double-quick? We gather intelligence behind the scenes, leaving no footprint: Like running one pass by a neighborhood so the informant can confirm the target house, the innocuous text message triggering the takedown of a narcotics runner, an unmarked plane circling high above property until the search warrant team arrives to knock the doors down, the black Otterbox wedged between the axle and the muffler of a car giving real-time vehicle location of our target.

Even as a freshly minted narc with minimal impact on the drug scene, my paranoia began ratcheting to new heights. We spent our waking hours plotting to take people down. On the flip side came the nagging fear that someone in the opposition might be looking to return the favor.

The sooner we rolled up Avila, the sooner I'd get answers. Invoking his right to silence or requesting an attorney wouldn't stop me. I'd be kneeling in broken glass until I knew exactly why he'd broken into my car.

Parra and I set up across the street from Avila's mom's house, his only listed address. There was a scant chance we'd see him, but it was our only lead. Parra's cell rang. He listened intently for thirty seconds, then flipping the phone closed and shot me a sideways glance.

"Go-time, Doggie. Avila's at the Economy Inn in a white, single-cab Ford truck. It's stolen. I'm callin' our guys."

I scrambled to put on Parra's old vest, which looked like a thick football jersey on me. My gear was all hopefully in Avila's truck.

I drove Parra's truck while he *quarterbacked*, his name for running an op. He pulled six guys from our team to converge on Economy Inn.

Ten minutes after Valentina's call, two unmarked *point units* were positioned in the parking lot as primary eyes on the room and the truck. Two *takeaway units* were stationed off the hotel premise to follow the truck out of the area. One takeaway if Avila turned left and the other if he turned right.

We never took things personally, unless it got personal. This was as personal as it got. Avila was about to ride the lightning and experience the full brute force of our unit.

As Avila left the hotel room and got in the truck, he took a glance around the lot, out of habit. But his tradecraft was nowhere near good enough to spot us. Putting the truck in reverse then hard slamming into drive, he lurched out of the lot tires screeching. The moment he left the hotel's lot, a silver Jeep takeaway unit lit him up with its lights and siren.

Avila took off. He took us all for a quick quarter mile vehicle pursuit around the block. He slowed down to a crawl, jumped out of his car, dashed towards a bunch of houses. His car kept going.

Avila's instincts were right on. He had no chance in a vehicle pursuit. More cops were going to converge. Police presence doesn't dwindle over time. Just the opposite. On foot, he had a chance that some out of shape, donut-eating-caricature-of-cop had the task of chasing him down.

Bright idea. Wrong cop.

As Avila hopped the first fence, his truck side-swiped two vehicles stopped at the intersection of Main and Pennsylvania.

Without any gear, save a vest and gun, I felt incredibly light as I pursued him. I never considered if he had a weapon. I lost Parra but I didn't care. Avila wasn't getting away. I kept pace with him over two fences, grabbing him as he tried to scale the third. It was a low budget chase, but all I'd be getting that day.

Cuffing him, I dragged Avila out of the backyard into the street. Parra was waiting for us in his truck. Pushing Avila into the backseat I jumped on top of him. No one saw us and we left without a ripple.

Marked units worked the crash scene like any other. They processed it like any typical auto accident where the driver takes off without leaving any information, a common event in California. The street units recovered the stolen truck as they normally would. The CNET crew returned to the hotel, hoping to find my stolen equipment. The room was clean. And so was the truck.

We had nothing.

Parra drove to the end of Lee Road. Ramshackle body shops dotted the road up to the stretch where it was submerged by the thick, muddy water of Elkhorn slough every winter. The prolonged road closures turned the area dull gray, dreary and desolate. Nobody went there. Nobody would hear you scream. If Avila took a ride to the end of Lee Road with sureño gangsters, his odds of returning alive would be well below one percent.

Are we gonna beat a confession out of this guy? Is this really gonna happen?

I didn't know what Parra had in mind and would never object to anything he did. He knew the ropes, what he could do and what he couldn't. He'd do what it took to solve this. Parra drove deeper into the thick brush like he knew the way.

"Hey, Parra, this ain't the PD."

Avila rocked back and forth, licking his lips as he scanned the area for a possible witness.

"Don't worry about it. Do something stupid . . . I'll shoot you," Parra snapped. I could smell fear on Avila.

"C'mon, Parra, you know . . . I'm cool. I'm gonna be straight with you. Be cool man. *Cálmate Parra . . . por favor . . . cálmate.*"

Parra said nothing.

I didn't want to make Avila feel better even though I wasn't sure what would happen next. I played the grim silent partner to a tee. I'd never met Avila, so no way he knew I was the son of a preacher-man. Unfamiliarity here in the back of a truck on a deserted dead-end road added just the right pinch of angst.

He should be worried. He didn't know what Parra was capable of, and I was capable of whatever Parra did by definition. I was in for a penny or a pound.

As Parra pulled the truck as far as he could into the thick brush and muddy Elkhorn mush, he said, "Here's the juice, Nando, you're gonna tell us everything . . . and I mean everything. If you don't, this will be your last worst really bad day."

Parra put the truck in park.

He pulled a pair of gloves from the glove compartment. A Mechanix glove, black, a white skeleton hand printed on, undoubtedly from the grim reaper collection. Inside the dimly lit compartment was a black .38 snub nose revolver. Not a display model. The paint lacked luster and the barrel all scuffed. Grips crudely wrapped with a dirty gray grip tape. Not our department-issued firearm. Not by a damn mile.

I've heard old vets joke about a throwdown gun—a backup gun cops had in case they had to plant one on people when something went sideways. Usually, something small tucked on your body somewhere. I wasn't sure if I was looking at one.

Parra slowly lingered as he put his gloves on. The glove compartment still open. The twelve-volt bulb spotlighting the snub nose. Avila didn't miss the presentation.

Parra said, "Good day or bad day, Nando. It's really up to you."

Avila glanced around the truck. No one around. Nobody would come to his rescue. He couldn't beg his way out of this one.

Avila spilled.

He'd been on a meth binge, breaking into cars for weeks. When he got to my van, he didn't know it was a cop's until he opened the toolbox and saw the police gear. Then he knew exactly how to move the police gear and get top prices.

Osvaldo Ramos hated cops and paid top dollar for any cop gear. He paid an extra premium for any cop's gun. He'd issued a bounty on cops in the area.

Parra knew the name. Aptly nicknamed "Grande," Osvaldo was the oldest brother of my high school chum Jeronimo

"Bugsy" Ramos and Mauricio "El Toro" Ramos. He was big even by American standards, at least half a foot taller than both his brothers, with a husky build.

An all-American family.

Grande was a scumbag, but he wasn't directly involved in Nuestra Familia business like his brothers.

Avila's story was no surprise. I'd had run-ins with Grande in my street-cop life. He was a great trophy, and taking him wouldn't interrupt the larger ONE investigation we had going.

Pulling slowly out of the gravel pathway, we crossed the city, driving through the Waters Alley so Avila could point out Grande's storage pad on the corner of Jefferson. Grande's home was a small box with an attached garage. The only access was through Waters Alley. Avila was shaking, slumped in the back seat trying to disappear inside his baggy hoodie. He hated being this close to Grande's house but didn't complain. He was jammed up and knew it.

"That's it . . . that's the house," he whispered.

"Which door leads inside?" Parra asked.

"The blue one." Avila perked up a little bit to get a clearer view. "Yeah, yeah . . . the blue one . . . for sures."

"Doggie, remember this for the legal: Brown shingle roof, white wooden walls, house number 115 next to the blue door facing the alley."

I never knew if Parra's tactic had been to scare Avila into a confession or if we'd have made him talk if it came to *that*. I didn't know how far we'd have gone, and I was glad I didn't find out.

Still, the vengeful part of me wanted to see how it went when it went too far.

Once Avila gave us eyes on the house, Parra drove straight to county. On arrival, we turned on our audio recorder to advise Avila of his right to remain silent and his right to legal representation. It was a nice touch. The Lee Road *field-trip* never made it in the report.

A narc's most important work never does.

CHAPTER
26

Search warrant service on Grande's house was fast and furious. He had two cameras pointed in opposite directions on Waters Alley. There wouldn't be any sneaking up on him.

We piled four-man teams in two vans. Grande's home was small enough that eight guys were tactically sufficient for the warrant. Entry points were limited to one door and a window, both facing the alley. This was good and bad. Grande had no place to escape that we knew of. No back door or window he could use to slip away. It also meant he had his back up against the wall literally and might initiate a ferocious firefight in a cramped space unfamiliar to us.

We lumbered out of the vans in full gear braced with M-4 assault rifles, a door ram, and a Tactical Halligan. We stacked up silently. I was first on the stack, so I'd be first in. I relished being No. 1 in the stack for the rest of my narc career. I wanted to be the first one through. If there was serious mayhem behind the door, I wanted the first crack. Nothing describes the rush you feel.

The man at the back of the stack squeezed the shoulder of the guy in front of him in a process coursed forwards to me. It was a universal signal that the person behind you is set. We were all set for go-time. The whole stack shuffled to the blue door at 115 Jefferson, ready to pound sand up the ass of anyone inside.

I fist-banged the blue door, shouting:

"POLICE. OPEN THE DOOR."

I heard a scuffling noise inside. No doubt now somebody heard us. They were moving. Maybe Grande was charging the door to greet us, but that was unlikely.

Our key guy, the monster of the group, slammed the ram through the blue door. Two padlocks and a security chain had no chance; the blue door splintered and flew open.

Parra and I were 1-2 in the stack and funneled into the empty garage. Though empty, tactically it had to be cleared. Within moments, the sound of scuffling erupted behind us. I wanted to turn and look but clearing the garage we'd committed to by entering it was essential. Any loss of focus could be fatal.

"Right side clear," I barked after checking behind an old couch.

"Left side clear," Parra replied.

In two minutes, we'd secured the residence.

In the living room, I found Grande cuffed face down on the grimy carpet. Hands behind his back with his shirt pulled over his face and head, Grande looked like a kidnap victim about to get popped. His chones were down to his knees.

"What the . . . ?" I blurted out a profane quip without thinking.

"He was in the bathroom pretending to take a dump," Ricky Royce said.

"I get that. But why the shirt . . . why is it over his head?"

Commander Royce was the undisputed leader of the unit and a twenty-year veteran. He'd spent the first decade at San Jose P.D. mostly in street crime units and then jumped over to California's DOJ. Royce had grown up in Lansing, Michigan playing hockey, giving him the advantage of having experienced and enjoyed aggravated assault and battery as an organized sport.

Standing over Grande he joked:

"That's my favorite old-school hockey move: the shirt over the head."

Photographing every inch of the house before searching, we made sure to photograph Grande the way Royce left him. Royce kept a copy for his personal collection.

The garage was full-to-bursting with swag. Grande was thoughtfully meticulous in separating and classifying stolen property before stashing it. One section of the garage had artwork, another tools and electronics. In the deepest darkest corner lay thirteen guns ranging from assault rifles to hunting rifles. The garage was like Walmart without *the greeter*.

In the fourth corner, tucked inside a toolbox, was *Grande's Queens*—the prized possessions of his stash. The box had a collection of law enforcement equipment and uniforms including a state parole jacket, a vest, handcuffs, a fireman's suit, and a pair of Danner boots.

Every piece of my equipment was in with the Toolbox Queens. My vest, cuffs, a pair of uniforms, gloves, helmet, and goggles were all neatly and thoughtfully stored together. Grande had an obvious love for all things law enforcement related. The collection contained his treasures. Lucky for me he had a thing for cop stuff. Otherwise, my equipment would have been dimed off for cheap within hours. Grande was never gonna move this stuff. Like Gollum in *The Lord of the Rings*:

It was his.

Two days after Avila broke into my car, we got my stuff back minus a new pair of sunglasses sacrificed to keep the gods of larceny happy. We had two guys in cuffs and solved a slew of burglaries in the process. Without informants' fingers on the pulse of the criminal network, the burglary of my van would have gone cold like almost every car burglary report.

CHAPTER

27

The battle between cops and Grande's family didn't end there. It escalated to a higher playing field when the FBI got involved. I'd known about Operation Northern Exposure (ONE) since my time as a crime analyst. In the interim, I'd gone through the academy, finished the FTO program, and patrolled Watsonville for eighteen months. The primary assignment for Parra and me was CNET, but we were also tasked to assist ONE whenever possible.

In three years, ONE hadn't moved an inch. That was by design. Some of it, anyway.

The primary target of the FBI Watsonville office was still El Toro Ramos.

The NF established a leadership structure that served not only as a trickle-down communication device but also as a trickle-up mechanism for collecting profits. The structure was designed to firewall NF top leadership from criminal cases. Green lighting, ordering a hit, had to be authorized by NF leadership inside the prison system. The order had to filter down to the Regiment Commander (RC), for execution by norteño foot soldiers.

Inversely, money collected by foot soldiers had to make its way up. Foot soldiers were expected to pay dues to the NF. The street commanders kept a percentage of the money collected as taxes, and they, in turn, moved the money to a location or account arranged by NF Generals who are the highest-ranking NF members.

The NF was the leadership body for norteño gang members. To be an actual NF member was extremely difficult and took years. You had to rise through the ranks by putting in work IE: Killing rival gang members and "earning" for the organization through robberies and drug sales. The more violent a young norteño gang member is, and the more money he earns, the faster he rises through the ranks. Street crimes are prerequisites to entering the NF graduate school.

NF members got made in a California Department of Corrections prison. The hope for the young norteño was to commit heinous crimes, gaining sufficient notoriety to hopefully get noticed after ending up in prison. Once there, with a big rep, he can earn his NF status.

Watsonville only had a little over 50,000 people, which is minimal by contrast to Bay Area cities like San Jose and San Francisco. But what Watsonville lacked in size, it made up for in loyal, hardcore gang members. Eight NF gang members considered Watsonville home. Depending on who you talk to, there were only between twenty-five and thirty actual NF gang members statewide at any given time. So in simplest terms, a third of the members of the Nuestra Familia came from Watsonville. The FBI had every reason to focus on the small agricultural town where the Pajaro River met the sea.

• • •

"We need a dirty call. Bottom line."

Doug had been a brick agent when I met him three years ago. Now he'd made supervisor for the FBI Watsonville field office.

The frustration in the room was palpable. For three years, FBI, investigators from CDC, Tony Reyes, and two WPD investigators had worked relentlessly on ONE.

The objective was simple: Get up on a T3.

Title III or T3 was short for the Federal Wiretap Act. We needed to get a wire in and listen to NF phone calls. We knew all the Watsonville NF members discussed criminal business by phone. We had hundreds of thousands of phone toll call records from targets. We could see calls made before shootings happened and right after. We could see phone calls made to high-level narcotics dealers. We could see the calls were made, but had no clue what was said. We needed a wire to get up on all the details that would allow prosecutors to indict NF members.

Getting up on a federal wire is especially arduous. The wiretap would only be granted if no other traditional law enforcement techniques worked. The last three years had been all about proving ONE had exhausted *all traditional investigative techniques.* It was a fancy legal phrase that meant:

We've tried everything and nothing works.

Surveillance was out. NF tradecraft and discipline was such that they could spot cops a mile off, and smell them from an even greater distance. Garbage rips were useless. Again NF tradecraft never permitted throwing anything with evidentiary value in the garbage. Members knew what had evidentiary value, and if they didn't they could be killed for their first oversight. Confidential buy-walks using informants were useless. Like traditional Mafia dons, NF leaders never handled narcotic transactions personally. Introducing undercover officers was out for two reasons. NF gang members never dealt with anyone they hadn't known since childhood. More to the point, an undercover officer discovered inside the NF would envy Kiki Camerena. Any undercover officer found would likely vanish without the slightest trace, but not before going through unspeakable pain and interrogation skillfully employed to find out as much about us as we knew about them.

"What about Casper? He still in play?" Reyes asked.

Reyes knew Martin "Casper" Zapatero was a Category I NF member. Casper was a made guy but on the lowest NF tier.

"Casper's in the wind, haven't heard from 'em in two weeks. I think he's on a meth binge . . . again," Doug said.

"We need him to make *the* call," Reyes said out loud what everyone was thinking.

"I know what we need Tony. You don't have to tell me," Doug snapped defensively. He was Casper's handler.

The room went painfully silent as everybody took a breath.

"I don't wanna start all over again," Reyes muttered, slumping in his chair.

Sitting around the big table in the FBI's office at our familiar weekly meeting, the team was losing heart. The investigation had dragged on for nearly four years, and *we had squat*. We'd amassed more than enough intelligence. We knew all the major players, the runners, the financiers for the organization, the women who made the money runs and bank deposits after collections, and the narcotic node quietly hiding in Visalia.

But we were missing *the* key ingredient to tip the balance that would allow us to get a wire: We needed a dirty call.

The dirty call had to be a dope order, a hit, or dope-money transfer. The easiest would be a narcotic buy. The informant called an NF member, ordered drugs, and we monitored the exchange. This would "dirty" the NF member's phone. That call would support the application for a wire on the dirty phone number. The trick was finding someone who could and would make a dirty call to a Nuestra Familia gang member and testify in open court about it.

Fresh suicide in a can, it was a very tall order.

Casper appeared to be a perfect candidate. An NF member who'd lost his taste for prison. Casper had a terrible meth habit. This was frowned upon by the NF but not fatal. Nuestra Familia members were the cream of the gang world, requiring their members to be unblemished. They ousted or killed norteño members who used heroin. Organizationally it made ruthless sense. Drug addiction was a vulnerability that could lead to betrayal. The NF were purveyors of narcotics but they despised addicts.

Of course, that was the story.

In fact, there were very few NF leaders on the streets, or in prison, that didn't use methamphetamine or other narcotics. It was too available, too potent, too effective, and too alluring.

Casper's addiction was next level. He smoked meth three to four times a day every day, a $60–$100 habit. The desperate make sudden ill-conceived, unsound decisions.

Casper was all that.

He dealt meth on the side to support his habit and skimmed from the NF money he collected. Skimming would get him green-lighted if the NF found out. With that kind of mud in his resume, Casper would inevitably fall from grace with the NF. He was hanging by a thread. We hoped he'd survive long enough to make *a* dirty phone call.

• • •

"Looks like Casper is gonna make it after all," Doug said.

"No way! Wait, I thought he got shot like, what, five times?" Reyes asked.

"At least five. He's lucky. I can't believe he's going to make it. I can't believe he's conscious."

"You paid 'em a visit?"

"Yeah. This morning."

All three of us were standing under an awning at the 76 Gas Station on Holohan Road. We should be having this meeting at some office with the rest of the task force but no one was eager to have *another* meeting about what went wrong *this time*.

"What'd he tell you?" I asked.

"He still had tubes coming out of his mouth. He's not talking. At least, not anytime soon. But he made his point. He gave me the finger as soon as I walked in."

"Are you sure it wasn't for the nurse?"

"Nice try. No, the last person he wants to see is me . . . or any of us. He's done, guys."

"I can take a crack at 'em," Reyes said.

"You can. Doesn't hurt. I won't be offended. But I don't

think it's gonna change his mind. He was barely on board and now that he's shot up, he's done."

Earlier that morning, Casper Zapatero was shot multiple times in the chest and left for dead on Highway 152 between Gilroy and Watsonville near the summit of Mount Madonna. Believing him dead, the gunmen left his body in the middle of the twisted two-lane asphalt road. The shooters did not attempt to hide anything. They'd left his body where it would be found quickly. They wanted Casper's death and the message it carried to spread muy rápido:

The NF handled business quickly cleanly no matter what.

No matter the rank. No one was safe.

But Casper survived.

A horrified motorist veered around Casper's bloody torso, narrowly missing him, and called 911. Meanwhile, his blood trickled to the ditch on the side of the road. When the ambulance finally arrived, Casper was half-gone, rallying long enough to give a Santa Clara County Sheriff's deputy a classic dying declaration:

"Pelogroso and Leon shot me. Pelogroso and Leon. Write it down. They shot me! *Por favor*, write it down so you don't forget."

With that, the ambulance whisked Casper off.

"I'm telling you, man, gangsters never die. I'd probably seen twenty of 'em shot. What, maybe two, MAYBE TWO? Died," Reyes said. "Goddamn roaches."

"I'm not even going to try to revive him as a source. It's just too much liability now. He's done. They obviously know what he'd been doing with us," Doug said.

"How'd they get him in the car?" I asked.

"I'm not sure but Casper's girl called me on the number he wasn't supposed to give to anyone," Doug said.

"Of course, she did. Did she know who you were?"

"I think she did. She asked: 'Is this FBI Doug?' How was I supposed to answer that? So, I asked her who it was. She said: 'Jenny, Casper's girl.' I didn't know what else to say. I couldn't admit I was FBI Doug. So, I just told her to tell me what she knew about Casper. It was one of those games kids play: 'You tell me what you know and I'll tell you what I know . . . . No, you tell me first . . . .' I thought it'd never end. She didn't know much, at least that's what she said. But she was home when Leon and Pelogroso stopped by earlier in the morning to pick him up. Something about getting the books in order in Gilroy. Maybe collecting money is my guess. She had a bad feeling all along, but Casper wouldn't listen to her and wasn't about to say no to those guys."

"She's probably in on the hit. She a hood rat. Rumor is she's hooking with Leon," Reyes said.

"I wouldn't put it past her. I warned him to not tell her anything . . . but he did. If she knew my name, she must've known everything else."

"She want to come in and talk?" I asked.

"I don't think so. After this, no one is going to ever want to talk to us."

Doug was right. Casper would never talk to us again. No secret meetings with the cops. His informant file officially tagged deactivated.

The Nuestra Familia got to him long before he could testify, and long before he could make a call. He never got close to being relocated and if he had, relocation wouldn't have helped. The FBI could make all the promises they wanted; unafraid of death or life in prison, the NF was infinitely better at keeping promises.

We were back to square one.

CHAPTER
28

After the *Casper Disaster*, Parra and I were split up.

They tasked him to work ONE exclusively, and I was detailed full-time to CNET. The one concession was I would assist Parra whenever he requested it.

Parra and the ONE group eventually got their dirty call, but not from Santa Cruz County. The FBI had task forces across Northern California, all racing to get up on a wire on the Nuestra Familia. The organization was a custom fit for a RICO (Racketeer Influenced and Corrupt Organizations) prosecution.

Under RICO, the leaders of the NF could be held liable for crimes they ordered or directed. The NF leadership sat atop a pyramid in their prison cells, collecting a massive fortune, while their subordinate NF street commanders relentlessly bludgeoned young, disenfranchised teenagers to carry out the NF's will. At the street level, the most insignificant infractions were punishable by death, while at the top level the leadership did whatever they wanted whenever they wanted.

When the wire went live, the floodgates opened, and investigators learned that Sacramento NF members got their marching orders from Salinas and Watsonville NF members. As soon as the Sacramento task force got a wire on one phone, they wrote another wire affidavit for another line, creating a daisy chain of wiretapped phones.

Before the first wire went up, task forces blindly grasped at leads and examined phone toll records without knowing the content. When the wires went live, voices became faces, whose words painted an ever-widening, detailed picture.

Operation Northern Exposure (ONE) rolled into Operation Valley Star, the Sacramento's task force's operational name. With multiple wire room monitors listening to the NF leadership 24/7, evidence for indictments piled-up like snow in a blizzard.

The cases were a snap to build.

A coded call for a five-pound methamphetamine order from an NF member was intercepted. The codes were never intended to be sophisticated and were almost too easy to crack. It would go something like:

> Voice 1: "Hey I'm going to need five *ventanas* down in Watson Friday."
> Voice 2: "Who picks it up?"
> Voice 1: "Same . . . Jimmy's primo."
> Voice 2: "Same place? The shop?"
> Voice 1: "Yeah, yeah. The shop."
> Voice 2: "Ya . . . okay. I'll send it with Li'l Spider."
> Voice 1: "*Orale' pues.*"

It didn't take Albert Einstein to figure out what *ventanas* were. Being the Spanish word for windows, glass windows are clear. When refined, high-grade meth looks like a pane of glass. Once crushed, they look like broken glass or shards. The only real question was whether five ventanas was five ounces or five pounds or maybe even five kilos of meth.

Prematurely taking people down created a massive risk to the whole operation. If people got busted, the NF could figure out that we were up on a wire or something. It would be a total laugher if we seized a massive five-ounce meth delivery. Every seizure was a calculated risk that could reveal the wire. The juice had to be worth the squeeze.

Li'l Spider magically got stopped by a random CHP unit. The soon-to-be public relations rock star CHP officer diligently searched Spider's ride and seized five pounds of methamphetamine. It would be the most dope that an officer would ever see in his entire career. We, of course, were not mentioned anywhere because we were never there. A textbook wall stop.

Li'l Spider caught charges for possession and transportation of narcotics. He was just a spoke in the wheel in the overall scheme of things. The beauty of being up on a wire was that the dope seizure was only the beginning of the pain. Every human link of the transaction chain, every conspirator: the NF member who ordered the dope, the girlfriend collecting the money, the NF member in prison who got some of the money in his account, the runner, and the suppliers—would all eventually get roped-in for conspiracy.

Within a few months of the wire going up, over three dozen federal indictments were issued against NF members and associates throughout Northern California for conspiracy to distribute narcotics. The indictments covered NF members inside and outside the prison system. Those who weren't inside were going inside and those that were in were gonna stay much longer, maybe never get out.

Mostly, the conspirators in the chain were charged for the same crime, i.e.: conspiracy to distribute narcotics. If there was an order to kill, the conspirators were all charged with conspiracy to commit murder.

The wire was the sledgehammer law enforcement unleashed on the NF. Charges piled up so fast when they finally came down some members thought they'd died and gone to hell.

They were looking at *forever* inside.

CHAPTER
29

Operation Northern Exposure and Valley Star hammered a massive dent in the body of the NF. It put key people away for extremely long periods and segregated NF leadership in prison walls for decades.

The NF Santa Cruz County regiment, however, remained relatively untouched; its leadership burrowed deeply into Watsonville neighborhoods. Worst of all, Mauricio "El Toro" Ramos remained in power. While federal wiretaps sliced through key NF leaders like a scythe throughout Northern California, El Toro slipped the ever-expanding surveillance nets. El Toro was the guy who managed to be in the exact center of a huge explosion where science tells us nothing happens. Meanwhile, everything slightly off-center gets blasted to bits.

Throughout the wiretapping of the NF, Santa Cruz County norteño gangs steadily gained strength and numbers. In 2005, Watsonville's person crimes hit a peak. Shootings and stabbings occurred almost daily. In statistical fact, they happened every other day, day after day. The extreme violence held the small city under siege.

Gang membership was lucrative, romantic, and generally attractive for many young people, and the youth ministry wasn't immune to the effects. The ministry continued to grow and students dedicated their lives to a walk with Christ. Meanwhile, some were walking a parallel track with the norteños.

Although understaffed, we compensated with dedication. We had an afterschool homework program. We took students on multiday backpacking adventures, stressing independence, resilience and self-reliance. All the activities, coupled with a discipleship program for those who wanted to take their walk with God to a different level, resulted in monumental spiritual growth among students. For many, this change carried through adulthood.

Despite the growth, I noticed some weekly familiar faces fading away. Joaquin and Santiago Quintero started going MIA at weekly services. During his first three years in youth ministry, I couldn't keep Joaquin away. He was a fixture at every event like the furniture. During the first few months of 2005, Joaquin attended every youth service. By year's end, he'd vanished.

• • •

WPD's pre-booking facility is an L-shaped room. The walls were painted a warm beige color to mask the cold, thick concrete walls. The facility could have doubled as a bunker or meat locker. A board with height marks for the mugshots covered one end of the longer wall. Opposite the board was a counter and a camera connected to a computer. Three five-foot steel benches were bolted flush to the side walls. Above the benches galvanized pipe cuff bars were bolted into the cement walls. At the other end of the room a small toilet nestled against the wall without doors or partitions, not unlike a prison cell. If you had to go, you had to go, but you were on full display.

Incredibly the booking room crapper was hands-down the most popular toilet in the building. Cops used it despite having to share it with arrestees because it was maintained regularly. If somebody "blew-up" the booking room crapper, the mess would be on full display and thus got remedied *tout de suite*. But most importantly, this humble little toilet was just outside of the actual police station and accessible from the parking lot. One could slip in, stealth crap, and depart incognito without entering the police station proper.

Any officer, walking into the station, during regular business hours, dramatically increased his/her chances of receiving an unsolicited and unwanted distasteful assignment. Administrative staff prowled the facility like rabid wolves, eager to pass off undesirable rotten work. Going into the office to hit the head meant you'd likely walk out with an even crappier neighborhood outreach project invented by some jumped-up captain. Better to poop in shame with the prisoners than end up waist deep in administrative filth.

I avoided the office like a scorching case of herpes. If I didn't go near it, I figured it couldn't get me. Out of sight, out of mind was Parra's mantra, but I liked mine better. On one occasion, nature obliged me to take desperate measures. We'd been on the surveillance from hell that lasted hours with no money shot and skipping the bathroom simply was not an option at this point.

A lot of narcs take great pride in their ability to pee in a bottle, a can, or your shoe while on surveillance, but I'd never mastered the art. I'd sprinkled freeway shoulders, country roads, brush, rose bushes, dead lawns, the space between parked cars, bridges, decks and docks . . . just about everywhere. But I couldn't pee in a bottle and let it ride shotgun next to me for hours. I don't care if it had a cork or a screw cap. It wasn't happening.

Warily I rolled into the station parking lot and beelined straight for the stealth stinker. My teeth were floating as I entered the booking room.

"What's up, Dan?"

Joaquin's voice startled me.

"Joaquin . . . ahhh . . . shoot. How you been?"

"You know. Okay, I guess. Like . . . I'm here . . . had better days."

"What're you in for?"

Eye contact with the arresting officer who I didn't recognize produced no reaction. A rookie. A seasoned officer would have clued-in on my question and slid the booking sheet over the counter for me to see. The rookie banged away on the computer and ignored me. A miracle occurred at that moment: I felt myself getting mad and I no longer had to piss.

"Guess I violated my probation."

"Didn't know you were on probation. How long you been on?"

"For, like a year now," Joaquin muttered.

He stared at the cement floor, shoulders slumped. I knew he was embarrassed and hadn't wanted me to see him in booking hands cuffed up behind his back, bolted to the wall post.

"Are you cuffed to the wall?"

"Yeah, I am. But it's . . . I'm cool . . . it's all good."

"You're a juvenile, Joaquin, you're not supposed to be cuffed to the wall. Is there some reason he's cuffed to the wall?"

When I turned to the young officer behind the counter my face said it all.

"No . . . I don't know . . . sir," the rook said.

I'd finally gotten the rookie's attention. Still, he didn't move to deal with the problem. He'd frozen.

"Alright . . . okay . . . I'm gonna take your cuffs off the wall and move them to the front, so you're a little more comfortable," I said.

As I scrambled for a cuff key the rookie turned into a lampshade.

"It's okay. Dan, like, I'm totally good."

"Bro, you're a juvenile. You shouldn't be cuffed this way. It's against policy."

Now I was yelling, hoping the sound might shatter the rookie's catatonic state, but he didn't react. His eyes glazed over as he tried to solve the ancient recondite mysteries of the booking process for juveniles.

Once un-cuffed, I instantly realized why Joaquin was dead-set against me touching his cuffs. Across the four knuckles of his right hand were the letters "NSSC." Now I knew why I hadn't seen him at youth service for months. He couldn't hide the tatts. NSSC stood for North Side Santa Cruz, the largest norteño gang north of Watsonville.

The city of Santa Cruz and the areas just outside its city limits were mostly controlled by sureños—the infantry branch of Southern California's Mexican Mafia, and the arch-nemesis of norteños. Because NSSC was severely outnumbered by sureños, they relentlessly tried to expand their control into the sureño-infested territories through violence. They needed violence to succeed, and to compensate for a lack of numbers they employed firepower.

I felt betrayed, angry and deeply disappointed. All the time Hope and I invested in Joaquin, the prayers, youth nights, camps, and the mission trips—all of it, wasted.

I couldn't catch myself in time to hide my reaction. Joaquin knew what I thought and expected it. Having NSSC tattooed anywhere on his body meant he was an active, functioning norteño gang member. Anyone falsely wearing these tatts (a poser) could be beaten or killed. Sooner or later, he'd have to put in work, if he hadn't already.

Joaquin was a natural leader and would rise to the top of any activity he chose. In the ministry, he could have been a pastor. If he worked at a brick-and-mortar store, he would eventually become an owner. He was driven. He'd pursue the top slot in any organization and had chosen one of the most violent chapters of the norteños. Joaquin pledged his life to NSSC. I knew he'd work to be one of the most violent and prolific gang members.

My anger and disappointment melted. Now I was worried. The half-life of prolific violent gangsters was not promising. The odds said he'd be locked up or dead in a matter of years.

"Joaquin . . . ." I exhaled audibly, not knowing what to say. I fiddled with the cuffs, glad for the clanking sound breaking the grim silence.

"I know, man, I know . . . it's . . . ."

He shook his head from side to side and stared at the floor.

It was a conversation two soldiers could have had across no man's land or two fast-friends saying possibly permanent goodbyes at an airport. Nothing left to say.

Our relationship was violently altered at that moment. The kid who spent countless nights at our home was no longer welcome there. As a norteño soldado, he'd taken up arms for the opposing side in a deadly ongoing battle.

I had one thing left. Prayer has great power in my life, but it required intense faith in the unforeseen and unforeseeable. I had to give the whole thing over to God. There in the booking room with my bladder at DEFCON 9.7 on the seismometer, the stealth toilet still unused, I wasn't sure what God would do. So I prayed:

God help him.

"You gotta be careful, I mean . . . out there. No one's gonna look out for you. You gotta be smart. You gotta . . . none of the guys will be there for you. Not really. They get the green light for you, you're gone and your homies will do you. They'll laugh while they do it."

"I know, Dan . . . I know."

"You need anything, you can count on me. Always. Maybe I'll see you in church . . . soon . . . I hope."

He stared at the floor and said nothing, quickly brushing his eyes with the backs of his cuffed hands. I walked out of the booking room, leaving behind a kid I loved and a stealth toilet I never used. His future was violently uncertain at best. At worst he was dead or locked up forever in the fullness of time.

I never saw Joaquin in church again.

CHAPTER
30

"It easy, bro, if the last name ends with an I-A-N or a Y-A-N, they're Armenian."

Day one at CNET for Tony Petrossian meant his first order of business was to inform me that he was, first and foremost, Armenian. Petrossian was the first of two new agents from the sheriff's office. We'd been waiting for him and Jake Peters to add as two new full-time narcs to boost our unit.

"Cool, bro. I didn't ask. But that's good . . . real good . . . I mean your nationality and all. Congratulations?"

I was messing with him. I'd seen him around a couple of times but always thought he was Mexican. I silently congratulated myself for not volunteering that, especially since I had no clue where Armenia was.

"I know, but like everyone thinks I'm Mexican and I'm not."

"Don't know much about Armenians, but good to know . . . ."

"You're Filipino, right?"

"Yup, born and raised there."

"You wouldn't want to be called Korean, Chinese, or Japanese, would ya? Because like . . . you're not. Right? Same thing."

Anyone else probably would have pissed me off. But Petrossian's brash intro felt rehearsed, like an ice-breaker he'd used dozens of times. Underneath it, he seemed lighthearted and genuinely glad to meet me. He'd asked around and knew my background. Anyone who puts that much effort into your first meeting had a good sense. I immediately liked the guy.

"I hate being called a chino, so you're absolutely right. I won't call you Mexican." I promised.

"Bro, I got tons . . . tons . . . of Filipino friends."

"Oh? So you know all the Filipino cuss words, right?"

"Yeah yeah, of course. Hell yeah. But I love the food more. Pansit, lumpia . . . man, they're all so good!"

"K, good to know. I'll bring some for you some time. But just so you know, bro, I got no clue about Armenia, not even where it is, dude."

I was completely unprepared for this conversation. Tony's done his homework and I hadn't.

"One way to remember: Mount Ararat is in Armenia. That's where—"

"Noah's Ark? It's on that mountain!"

Starting to hit on all cylinders, I proudly interrupted him with the one piece of trivia I had in my kit.

"Yeah . . . there you go, bro. I heard you were religious. So are we Armenians."

"Good to know."

I was out of intellectual ammo and could only hope Petrossian couldn't hear me start to mentally dry-fire.

"You just gotta remember, we celebrate Christmas on January sixth, not December twenty-fifth. Using the Julian calendar, it's the most traditional date for the birth of Jesus. Russian and Greek Orthodox do it that way too."

Like that, I became intrigued with the Armenian church. Church history was one of my favorite classes. I remembered that early Christians celebrated the birth of Christ in January before the Romans conveniently and forcefully merged it with the winter solstice.

"Nice. Nice. What's Armenian food like? I've never had it."

Petrossian smiled. "Meat and vodka, bro. All you need to know. Meat and vodka, dude. And all you can hold."

Five minutes after we met, I knew Petrossian and I were bros.

• • •

There are square cops and there are cops. The squares know the law and are competent and professional in enforcing it. Their reports read like a manual. They're the classic recruiting poster professionals. The ones you want to represent your city on camera or in the papers. If my mom needed a police officer, I wanted a square to respond. They'd do an amazing job documenting her statements in detail, making the appropriate notifications, and following protocols. All nice and neat.

The other cops become cops to do one thing: to find the worst elements in the underworld and snuff them out. In some shops, they're known as hunters. In reality, the line between excellent hunters and the criminals they hunt can be razor-thin. They are made of similar cloth, woven for diametrically opposite purposes. Hunters despise street crimes and violent criminals, especially those whose prey consists of the weak, the meek, and the innocent.

Hunters are society's wolves. They guard civilization instead of feeding on it. Unsupervised they can become death squads of incredibly corrupt gangsters with badges as what happened with the Jaguar Unit in Mexico City and Rio de Janeiro's 7th Military Police Battalion. Carefully managed and rotated off the line systematically, hunters are the backbone of effective stable law enforcement all over the world. Their efforts are never heralded in ceremonies or in the media. Parra was a hunter. I wanted to be one.

Then there was Petrossian.

It didn't take me long to learn that the Armenian mob was a very potent but discreet force, especially in Southern California. They were old school criminals who'd been in the game back in Armenia for centuries.

Armenian crews specialized in extortion, murder-for-hire, racketeering, drugs, gambling and prostitution. If it was a crime and it was lucrative, they had a piece of it. But unlike the flashy John Gotti types who wanted to be a face and talk about crime, they did crime . . . lived and breathed it for generations.

Petrossian often alluded to cousins and friends mobbed-up in Armenian organized crime. I never knew the extent and didn't want to. In the final analysis, I didn't give a damn if he was by-the-book loyal to law enforcement. I knew he'd be loyal to me when it counted.

That was enough.

It was everything.

Most movies and TV shows get it wrong because they want to. Unit loyalty and integrity far outweigh patriotism, truth, justice and the American way . . . whatever that is. The truth is battleships slide beneath the waves, their heavy guns blasting to the last moments, eighteen-year-olds charge machine guns and throw themselves on live grenades, sniper teams rope into hot zones and die shielding other army units. They die out of fierce, unbreakable loyalty to each other. Period. Later politicians and spin doctors dress it up and call it something else.

Petrossian wanted to cultivate informants. He had a couple of inherited CI(s) but he wanted his own, so he and I hit the streets. You could find street dealers all over the county, but the wire told us early on that major dealers ran their dope through Watsonville.

The big dope always came through Watsonville.

I'd graduated to driving Parra's old pewter unmarked GMC truck. He'd custom ordered it, with every amenity: leather seats, a roomy second row, four-wheel drive, and power everything. The only thing it lacked was a nice flip-down composting toilet so I'd never have to stop or go to the office again.

Petrossian and I rolled through the usual spots where drug deals transpired. Streets that touched the levee and the railroad tracks near the recycling centers were fan favorites. The plan was: (1) Find a street dealer, (2) Crack the dealer for possession with intent to sell, (3) Find the supplier, (4) Crack the supplier, (5) Climb the chain as far as possible.

Although we were hunting, it was just a day to hang out and maybe find something good. I said, "I gotta grab a Monster real quick. I'm laggin'." I'd started feeling the afternoon lull.

"Perfect. I need a Red Bull. God they're so fine with vodka. We call it the *Armenian Rush Hour*. But it's gotta be later."

Petrossian laughed as we slow-rolled through the busy

five o'clock Watsonville cross-traffic to the 7-11 on Lake and Lincoln. As usual, the 7-11 lot was jammed. I rolled through the lot, waiting for a parking spot to open.

"Hey, bro, you see that?" Petrossian said.

"Whatcha got?"

"Those guys are about to do a hand-to-hand."

"Which one?"

"Between the blue truck and the white Honda. Done deal, done deal! The guy is walking away now."

"Alright, I see the guy. Gray shirt, red hat . . . right?"

"Yup, that's him."

"Okay, bro, who you wanna nail? The car or the guy walkin'?"

This decision was critical. Nail the buyer, and we are moving down the chain. Tag the seller and we're moving one step up the chain.

Petrossian was a great cop despite his youth. Great cops perceive huge amounts of information that is both nonverbal and difficult to articulate. Often labeled as instinct or gut feelings, it's a highly refined perception of subtle tells and details most people miss.

It's what separates good cops from great cops.

"The Walker." Petrossian had zero hesitation without seeing the actual hand-to-hand buy.

The Walker kept looking around, scanning his surroundings out of habit, a street-pro. By contrast, Car Guy was an obvious doper who'd just scored. Car Guy stared lovingly at his lap, unwrapping a bindle like a kid on Christmas morning. Aching all day for a fix, nothing could distract him.

The Walker paid close attention to every car driving by. On

the lookout for the three C's: competition, customers, or cops.

"Get closer, bro," Petrossian said.

Petrossian cracked his door as we closed on the Walker. The Walker had four dots on the corner of his right elbow. Even better. We were ten feet away. The Walker sensed our presence and shot us a look. We'd done everything we could to not look like cops but despite Petrossian's heavy beard, my scraggly nappy long hair, our buttoned-to-throat Pendletons—the Walker bolted.

The Walker's instincts were also honed-in.

Petrossian shot out of the truck like it was the starting block for the Olympic tryouts. Both men rounded the corner to Lincoln Street vanishing behind a grove of overgrown shrubs.

I jumped from the truck, then a dozen strides into a full sprint realized my keys were in the ignition. Attempting to stop dead, I slipped, fell on my ass, popped up, raced back to the truck, yanked the keys from the ignition, hit the lock button, and double-timed it northbound on Lincoln.

Petrossian and the Walker long since left Lincoln in their wake. They'd blasted into Waters Alley. When I got there, Petrossian had reached top speed, his Pendleton now unbuttoned, flapping like a cape, pumping his arms like a sprinter. I spotted the blurred image of the Glock in his right hand.

Petrossian and the Walker were evenly matched. Without bulky vests, radios, uniforms, and a fully-loaded utility belt we'd both catch him eventually. In our twenties, both of us like Malinois police dogs had never lost anyone in a foot chase.

The Walker rounded the corner turning right onto Jefferson and out of my sight, with Petrossian five seconds behind, and me, fifteen seconds behind Petrossian.

"Get on the ground. Get on the ground!"

They were screaming voices I didn't recognize.

I, too, rounded the corner, wielding my duty weapon in my right hand. When I finally broke the corner, I saw six uniformed WPD officers with their guns pointed at our suspect and Petrossian.

"Get on the ground . . . NOW."

A uniformed officer was pointing his gun directly at me. I instinctively ducked waiting for the bullet to buzz past.

"BLUE, BLUE, BLUE!" I yelled.

A uniformed officer lowered his weapon. We recognized each other.

"I'm a cop! I'm a cop!" Petrossian yelled.

He lowered the gun to his side away from his body. Short of dropping the gun, it was the best way to signal he wasn't gonna point it at anyone. He looked exactly like a young soldado gangster, richly tattooed arms, a standard-issue gangster buttoned-to-the-throat Pendleton, chasing another vato with a handgun. Having zero visible police identification, the uniformed cops kept their weapons on Petrossian until they'd proned him out fully face down on the pavement.

When the dust settled, we realized how lucky we'd been. A small team of uniformed officers was serving a warrant on Jefferson, on the same block and at the exact time we were chasing the Walker. We could have easily been killed. Nobody knew Petrossian, we didn't have radios, police identification, or any tell-tale marks on our bodies. We weren't following the officer safety protocols they teach in narc school. By definition we were reckless. But that's how Petrossian and I operated.

Our wild reckless street-rips energized both of us. Everything we did was a rush. The adrenaline high is incredibly addicting and eventually infected every aspect of our lives.

CHAPTER
31

Some narc officers love undercover work. They're excellent at it, literally letting the life absorb them. They play the thug-life part all day and sometimes into their days off. Other narcs avoid undercover work preferring to be the behind-the-scenes investigator setting up cases, arranging deals, and running complex surveillance on which all great narcotics work ultimately depends.

I wasn't a great undercover narc. I gravitated towards case agent work. My shelf-life at CNET was three to five years. The chance to work undercover would probably never come again, so whenever I was asked to go under, I jumped on it.

• • •

Driving the grandma mobile, (1999 white Dodge Caravan), north on Highway 101, I wore my go-to undercover couture:

A black hoodie and the baggiest jeans I could find in my closet that morning.

Is it Marsh or the exit one after that? I should know this!

I took a chance on Marsh Street with two plain cover cars following me, hence the added pressure to make the meet location without looking like an idiot.

Two vans were already embedded in the parking lot of the Century Park Theaters in the city of San Mateo. The first van had three guys designated as the *undercover rescue team*, all guys from my crew. If anything went sideways, I wanted CNET guys I knew rolling up to save me. Unspoken Rule #1: When your life is on the line, no one better to rescue you than guys who know you best.

The second van carried two FBI agents, operating the latest-super-amazing-out-of-this-world "awesome-ist" camera system the federal government could afford. The buy money and the prosecution ultimately belonged to the feds.

I'd met Townie through a mercenary informant from San Jose. Mercenary informants work solely for money. They are not working off massive prison time they'd otherwise face but instead offer their services to the highest bidder. They serviced local police, task forces, the feds, and even rival drug dealers.

For mercenary snitches, it was all about the money

Unspoken Rule #2: Never trust informants, especially mercenary informants. They'd do anybody for money and they made no bones about it. This also made them treacherous to control, because any leverage you had was only as good as their next cash offer. They didn't take Visa or Mastercard and had zero fear of a lengthy prison term for noncooperation.

Townie was a young up-and-coming drug dealer. A couple of two-ounce deals later and Townie told me he lived in Daly City and wanted to move our dope deals closer to home. I reached out to Aleti Hisatake, a narc from the San Mateo County drug task force. Aleti, in his forties, was a large Samoan even by Samoan standards. An intimidating figure, Aleti was soft-spoken and had been a narc for almost a decade. He knew the game. Legend had it that he'd been a star running back for the University of Hawaii, but I decided he was too big to question stuff like that.

Aleti agreed to be the case agent for Townie's developing case and pulled an FBI agent from his task force to work the case, bringing in more funding and better equipment.

Aleti peeled off and parked on a street curb while I eventually navigated the theater's huge parking lot. It was the perfect meet spot. Thursday nights meant the parking lot was peppered with just enough cars for all the narcs to blend in. But it wasn't too crowded and wouldn't be problematic if I needed rescue.

I rolled the grandma van into a spot where I could see Aleti's Dodge Durango from my rearview just as my phone started vibrating.

"It's me, Aleti."

"This spot good?" I asked.

"Fine for me but the FBI guys say they can't see you."

I wanted to tell Aleti some snarky joke about the FBI and blindness but decided against it. They'd paid for the party. Cracking jokes at their expense wasn't on the menu for the evening.

"I'm not sure where they're at, so you tell me where to go," I said.

"They say, move two parking spaces to your right."

The grandma van groaned and shuddered as we moved into position and shut off the ignition. I scanned FM stations trying to find an alternative rock. Townie loved hardcore gangster rap.

I didn't. I intended to listen to music I was familiar with and liked. Tuning the station to crap Townie liked was a tell. Tells got you shot. Tells got you shivved or your throat cut. If you were really lucky the only thing a tell did was blow up your undercover gig.

Undercover work is paradoxical. Great UC operators never pretend to be something they're not. If you're not into cars, then don't pretend you are. If you know zilch about guns, don't act like you do. Be what you are and what you know. A target may quiz you. The slightest hint that you aren't who say you are can get you killed. It doesn't matter what the subject is; better to say you don't know than pretend for a second that you do.

You gotta have a frame and stay in it. Your script has to be first nature, not second. You have to know it and breathe it. It's gotta be you. You've gotta be able to run your script forwards and backwards with total confidence. Hiccups trigger self-doubt, self-doubt reeks of a fake.

A Fake = A Cop.

Two minutes later, Townie rolled up behind me in a black Chrysler town car with brilliant chrome rims. Standard issue, look-at-me-I'm-Capone-in-training car.

Townie wasn't alone, a first I didn't like.

"He's here. There's a passenger. Hispanic male, twenties . . . can't see him. He's slouching real low," I said.

I hoped my crew could hear me on the wire.

Townie got out and jumped into the passenger seat, just like he had half a dozen times before.

"What's up with you?" Townie's favorite greeting.

"Nothin'. What's up with you?"

"Same ol'."

Townie pulled a meth pipe from his jacket. He'd asked me to smoke meth before but I'd used my stock excuse about my tight schedule:

I gotta be back in Santa Cruz pronto to close out some more business.

This time Townie destroyed that excuse. He said, "We got a few minutes before the dope gets here."

He held the flame to the bulbous end of the pipe and a thick white vapor bled off as he inhaled.

"You serious bro? Now? I got twenty-one thousand right here? 21K! And you're gonna smoke meth? Is-we-is or is-we-ain't? This gonna happen or no?"

I'd given clues to the hungry fish on the other end of the wire. I was sending the surveillance folks a huge half-dead salmon. The clue sheet should read: Dope is not there. A delivery person may show up bringing a grand total of three bad guys to the party. And now, Townie is making me smoke meth.

Taking the paper grocery bag of cash from in between the seats, I tossed it on Townie's lap. I said, "Here . . . it's all there, count it. I'm not lyin'."

"If you ain't hittin' the pipe with me, I'm gonna start thinking you's a cop,"

The meet was going to the place all narcs fear.

"Bro, I don't give two shits what you think. I'm not gettin' violated for you. I'm months from being off probation . . . know what that means? Do you? They can roust me whenever for whatever . . . pretty much. I get pulled over? They piss test me? I piss dirty . . . then what? I'm done, is what. The crew I sling with doesn't like to use guys with sheets for transport-buys. I had to bust my ass to move up into this spot. I ain't about to ruin that. Truth, bro . . . I ain't goin' there. Not for nobody. We doing this or what?"

"You know you need me, right? You gotta make nice," Townie said.

"Look man, I'm here for business. I've got money. Hell, you've got it, right there . . . you've seen it. I'm all about makin' money, not friends. No offense. You don't trust me? Don't do business with me. You wanna make money? Let's go . . . make this happen."

It felt like I was shoveling sand against a rising tide. Putting it all on him was a Hail-Mary move. Either it would work or I'd crash and burn.

The dope game runs on leverage and I needed Townie to think I had tons of it. The truth was Townie was connected way up the line. I could talk the big game pretty well, but I was a kid struggling to stay in my frame. Townie was the real deal, a true well-connected dealer.

In the months I'd bought from him, he'd delivered decent weights of cocaine, all of which looked chipped off a brick. Today's deal was two full bricks: two kilos of cocaine, our biggest to date. Feds would charge on two kilos. It was a buy-walk. The money would be paid, and Townie and his passenger would walk with the $21,000.

Townie sank into the seat letting the meth hit.

I waited, knowing I'd made it to the part of the conversation where the next guy to speak loses . . . .

Townie snapped to and began counting the money out loud as part of his obligatory display of due diligence. No respectable drug dealer trusted anyone else's count. Townie played the part but no way he could accurately count twenty-one grand stacked in bundles of five thousand, all in hundreds, and wrapped in rubber bands. I'd never shorted Townie and he knew he could trust my count. The rest was for show.

"K . . . the count is good. Alright. I'll be back," he said.

Townie slipped out of the van.

"Money stays here."

Unspoken Rule # Whatever: Never, ever, let the money walk.

Townie shot me a disappointed look but left the lunch bag on the passenger seat. I was doing my due diligence.

Walking to his car, Townie popped the trunk and walked back to the van a few seconds later with a two-kilo-looking bulge wrapped in a shirt. Opening the door he laid the shirt on the seat, unwrapping it to reveal two full bricks of coke with a red scorpion symbol on the wrapping.

"We good?" he asked.

"Sure are."

I reached over, covered the bricks with the shirt, and moved the bundle to the floorboards of the granny van, where I'd stashed the money.

Reaching across the seat I shook Townie's hand.

"Good doing business with you, bro," I said.

"Alright homie. K. Til next time."

His handshake was weak.

Despite the built-in tension in our dope deals, Townie and I liked working together. We were both prompt and kept our word, qualities hard to find in the dope game.

I almost felt bad for Townie. You could stick a fork in him

now cuz he was done. He was bought and paid for. The weight he'd sold me and his prior felony conviction would buy him a decade in federal prison.

Unless.

A block away from the freeway on-ramp to southbound Highway 101, I noticed the wigwags of the patrol car behind me. I punched in a call to Aleti but he was busy running the ongoing surveillance of Townie and his passenger.

Thankfully, Petrossian answered.

"I'm gonna get pulled over. Un-flippin'-believable," I said driving past the on-ramp.

"By a marked unit?"

"Yeah. Send someone over. We'll be on Marsh. I think it's Marsh. Same exit I took, just the other side of 101."

"Alright, bro. Stay cool. We on the way. I'll call boss-man."

The marked unit's siren chirped meaning the driver wants me pulled over now. I pulled to the roadside in the open. The takedown lights came on at max brightness: headlamps, spot-lights, and white lights from the light bar. I barely made out the silhouette of the female officer approaching on the passenger side.

I looked like the scumbag I was supposed to be, complete with two kilos of cocaine on the floorboard. I had a loaded hand-gun on my waistband and a spare magazine in my pants pocket. My only ID in my wallet was a fictitious driver's license under the name Joffrey Bautista. The female officer would have no way of knowing who I was or what I was doing.

The stop had "Accidental Death and Dismemberment" flash-ing in neon. My first words would set the stage.

Or set it off.

I spoke slowly and clearly through the passenger window.

"Just so you know, I'm a police officer and I'm working right now," I said.

For a second she was visibly startled.

"SAY THAT AGAIN."

She barked out the words in her strongest authoritative tone.

"I'm a police officer. I'm working undercover."

She stared hard at me for what seemed like a small eternity, struggling to process the words, then looked back at two sets of headlights approaching us from behind her patrol car. Another cop's nightmare: *Bad guys with backup,* a scenario that wasn't in the academy training manual. She was now being forced to crush-process a ton of conflicting information in her head on the fly, and get it right.

I gripped the steering wheel like my life depended on it.

Don't make any sudden moves. Scratch that. Don't move at all. Does she think I'm lying to buy time? Does she think she's gonna get whacked?

"The cars are with me . . . they're cops," I said in my best level voice.

"Keep your hands on the steering wheel." She unholstered her weapon, pointing it at the dirt.

"Okay."

I'd never considered moving my hands anywhere.

The young officer marched back to her vehicle, yelling at our guys in the other cars to stay put. I heard murmuring back and forth, but it was so bright I couldn't see details. Finally, I caught the silhouette of someone raising their right hand, waving what could have been a badge.

It was a long minute before the young officer got in her vehicle, snapped off the takedown lights, and peeled back onto the roadway roaring past me.

Petrossian appeared at my window.

"Sheeeeee-ittttttttt. We're clear. Let's go."

CHAPTER
32

Two weeks later I ordered five more kilos of cocaine from Townie. This time the meet was at his other favorite location. I perched in the surveillance van with two FBI guys, watching the parking lot of the shopping center off of University Avenue in East Palo Alto.

My phone started ringing as Townie rolled up in his Chrysler made-guy town car. I didn't answer, watching as three unmarked cars began casually stalking him, and disguising the takedown to the last second. It reminded me of sharks slowly closing the circle on a wounded seal in deep water.

With machine-like precision, the first unmarked blocked the front of Townie's car as the second blocked the rear. A van roared up stopping ten feet from Townie's door. In two seconds four heavily armed men popped out and had Townie at gunpoint.

He exited the Chrysler hands up, but without thinking lowered one hand to keep his saggin' jeans from hitting his ankles. The result was a volley of screams and multiple conflicting commands from the takedown team. Eventually, Townie dropped to his knees and ultimately on his stomach. He loved guns but wasn't the type to throw down on cops. Outgunned, overwhelmed, defeated, and dejected, he went down like a lamb.

Aleti quickly chatted him up giving Townie the ten cent tour: He was nailed, caught red-handed with five kilos of coke in his trunk. Then came the come-to-Jesus money-shot to determine whether Townie would flip and work for Aleti and the FBI. Townie was young and sounded soft, but he bowed up, refusing to cooperate and lawyered up on the spot. I was floored. We'd underestimated this guy.

Maybe.

We'd hedged our bet that Townie wouldn't flip by creating PLAN-B to turn up the gas in case Townie had a good sense of self-preservation. Stamped cocaine bricks with cartel marks are moved by Mexican nationals one degree away from the plethora of Mexican cartels. Perhaps Townie had a lot more horsepower under the hood than we thought. His refusal to flip triggered PLAN-B. A warrant entry team hit Townie's home in San Mateo tossing it from end to end.

"We got three more kilos of cocaine and three handguns. I'll call when I'm done." Aleti sounded excited on the phone.

As I turned on my right turn signal and merged southbound onto Highway 17 for Santa Cruz, I couldn't help feeling a twinge of remorse for the guy. One way or another, his old life was destroyed. His life going forwards would never be the same.

If not me, somebody would've done it to him. Maybe getting arrested will be a turning point in his life?

You tell yourself things to justify betrayal.

Sometimes it helps. Other times not so much.

CHAPTER

33

The Santa Cruz County Superior Court facility is an ugly building. The walls are made of huge, prefabbed slabs of dark gray concrete bolted and fitted together like a massive crossword puzzle-picture with pieces missing. There were no attempts to conceal mistakes. The courtrooms tend to be as cold as the justice dispensed inside.

I walked into Department 5 and dropped into a seat on the left side customarily occupied by cops and district attorneys. Depending on who you ask, this is where the good guys sit. The opinions that run counter to this notion come from surprising sources. Santa Cruz County is famous and infamous as one of the nuttiest counties in what is generally considered the nuttiest state in the union.

Department 5 had plenty of open seats hosting only the bailiff and the court clerks when I arrived. Gina, Joaquin's mom, was sitting on the (right) defense side of the courtroom. I'd met her several times when I'd pick up Joaquin for youth service. Always cordial, she'd never warmed up to me and I never took offense. She didn't like cops and I wasn't going to change that any time soon.

Joaquin sat at the defendant's table with his attorney, wearing the county issued fluorescent orange jail jumpsuit. Mr. Ever-Popular with the Young Ladies and His Norteño Homeboys was all alone now, awaiting sentencing that would change his life permanently. All his gangland fans apparently couldn't be with him that day because they were either at a piano recital or taking their handsome lessons. In his darkest hour, sitting at the bottom of his emotional barrel, Joaquin had his mom and a reluctant youth-pastor-turned-narc in his corner.

After a lengthy jury trial, Joaquin and another NSSC gang member were found guilty of gunning down an innocent man in Live Oak. The prosecution accused Joaquin and his co-defendant of driving around, hunting for rival gang members. The prosecutor averred that when they found a victim—who by all accounts did not have any gang affiliation, but by a tragic twist of fate happened to be wearing a blue shirt—Joaquin stopped the car and jumped out with a bat while his passenger pulled a gun and shot the victim three times.

After the victim collapsed, the passenger approached the victim and shot him in the head two more times for good measure while Joaquin acted as the lookout, making sure the shooting went off as planned.

The prosecution alleged that Joaquin hosted and prompted this killing as an initiation for the passenger. No doubt he did. He was a natural-born leader. In the youth ministry or the norteño gang world, Joaquin had followers.

Both defendants were seventeen years old at the time of the shooting, but both were tried as adults. Now they'd be sentenced accordingly.

The judge entered the courtroom and efficiently went through the procedural reading of the documents associated with the conviction. At the end of all the banter between the attorneys and the judge, Joaquin got fifteen years in state prison.

I expected a harsh sentence, but still I was stunned. Gina sobbed.

Joaquin turned towards me while the judge continued to dollop more legal cherries on the cake of his sentence in the form of additional instructions for the clerks. His eyes betrayed the panic and raw fear he felt.

"Do something," he whispered.

I shook my head slowly from side to side. He knew well enough nobody could do anything for him. It was impossible at that moment for Joaquin to see he'd been lucky to get fifteen years given his co-defendant got thirty-two. Telling him how lucky he was would have been like handing him a Band-Aid after he'd just been gut-shot with a 12 gauge.

But it was true.

Cuffed and shackled, Joaquin hung his head. Shuffling and looking back at me and his mom, he vanished into the tombs of the courthouse, a ward of the state for a term nearly as long as he'd been alive.

I've seen many people sentenced to decades in prison and felt nothing. I felt zero remorse for Joaquin. He'd helped kill an utterly innocent man for absolutely no reason whatsoever. Maybe he hadn't dropped the hammer but he was culpable. Some kind of justice had to be served, even if imperfect.

But I did wish everything had been different. I wished he'd never got into gang life. I wished I'd done more to intervene when I first saw those tattoos on his knuckles in the booking area. I wished I had dropped everything and just focused on him, visited him at home, and prayed more. All gone now, none of it mattered.

Not anymore.

The next time I'd see Joaquin, he'd either be grown to manhood or on the cooling board in the morgue of the state penitentiary. Straight up or straight down.

I prayed for his rehabilitation, whatever that word means. In reality, I knew better. Rehabilitation was highly unlikely, given the official purpose of imprisonment in California is punishment. Prisons are gladiatorial colleges that routinely grind boys into iron-hard master monster criminals.

Joaquin was just more meat for the grinder.

PART SEVEN

---

*The weapons I fight with are not
the weapons the world uses.*

2 Corinthians 10:4 (NIRV)

CHAPTER

34

On the second floor of a small two-bedroom apartment, bright afternoon light filtered through the curtains, filling the room with warm earth tones. It was unusually warm in Capitola and beads of sweat trickled down Verde's temples as he took a drag on an unfiltered Camel. The smoke danced lazily through beams of buffered sunlight. We sat opposite each other. Two poker players with no cards in sight.

A clash of the stoics.

I'd raised him. Verde had to call or fold. The heat of the sun scorched my left side but I couldn't move. This was the break-point in our conversation. The next guy who spoke or moved would lose. My roasting flesh would have to wait.

"This is your lucky day, bro, you know?"

"Ha! How you figure that?" Verde asked.

Verde was born in Mexico but he'd bounced in and out of the US since he was six. Although he spoke fluent English, he had a strong Latino accent and frequently slurred words together and rapidly spewed them out. Deciphering his fluent English was a challenge.

"Somebody else hit you? It'd be a done deal. You'd be done. In handcuffs. Leg shackles. Shuffling in that orange suit, on your way to *la pinta*. No deals. No negotiations. Your Miranda rights. Cuffed, stuffed, booked, and cooked."

"You can look at it that way, I guess. But then, maybe they send me back to Mexico and you'd never see me again. So you, maybe you got nothing."

"Or maybe I'll just have you frozen in state prison. Or get you federal time in South Dakota. Do you really want to spend ten years playing handball with a bunch of *pinche cholos* with your *cajones* frozen to the inside of your leg? I don't care if you win the Nobel Prize. You gonna get it right there in your cell cuz you're gonna do 85 percent of the federal time you catch bro."

"85 percent?"

"No joke. You know this. 85 percent of ten years. At least. Maybe twenty if I find the right prosecutor."

"And you say it's my lucky day?"

Verde's tone dripped defeat.

The cigarette teetered on his lower lip. He'd given up puffing.

We both knew he was playing a losing hand. The only decision remaining was *how* he'd fold.

•　•　•

Verde's picture complete with the hokey blue DMV background hung in my cubicle for eight months. He was a phantom dope dealer, fast, smart, ghostlike. No one had touched him. At twenty-six, Verde was over his skates and in every sense a worthy opponent. His moniker within my unit came from his striking bright-green eyes contrasted with his fair skin. Interesting people often have nicknames and this guy was interesting almost no matter how you looked at him.

I'd first seen Verde through a grainy monochrome monitor in a surveillance van packed with high tech goodies. The white van had a periscope. It had been loaned to us by the High-Intensity Drug Trafficking Association, dubbed HIDTA. A federally funded agency provided support services to narcotic teams working in High-Intensity Drug Trafficking Areas. The HIDTA techs sent us cool, state-of-the-art equipment right out of a James Bond movie, and analysts to help local, state, and federal agencies in the drug war. The van was one of thirty surveillance vehicles stashed in an unmarked warehouse the size of a football field in a commercial district in South San Francisco. The Costco for all things narcotics.

I spotted Verde exiting a Chevy Silverado and walking into our target's house carrying a shoebox. A stupid thing to do really, who carries shoeboxes around ceremoniously? I always wondered why he didn't have a toolbox or maybe some kind of rolling kit box used by service technicians. With overalls and a name tag, he'd be virtually invisible to the neighbors and untrained eyes. Ten minutes later, he'd sauntered over to his car, and drove away leisurely.

Sans shoebox.

The team had posted up at Zero-Dark-Thirty that morning prepping and watching the house before serving a search warrant. Verde was a new face that wasn't on the menu. After hitting the house, we found Verde's shoebox with half a kilo of cocaine inside. The Target caught charges for the cocaine, and almost immediately fingered Verde as the supplier. He gave us just enough information to identify Verde by pulling his DMV records, but no more. No way would the Target even make a phone call to Verde, let alone do a controlled buy.

"The guy's in with the Sinaloa Cartel. Nah-nah . . . no thanks . . . uh-uh . . . I'll do the time. Thanks anyway . . . ."

The Target was immovable.

A case against Verde had to go on the back burner. After we grabbed his shoebox, Verde became my obsession. He had been arrested once before but this had made him more elusive and careful. He had no listed address, fixed or otherwise. No next of kin. His vehicles were registered to a post office mailbox under someone else's name. His phone number changed every few weeks, which meant he used burners. A seasoned pro that'd been burned once and was gonna be ten times harder to brace.

Then Verde got shot. His luck got worse and ours got better.

Walking back to his Chevy Silverado from the Quick Stop on Porter Drive in Pajaro, Verde was greeted by two young gang members probably from Salinas, since their car was stolen in Salinas. Jumping out of the car, the youngsters launched multiple rounds in his direction. Word was Verde owed money to a high-ranking NF member from Salinas and the NF were a lot better at skip tracing than we were.

Verde took two rounds in the shoulder and another to his right arm. The shiny Silverado was also wounded non-fatally, taking a stray bullet to the driver's door panel. The Monterey County Sheriff's Office towed the truck to retrieve the bullet. Both surgeries went well.

Petrossian and I creepy-crawled the truck at the tow yard,

betting Verde would want his brand-new shiny slightly-wounded Silverado back. Up under the engine block, we planted a vehicle tracker to encourage the ever-shy and reclusive Verde to invite us to his home.

• • •

"It is your lucky day, bro! Not everyone gets the chance you're gettin'. I know what you can give us. And here's the thing, lucky for you, I don't hate you. I can work with you . . . ."

I parsed my words carefully to avoid sounding overeager.

Verde calmly processed everything, keeping his head down. We'd just caught him dead-bang with three kilos of cocaine in his bedroom, not to mention the loaded Colt 1911 .38 Super with gold grips and scorpion inlays wedged under his mattress. How many firearms does a convicted felon get to possess?

That number would be right around zero.

No sense sugarcoating it. Verde would have to snitch. He'd have to betray his lifelong friends in the ultimate act of self-preservation. Nothing noble about it, his freedom or someone else's, but somebody was goin' and he got to choose who.

He adjusted the cigarette from his teeth back to his lips and took a deep long puff as if more nicotine might clear his mind.

There were no easy answers.

Behind Door #1 and Door #2 Verde had his choice of prisons. One featured bad food, a room with no view, nervous showers, fences and guards. The other prison, inside his mind, would surround him with guilt, fear, and isolation for the rest of his life.

CHAPTER
35

It took a while. But eventually Verde wised up, agreed to flip and work for me. He would make the phone calls and do the controlled buys that the Target one level below him had refused to make. I realized working with Verde meant we'd need lots of cash. This guy didn't move plastic baggies of dope. I wasn't sure what his upper limit in kilos was. But it would cost serious F.U. money. F.U. money was the kind of cash my task force didn't have and couldn't get. For a job like this we needed "Uncle." Reaching out to the feds, I got Harris.

Harris wasn't your typical FBI field agent. The tall African American loved working cases in the field. He wanted to interview sources, build cases himself, and take out entire criminal enterprises. Verde thought he'd died and gone to heaven. He was barely able to contain his excitement when he first met Harris. He was enthralled by all things FBI: the logo, the dinky badges, and all the lore associated with the Bureau.

"You guys don't get how it works."

Verde was visibly jazzed as he spoke.

"Tell me, then huh? How's it work."

Harris didn't have to pretend to be interested.

"It's not just one guy. There's many sources. I call a guy if I need something. That guy doesn't have it right away but he calls someone else. It's not like old school, the old days. No one guy, one place. Not a . . . si, not a supply chain. It's lots of people. It's like . . . like . . . ."

"A network?" Harris asked.

"Bingo! Si. Si. A network . . . hahaha, yes, good word . . . network. We got us a network."

"So how do we get into this network? Like who's in it? How do we get inside this? Follow them?"

"All you need is to be with me. I'll take you. *No tengas miedo* . . . don't worry. You won't regret your decision . . . working with me."

Verde sounded like a car dealer who'd just clinched a sale.

I couldn't tell if we'd just bought a vintage Ferrari or a 3-cylinder diesel Yugo.

• • •

Harris and I parked strategically to cover both sides of the Mountain Valley Shopping Center in Salinas. The shopping center tucked away on the corner of Williams and Bardin, hosts about half a dozen Hispanic retail shops ranging from restaurants, cell phone stores, and laundromats. Good cash businesses mostly.

I parked my granny-van two rows away from a McDonald's. Harris's intimidating size would make him stick out, so I had him cover the Bardin Street exit, away from the target location.

244 / WEAPONS OF OUR WARFARE

Mi Lindo Nayarit looked like any other unassuming Mexican restaurant tucked in the corner of a shopping center. Known for their seafood, Verde assured us that Mi Lindo served the best *siete mares* (seafood stew). And addition to the great *siete mares*, Mi Lindo was also a hub for high-level drug dealers, like Verde.

"Give me time to eat . . . maybe get a cerveza or two. I promise you, I'll get you a *mejor* connect within an hour."

Our operation wasn't official, which meant we'd foregone having an operation plan and a supervisor overseeing our activity. Verde wasn't wired, because we were sending him to meet and greet, not buy. Verde's only rescue team was me and Harris. If things went FUBAR, there was a real chance we'd never get there in time. On the other hand, the risk was relatively low and everyone knew it.

Verde sauntered to Mi Lindo in his classic cocky style. Before entering, he paused, turned my direction, shot us a big smile, and saluted. He'd wanted me to know he'd spotted me a mile off. I felt angry and nauseous instantly.

"Arrogant prick . . . ." I mumbled to no one. "Guy's brash. Overconfidence like that'll get him killed."

Even as I said it, I realized I liked working with Verde.

"Okay . . . he's in. He walked in the restaurant," I announced officially on the encrypted hand-pack radio I got from Harris.

"Copy." Harris's voice cracked over the encrypted channel.

"You see that? The *pinche cabrón* gave me a little salute just before he walked in. He's gonna get killed."

"Hope not . . . not today . . . not while we're here." Harris chuckled.

Verde texted me:

"In boss. 10-4?"

"K."

Thirty minutes later he texted:

"3 guys. Clean-head. Blk shirt. Follow them. $$$"

"Harris, just got a text from friendly. There's three guys to look for. One with shaved head and a black shirt. Don't know who they are but he's all excited."

"Copy."

I used binoculars to peek into the restaurant but it was useless with the reflection on the windows. The video camera was zoomed in directly on the door of the restaurant. We couldn't miss anything that came out.

Three men walked out of Mi Lindo a couple of minutes after Verde's text. They stood in front of the store, pausing a few seconds to scan the area, almost like they were posing for a surveillance photo shot from a long lens.

All three were Hispanic males in their thirties and clean cut. They were not typical thugs. They could easily have been salesmen selling prepaid phones. There had to be a reason why Verde alerted us to these three guys.

After the brief money-shot, all three got into a late model red Jeep Cherokee. The jeep was plain, unassuming, all stock, with absolutely nothing noteworthy about it. No mafia staff cars for these guys.

Squinting through my binos I called out:

"Okay, Harris. The plate number is 9DDKP75 . . . red Jeep Cherokee. They're all gettin' in."

"Copy," Harris replied.

A few moments, his radio squelched again.

"You wanna follow 'em?"

"I do but we don't . . . nah, I don't think so. We don't have enough units. Gotta be done right or they'll get onto us. Let 'em go," I said.

Two unmarked units trying to discreetly follow an innocent person would be tough. Tailing savvy criminals with anything less than four cars would be nearly impossible and downright stupid. We'd get made.

"We got the plate. That's a start," I said.

The Cherokee drove out of the parking lot, vanishing quickly from sight.

Another half an hour and Verde walked out, looked in my direction, flashed a big smile, and shot me a thumbs-up.

"That's gonna get him killed!" I mumbled involuntarily.

Again.

We met Verde three blocks away, behind a grocery store for a quickie-de-brief.

"Did you get it, did you get it?" Verde could hardly contain himself.

"Yeah, yeah. We got the plate. What's up with those guys?" Harris asked.

"Oh, man. Oh, man. You guys are sooooooo lucky! Who-de-man? Am I good or what?"

Verde's enthusiasm was contagious at least for me. Harris wasn't as entertained.

"C'mon, bro, what's up with those guys?"

Harris's tone was demanding.

"Okay, okay. Lookie here . . . ." Verde went serious motioning us to huddle around him like the QB at the homecoming game. We ignored him. Verde sighed, realizing we were unwilling to enjoy the moment. Realizing we weren't going to budge, he continued.

"Those three guys are major—I mean, major—players. The guy with a shaved head is a *Boss of Bosses*. You know what I mean?"

Harris and I nodded like we knew exactly what Verde was talking about but I knew he, I, and "we" didn't know anything.

"That guy makes his phone calls to Mexico. *Directamente* bro. He moves major weight or nada, nothing less. You need ten keys? Boom. He'll have it for you in an hour! *Sabes que?* Know what I mean? Them two other guys work for him. They run around, collecting the money, and put in whatever work he needs them to do. You just saw the biggest movers in Northern California."

"So can you buy from them? Do you have their numbers?" Harris asked, struggling to get at the bottom line.

Verde laughed explosively right in Harris's face, catching me off-guard because I had no idea why. Harris instantly started giggling as though he understood. Despite all the merriment, I was positive for the second time in less than a minute Harris was just as lost.

"You don't order from them guys like that. You think them guys take orders? Like takeout enchiladas? Or deliveries in their little *carritos*? This ain't pizza they're sellin'. They don't make no deliveries, bro. Man, you got tons to learn. These guys? They're pros!"

Harris quit laughing as quickly as he started. Verde's tone was grating on him. Maybe it was Verde's high-speed slurred language, but the sarcasm wore thin in a nanosecond and Harris was about to snap his neck.

Verde, sensing something, toned it down.

"Okay, so here's what I mean. Those guys? The Big Boss for sure? They are clean, man. Them guys never get their hands dirty. NEVER."

"What'd you mean c-l-e-a-n?"

Harris's blood was still visibly up.

"They're *limpio . . . todo . . .* clean. They only handle money. They never EVER have dope on them, in their house, or their cars, *nunca.* They're untouchable. They never risk getting arrested. They got people that put in all that work for them. Their people handle *todo el negotio.* You know? All the business. They don't touch nothing. Some of them guys way up? They never even talk on the phone, bro. Not any phone. Not ever. They don't talk with more than one dude at a time cuz they don't want nobody hearing what they say, and they don't want nobody listening to what they're bein' told. These dudes are TIGHT."

"This Boss of Bosses? What's his name?" I asked.

"I don't know his name. I don't know anybody who does. Everybody calls him El Pulpo . . . You know what that is? *Sabes que es un Pulpo?* The Octopus . . . the fish with all them arms?"

"Why . . . what's the . . . why the name?"

Harris leaned in, clearly intrigued now.

"They call him that since he was young for two reasons. *En el negotio . . .* in the business? He reaches out everywhere at the same time many ways and directions. *En la lucha,* in a fight? Once he get ahold of you? You ain't leavin' till he's done."

I noticed I was leaning in to listen. He was right; we should have huddled.

"You guys gotta do homework! These guys? *Estan grandes* . . . you know, *grandes*? These are big ones . . . major players."

"Got it, bro."

He had me and Harris on the edge of our seats and we weren't even sitting.

"I tol' you. I tol' you . . . isss your lucky day. Yeah, man! I gonna make you guys famous."

It didn't feel like Verde was playing us. He'd bragged incessantly about his mad skills as a high-stakes poker player. That always seemed hard to believe given he appeared to wear his emotions on his sleeve every second. Then again, maybe his frame and his game were diabolically good, which meant Harris and I were getting royally played by a guy who used displayed emotion like an invisible cloak.

I wasn't sure of anything.

CHAPTER
36

All criminal investigators need to deconflict. They need a sure-fire way to make sure that nobody else is investigating the same people or watching the same house. For a narc, deconfliction is a sacrament. Illegal narcotics networks span county, state and even international boundaries. Large wide-ranging investigations are bound to collide. Movies and TV are filled with colorful tales of undercover narcs unknowingly buying drugs from other undercover narcs posing as dealers. These conflicts have the potential to become deadly if they go wrong.

Deconfliction centers are also a way various agencies stake their claim to targets of an investigation. The public isn't generally aware that cops, especially hard-charging ones, jealously guard and fight over cases like birds of prey over their kill. Street cops even go so far as to not update their activity by radio or computer terminal when they're on something they don't want other cops to get in on right away. It's part of the move aside and let the big dogs eat mentality.

The first real police to post a target with the deconfliction center typically have investigative priority. Not unlike lenders who secure their loans against real estate by recording the liens at the county recorder's office so everybody else knows who's in the first position. The first lender to record their lien normally gets the first bite of any sale proceeds. For narcotics investigators it's the official way of telling other narcs:

Back off, we're first. This is ours.

Calling the Northern California Deconfliction Center and giving them the plate of El Pulpo's red Jeep Cherokee got a bite from a narcotic investigator from the Los Angeles County Sheriff's Department within ten minutes. The investigator had an informant inside a boutique Pasadena auto shop that specialized in installing sophisticated hidden compartments. Every time the informant installed a hidden compartment, he tipped the LASD investigator and gave him the plate. The investigator then called the Deconfliction Center and dumped the license plate info in the database.

It was diabolically brilliant. The investigator had no idea who owned or drove the vehicles. He didn't need to. He knew that the vehicles had hidden compartments. El Pulpo's red Cherokee had a very sophisticated hidden compartment installed at the Pasadena boutique auto shop. We knew it to an absolute certainty and we had an idea where it may land.

• • •

El Pulpo went from being *on our radar* to a bonafide investigative target as a result of that deconfliction check. Harris, Petrossian, and I, along with a couple of other guys from the unit, rotated waiting for the Cherokee. We didn't know when El

Pulpo or the red Cherokee would show up, so we waited in the parking lot just outside of Mi Lindo hoping by mere chance to get lucky. As careful as El Pulpo was, he committed the cardinal mistake many organized and cautious criminals make:

He had geographical public patterns and habits of criminal activity. We had no idea who he was, but we knew the car he'd used was modified for hiding things and we had every reason to believe he'd use the car again.

The second day staking out Mi Lindo, the red Cherokee pulled into the parking lot. Inside was the same crew, minus The Octopus. They parked several stalls away from Mi Lindo. Both were well dressed, one with a black North Face jacket, the other, a brown suede jacket. They walked confidently across the lot and into Mi Lindo like they owned the place. Perhaps they did and we hadn't traced that financial line.

We had a narrow shot, and a tiny slice of time and opportunity to slip a tracker onto the jeep. The moment the pair entered Mi Lindo, Petrossian rolled through the parking lot, stopping the van behind the Cherokee. Almost simultaneously, Harris drove down the same row parking his car behind the van, covering the sight gap between the van and the Cherokee. Harris hit the hazard lights to divert other vehicles around him. To passersby, he was just another motorist with some auto-related issue or maybe just waiting to pick someone up.

Harris's blocking move enabled me to quickly yank the side door of the van open unseen. Petrossian had skillfully positioned the van a mere foot from the Cherokee giving me just enough room to slip between the vehicles and dive under the jeep. Wearing a miner's headlamp, I found my favorite spot for the vehicle tracker and placed the black, anodized plastic GPS housing on top of the tire axle.

The powerful magnet audibly snapped against the steel. The magnetic lock on the tracker was so strong I had to work the tracker towards the middle of the axle because I couldn't easily pull it free to reposition it. Unless experts dismantled the Cherokee, no one would ever find the tracker, even if they searched.

I'd slipped out of the van, under the Cherokee, and back in the van in less than thirty seconds allowing Petrossian to drive off with Harris discreetly in tow.

We'd gotten deadly good at what we dubbed *quick-slap* operations. Daylight moves like the one we'd just pulled off in a public parking lot for a string of highly active businesses were high-risk at best. But it was either take the chance or lose the investigative lead. We had no other path forwards. We've done *quick-slaps* successfully a handful of times before, which gave us the confidence to go for it with a potentially high-level target like El Pulpo. All three of us relished high-stakes, dangerous moves.

I refreshed the tracking software on the laptop while Petrossian drove. The tracker signal strength was four bars out of five and the battery registered a full charge.

We were good to go.

Forty minutes later, both men walked out of Mi Lindo and headed straight to the Cherokee with no stops for a photo op. They exited the parking lot onto Williams Avenue. I clicked on refresh. The icon for the tracker blinked on Williams indicating that the Cherokee was moving. Ten seconds later, the icon blinked two blocks further down the street.

The tracker was golden.

We were partially up on El Pulpo, but lightyears from a wire or a solid case.

CHAPTER
37

The Cherokee was a busy sport utility vehicle. It started moving just before 1100 hours and for the rest of the day it stopped at little taquerias all over Santa Clara, San Mateo, and Monterey counties. At day's end, the plucky Cherokee went to bed in the garage of a two-story, single-family home on the east side of San Jose. The home was in a nice, neat neighborhood with an active neighborhood watch program, which made our surveillance tricky.

The pattern repeated nearly every day:

The Cherokee arrived at the house and went into the garage just before 2200. About three hours later, the lights inside the house turned off. Somebody was up 'til 0100 nearly every night. Not illegal but interesting. There were no other signs of activity. No one went in or out until the garage door opened every morning. Garbage runs didn't give us anything. The lack of actionable intelligence was uncanny, impressive and frustrating. I had hoped to see El Pulpo walk out and jump in the jeep, but he never did. We never saw him.

He might as well have been dead.

The Cherokee was predictable and busy. It conducted a three-hour road trip to Atwater like clockwork, and then stopped on Spruce Avenue without fail, every, single, time. The first road trip usually occurred on a Tuesday or Wednesday. The second trip of the week was *always* on Saturday. We had to get inside what was taking place on Spruce.

We formed up a full team on Saturday, which was normally our day off. As much as we loved our families, most of the team volunteered. Everybody wanted to know what the Cherokee did on Spruce and there were more than a few side bets. In addition to the tracker, we had eight mobile surveillance units and fixed-wing surveillance, courtesy of the CHP.

The garage door to the East San Jose home rolled up at 1140 hours. The *spotter* in the plane couldn't tell how many passengers there were. Within five minutes, the Cherokee headed southbound on Highway 101 towards Gilroy. It stopped at a gas station in Gilroy before heading east on Highway 152 to Atwater.

Three surveillance units drove well ahead of the Cherokee, which is one of the best ways to follow a vehicle provided you have one or more units behind or above the target. Nobody thinks cars ahead of them are monitoring them or following them. On arrival at Spruce, surveillance units were already embedded on the block. This was a bit dicey because no one knew exactly which house the Cherokee would land on and our team could've posted up directly in front. But the three units we embedded were top narcs. They could hide in plain sight no matter where the Cherokee parked.

The Cherokee's driver found an open spot on the curb parking on Spruce instead of a driveway. The guys were savvy. The actual house could not be deduced from where the Cherokee parked. It could have been anywhere on the street.

The aerial spotter reported the driver exit the Cherokee's driver side and got into the backseat.

"Driver out of my sight."

Street unit (Nora 14) cut in: "Don't know what he's doing in the backseat, but he's still there. He's moving around. Standby."

"Copy."

Nora 14: "Okay . . . driver is out. He's got a black backpack. Yup, like a Reebok backpack."

"Copy."

"Alright, he's got it slung over the shoulder . . . he's crossing the street . . . walking up a driveway of a house. Standby for numbers." Nora 14 paused. "Can't see the house number . . . . It's a white house, blue trim, fifth one east of the intersection."

Nora 14, with the best view of the action, took lead on the radio while the rest of us stood by. "He's at the door . . . looks like he's using keys. He just walked into the house."

I waited ten minutes before sending another surveillance unit to drive past the address. Nora 14 guided the roving unit to the house the driver entered.

It was 1138 Spruce Avenue.

Our *new* target.

•   •   •

Two weeks after Nora 14 cinched the address, Petrossian and I were back on 1138 Spruce. We weren't needed but wanted to see the warrant service go off. The Merced County Narcotics

Task Force sat poised to serve a warrant on the home as we watched.

With the help of our auto-tracker, with only eighteen hours of battery life remaining, the Merced Team knew the Cherokee was back on the street and following its usual pattern, thus triggering the pre-planned warrant service.

With a long telescopic lens, I snapped photos of the team as they made entry through the front door of 1138 Spruce. Petrossian played the role of an inattentive petulant teenager to perfection, scrolling through a blur of FM stations, and singing along with oldies from the 1960s. For a guy who was no-way old enough to experience the 60s first hand, he had an impressive familiarity with the music from that era and was using it to drive me nuts.

About ten minutes into the warrant service, two guys from the team walked out of the house carrying equipment back to their cars. The warrant service was over and we had to leave. No one could know we were involved in the case even though we'd created it. A connection to Santa Cruz County, in any way shape or form, whether by personnel or documents in the warrant, would silhouette Verde, suggesting him as the source. We were playing the Game at the level where cartel managers would not require complete proof. They would tie off any *suspected bleeders* the old fashioned way. Verde would either be killed gruesomely and publicly or vanish without a trace. His death was the ultimate insurance whether he was the source or not.

The Merced Team wrote the warrant for 1138 Spruce. They did their independent surveillance. They added calls-for-service records on the address and pulled criminal histories for everyone that had ever lived there. All of it was designed to paint the picture that *they*, the Merced Team, had been investigating the house for a long time and had acted upon the fruits of that investigation.

Concealed inside the sealed portion of the warrant were "The Dirties" on what really happened: Verde, the auto-tracker, the San Jose house, the hidden compartment in the Cherokee—all of it, courtesy of California's Evidence Code, would remain secret.

The Merced Team seized seven pounds of methamphetamine and almost a quarter-million dollars cash from the house. But there was no trace of El Pulpo, who hadn't been seen again since coming out of Mi Lindo. If not for the photo we took that day, one could easily believe The Octopus was a figment of our imagination.

CHAPTER
38

Six months after the Merced Team hit 1138 Spruce in Atwater, my entire team was deeply involved in working a wire. The target phone number was El Pulpo's personal cell phone. It had taken Verde a few weeks, but he eventually pulled off a face-to-face meet with El Pulpo at a massive quinceañera in San Jose. The Octopus never dealt directly with Verde; instead, he introduced Verde to one of his reliable dealers.

With the leg up, we bought quarter pounds of methamphetamine from the dealer. I wrote search warrants for the dealer's phones. The phone records were analyzed by the FBI courtesy of Harris. The analysis inevitably led to El Pulpo's phone and at long last, a name.

Ramon Dominguez, El Pulpo, was a *legit businessman* on paper. He owned three restaurants: two in San Mateo and one in San Jose. I ran his name in the Deconfliction Center and immediately got phone calls from a slew of agencies. After scheduling a meeting with all the agencies who had an open investigation on El Pulpo, it seemed like everyone who was anyone in federal or state law enforcement had at one point investigated him.

DEA, FBI, BN&E, and the county narcotics task forces from Santa Clara and San Mateo had all taken a crack at El Pulpo. None had an active informant inside his organization, so inevitably their investigations were stillborn.

Harris and I had Verde.

In the meeting, we all agreed we had sufficiently exhausted all traditional investigative means. The raw number of agencies who'd tried and failed tended to prove this fact irrefutably. This meant we could attempt to convince a judge we had to get up on a wire and would very likely succeed. So we hashed out a plan:

I'd continue to manage Verde. I'd also write the bulk of the probable cause recitations for the wire, and Chachi, a Bureau of Narcotics Enforcement (BN&E) field agent out of San Jose, would write the rest of the affidavit. Chachi, whose actual given name was incredibly difficult to pronounce, was hands down the most likable agent in BN&E. Always well-groomed, clean-cut, and dressed impeccably, the guy looked like a poster boy for GQ Magazine.

Chachi also had the thickest, most current case file on El Pulpo. No one understood The Octopus's sophisticated network better than Chachi, making him the perfect candidate to write the wire affidavit.

Within two months, the DEA's wire room in downtown San Jose was crackling with energy. The wire room occupied the entire fourth floor of an unassuming building at the corner of First and Santa Clara Streets. The room had no distinct features apart from the windows being completely blacked out. Ten computers were lined up flush to one wall. On the other side of the room was a large org-chart with El Pulpo on top.

The computer screens had sheets of printed paper taped over them, to remind the wire monitors: *to minimize at least thirty seconds during all privileged calls.*

In other words, if someone on the phone is talking to their priest, lawyer, or spouse, we had to minimize: stop listening for at least thirty seconds. After thirty seconds, the monitor could check back again to make sure the conversation hadn't switched to a criminal nature.

Our Santa Cruz team immediately volunteered to augment the street surveillance team. While the wire was up, a surveillance team had to be ready at all times. Being on a surveillance team was either feast or famine. You were either darting from one side of town to another just to catch a glimpse of a meeting or sitting in some dingy office bored as hell, waiting for something . . . anything to happen.

El Pulpo was different.

True to his name and his nature, The Octopus was constantly moving and reaching out to do multiple things seemingly at the same time. He had two kids and a beautiful young woman at home. He also had several girlfriends he visited regularly. El Pulpo was a workaholic. He held conventional business meetings by phone on the way to drop off his kid at soccer practice and directed his employees to transfer money well past midnight every night. His conventional business enterprises consistently generated income. Just trying to keep up with his legitimate business activity was exhausting.

Our resources were fraying around the edges as the wire surveillance case expanded. We'd started by listening to one phone line and a few weeks later, we were listening to three.

Despite everything we did, El Pulpo stayed legally clear of viable charges. Like the best classically disciplined criminals, he'd never discussed illegal business over *any* phone. If we were up on thirty wires, it wouldn't matter. The Octopus conducted meetings in person and worked out details face to face.

On the few occasions where we believed he was discussing illegal business, his language was so vague and coded that it was difficult for the wire monitors to decipher what he was really saying, and it would be next to impossible to get a jury to buy the decoded version even if we could put it together. It would take us months to decipher El Pulpo's coded language and we didn't have months. Despite all the agencies working the case, the financial power and the physical resources they brought to bear, our entire effort was still skipping harmlessly across the placid surface of what would appear to a reasonable jury to be a legitimate lake. We were stretched beyond capacity and couldn't prove anything directly against The Octopus.

As a result, we began legally burning down people working under El Pulpo, hoping that one or more might give us a long shot. They were all caught dirty handed: holding narcotics themselves or directly ordering someone to move dope. The organization was designed to firewall off the top people in this fashion. They were paid to take the heat, go to jail, and carry the weight.

The El Pulpos in the cartel generally skate. Our best case against him was weak and circumstantial at best. Despite enormous effort and resources being poured into the investigation, none of it was sufficient to convict him with a well-paid team of attorneys on his payroll and a jury admonished to only convict based on guilt beyond a reasonable doubt.

• • •

In the end, we got El Pulpo for marijuana cultivation. Considering the breadth and depth of the horrendous narcotics importation and distribution he was engaged in, it was a literal joke. El Pulpo had two large marijuana grows in Marin County and for some obscure reason, he was fond of his grows. He tended these grows, met with the managers on-site, and talked endlessly about harvests over the phone. Basically, he violated every security commandment he lived by in the more serious areas of his criminal enterprises. Perhaps he knew the exact degree of legal exposure he was facing—being almost nothing, and just decided to chance it.

Upon *conviction*, El Pulpo's attorneys worked out a sentencing deal calling for three years of probation and *no time served in jail*. Some of his cohorts got sentenced to significant time, but they were all quickly and seamlessly replaced. El Pulpo's enterprise didn't miss a beat. In exchange for a slap on the wrist, El Pulpo gained access to the affidavits and all the reports written during the investigation. Our names, mine, Chachi's, Petrossian's, were everywhere. He learned all about CNET's involvement, our surveillance of his home, businesses, our rendezvous in Salinas and Atwater—all of it now belonged to The Octopus.

The details of Verde's involvement were sealed, but it was a relatively simple matter for El Pulpo and his intelligence network to figure out who snitched.

We'd taken a shot at taking El Pulpo down and missed. Now he had the upper hand and would be ten times harder to catch in the future.

Verde was a dead man walking. His only chance was to go into the witness relocation program with the FBI. El Pulpo, his children, and his children's children would be avenged no matter the cost or the time.

Verde was a good as dead, so when he declined the FBI's offer of relocation, I had to be extremely calculated around him. I documented every conversation to make sure I protected our interest when something happened to Verde. Our conversations were never the same. There was an oppressive, deadly pall hanging over every interaction we had with him. Everybody knew why. Verde would never get old. He'd die a brutally violent death at the hands of people who would revel in his suffering.

The text message from Verde said: "Got 2 kilos"

This wasn't the plan. *It was supposed to just be a meet.* Carillo and I scrambled to try and get a marked unit to stop the target vehicle. Reggie Carillo was a California Highway Patrol officer. Although CHP officers can be great officers, city cops and sheriff's deputies typically don't consider them *real police*, and at times for a good reason. They are traffic wardens who often can't handle actual police work. But Carillo was hardly a typical CHP officer. He was a savvy cop by any measure who'd done more undercover assignments and narcotic cases than most of the narcs in our unit.

Verde sent the dope broker to Salinas, giving us just enough time to get a marked Highway Patrol unit to stop the Expedition on Davis Avenue in Salinas. The dope broker of course had no driver's license (which is a lively art in California) nor any insurance or valid registration. The Highway Patrol officer cited the broker and towed the vehicle per yet another handy provision of the California Vehicle Code. Meanwhile, the dope broker and Verde were left afoot and forced to walk away from the traffic stop. Two kilos of cocaine still tucked in the Expedition as the tow truck hauled it away.

• • •

"Eighteen grand would fix this. If this guy comes to my house again, I'll kill him myself! I don't care what happens! I'll kill him before he kills me. You . . . you guys ain't leavin' me no choice. You don't give me the money . . . I gotta do what I gotta do! These guys don't care what happened. They sayin' the two keys were on me. My problem. I gotta break into the tow yard and get it back or pay eighteen grand. Period."

Verde was ranting alright, but I could tell he was serious. He was incredibly pissed and I couldn't blame him.

"Bro, bro, relax. Bro, we'll figure this out. Nobody's gonna kill anybody."

I was desperate to cool his jets.

"Easy for you to say . . . yeah . . . cuz nobody visited your place. Right? You're good to go. You go home. You're safe. They don't know where you live. No problem. Nobody trying to collect money from you."

Verde didn't know I got a *social visit* two weeks before he did. I hadn't told him.

I never did.

• • •

Three young men in their twenties parked their white Honda directly across from my house in Capitola. I spotted the car the second I walked out the front door. Hondas are vehicles regularly utilized by gang members and one of the all-time favorite cars to steal in California. I'd pulled over more Hondas than I could easily count during my tenure as a street cop.

This isn't good. These guys aren't from here. They're sittin' posted up in their ride staring at me.

If I had any doubt about their intentions, the backseat passenger closest to me pointed his index finger at me and simulated firing a gun. My body acted instinctively before he could put his hand down.

My Sig came out of my waistband and partially into firing position. It was pure muscle memory. I couldn't have stopped myself if I tired.

How'd they find me? They know where I live . . . who I am. Who sent 'em?

Several names ran through my head in a blur, falling away as fast as they came to mind. The process of narrowing the possibilities down to Ramon Dominguez, El Pulpo, took less than a second. But standing in front of my home with my wife and child inside, seconds away from the prospect of a pitched gun battle with three designated shooters, was one of the longest seconds of my life. Every preemptive instinct in my body told me to send a hail of 9mm rounds into the Civic. But a moment of clarity prevented it.

I walked into the house and called dispatch.

"Three male subjects. White Honda Civic. Parked directly across the street from my house. One subject pointed their index finger at me simulating a gun. I don't recognize any of them. No actual weapons were seen. No words exchanged."

No actual crime was committed.

Despite my profession and my background, I was as vulnerable as any citizen in that moment. Capitola patrol units were at my house in minutes. The Civic stayed put, proving they were well-schooled. They knew no one could touch them. The trio of homeboys stayed in the car, taking turns glaring at the house, even after the marked units arrived.

Capitola city cops rousted the trio from the car, took photos of all three, and asked them what they were doing. They all denied doing anything wrong. None of them provided any plausible excuse for being on my street, in my neighborhood, across my house. But that was exactly the point. They didn't have to provide any reason and they knew it. Mr. Finger Shooter in the back seat didn't even deny simulating firing a gun.

"Just playin' around, man."

The guys weren't smart. Without a cheat-sheet, none of them could pass a urine test. But they knew how to follow detailed orders. Mr. Finger Shooter was carefully schooled as were the other two. They'd been told exactly what to do and how to do it by people who understood how California criminal law works and the limits they could go to with absolute impunity. The car had been swept clean of anything that could result in an arrest. The trio was carefully picked so no wants warrants, hold, probation or parole terms would come up.

They weren't hiding. They didn't run or try to leave even though they knew I'd call the local cops. They wanted me to know they'd come for me. They weren't afraid. Not of me, who I worked for, or the Capitola cops. It was lawfare at its very best, using California's codified criminal law to terrorize and intimidate.

Legally.

Failing to find or develop any reason to arrest any of them, the cops released all three. It was something that happened every day thousands of times a day to average citizens all over the state who turned to the police for help. They got nothing, nor did I. For weeks after the visit, guys from my unit took turns spending the night in cars, guarding my house. I didn't ask, they insisted. They knew it would make Hope feel safer, and it did.

The *visit* was another reminder of how and what cops care about in the end. Unit integrity is everything. Cops typically don't fight, die and sacrifice for God, country, or the American Way. Nor do they live to glorify their so-called superiors. Not a single administrative staff member from my department offered any help whatsoever. But the guys on my team stayed all night, night after night, on their own time to guard my home. We took care of each other . . . always . . . no matter what.

When it's nut-cutting time, the only thing cops can truly rely on is each other.

The guys sent to my house were trained and prepped to deliver a clear message: We'll get to you whenever we want. We know where you live and we'll find you no matter where you go.

The Octopus had reached out and gently tapped me on the shoulder to deliver a personal message.

Received and understood.

• • •

"I can't give you 18K. And let it just go? There's just no way that can happen."

The words tasted bitter coming out of my mouth but I had nowhere to go. Nobody up the chain in my shop would let us toss eighteen large at an informant for business losses.

Despite real ongoing threats to his life, Verde kept his word. He'd promised big cases and he delivered. Harris wouldn't work with Verde any more courtesy of the FBI's longstanding aversion to having sources shot out from underneath them, especially after they declined relocation. The FBI doesn't want dead sources on their watch. The FBI fears embarrassment at an institutional level perhaps more than any other law enforcement organization in America.

Verde didn't need to give us any more cases. If he ignored my phone calls, I would have never pursued him. He had paid up in full and more. But a funny thing happens when you work with someone as closely as I did with Verde. For almost a full year, his words formed the impetus for nearly everything I did and not just me.

A deep bond developed between us. We were on the same team . . . our team. Verde repeatedly risked his life for me, Carillo, and Petrossian, and I'd have done just about anything to keep him out of harm's way.

"They want the two kilos of cocaine or $18,000. And they want it by tomorrow."

Verde's tone was clear and level. This was life and death for somebody.

"But it's not your fault. The guy didn't have his license. It was his car. He screwed up . . . got pulled over."

Even as I said it, I knew the answer.

"They don't care, Dan. They don't give a shit. They want the money. That dope was mine when we left the dealership.

Man . . . they know where I live. They visited last night. These guys ain't playin'. *No mames*, they're all about the money. *De veras mijo.*"

I felt the desperation in his tone. Verde was scared. The usual carefree, I-can-beat-the-world bravado had vanished. It's one thing to wage war in the streets and a whole different game when your enemies come to your home. Your sense of security is shattered. Peace, as you've known it, is gone sometimes forever

"Wait—did they get the Expedition out of the tow yard?" I asked.

I felt a fiendish plot coalescing.

"Should still be there . . . they're sayin' for me to get the Expedition or the drugs from the car. They're layin' it all on me. It's my problem. You can't argue with 'em. They don't believe in coincidence. It's the money or the drugs. Or else get ready for the pain."

"Bro, I'd give you the money, if it were mine to give. But we can't. There's no way the higher-ups would let that kind of money just walk away."

Saying it again just made me feel worse.

The room went silent. Carillo and I wanted to help Verde put a scheme together to get him out from under.

"I got an idea. What if we got dope from property? Legally, I mean," Carillo said. Carillo's idea, especially the legal part, felt like fresh cool air blowing into the room. I had started to contemplate all things legal or illegal we might have to do, and I was glad we weren't there yet.

Carillo continued, "We put the dope in the Expedition. The broker picks it up . . . he gets jammed. Boom! We seize the dope.

Verde's not in the equation. It falls back on the broker. They jam him up for the loss and you're out. The blame shifts. You're clear. The broker goes down."

Carillo could be diabolical at times and this was one of them.

"Bro, it's brilliant. But no way we can get this approved. What if we lose the dope?"

I played devil's advocate hoping Carillo was even more diabolical than usual.

And he was.

"We'll put a tracker on the Expedition. We'll know where it is no matter what."

"Jesus I like it. But the boss, I don't know. The broker could move the dope the second he drives the car off of the lot . . . and it's gone."

"Wait! Wait a minute! What if we put a fake kilo inside? Not real cocaine . . . fake stuff?"

Verde eyes had gone so wild as he spoke, he looked rabid.

"What do you mean? Fake cocaine?"

I was playing catchup now given Verde had proven even more diabolical than Carillo.

"*No mames* . . . I can fake a brick of cocaine faster than you can say it . . . part of my craft. Oh, man. I can make a brick of cocaine, no problemo . . . and it'll look real. One hundred percent authentic . . . *puro* . . . believe me. I've done it many times. Stepped on bricks hard before and no one ever knew. That's how you make five grand into ten *mijo*."

Verde spoke with the old energetic spark absent for weeks.

Stepping on drugs diluted their purity but radically increased dealer profits. Bricks of cocaine cross the border from Mexico as close to one hundred percent pure as they can be, and then the coke gets stepped on. The cocaine is mixed, and diluted, with other substances that look like cocaine. The cutting agents range from baby laxatives to detergents. It's far from an exact science, but the best dope dealers can step on their dope without a noticeable loss of quality. They use high quality cutting agents such as caffeine to preserve the stimulant effect of cocaine, or anesthetics that have the numbing effect of opiates.

If Verde claimed to be an expert I had no reason to doubt him. He never lied about things like that.

"You sure it'll look good? They'll be able to tell, you know. They got ways to . . . ." Carillo said what I was thinking.

"I been doing this since I was twelve . . . twelve, man! I can do it in my sleep. You'd never be able to tell even with a chemical test. Don't worry man, I promise. It'll be good! The best! *PRIMERO!*"

Verde was back in true form.

"What about the kilo stamp?" I knew all the full bricks were stamped because it pays to advertise in more ways than one. The stamps were proprietary and custom made. "It's not something you'd pick up at the local stationary store or Office Depot."

"Man . . . you need to believe in me, Dan. I gots this. You wait. It'll be good. I'll work it up today. It'll be good to go tomorrow. Good as gold . . . better even."

Verde hopped into his truck reborn, rolled down the windows, and blasted narco-corridos as he roared away, waving and laughing.

We stood in the street watching until he disappeared.

CHAPTER

40

The broker met Verde two blocks from the tow yard and immediately took control of the operation. Verde had to go into the tow office alone. He owed the money, so he had to take the risk. If the tow yard called the cops, Verde would take the pinch.

Verde dutifully objected to the role he'd been assigned by the broker, playing it to perfection. We'd set it all up the night before. The broker had no clue Carillo and I had already met with the tow yard owner, scouted the Expedition, and planted the backpack inside. The tow yard owner seemed honest enough, readily agreeing to let Verde in as long as he didn't take anything else but the backpack. Interestingly, the owner didn't insist on knowing what was in the backpack. It wasn't his first rodeo either.

Entering the tow yard like a boss, Verde retrieved the backpack from the Expedition. We made sure it was the very same backpack that held two real kilos of cocaine days before. Now, it held two bricks of creatine powder, each weighing exactly a kilo, both with an authentic crown stamp. The bricks looked indistinguishable from the two bricks of real cocaine sitting in CNET's property cage.

We watched as Verde confidently strolled down the street and hand over the backpack to the broker. The broker immediately checked the backpack for the bricks. It went perfectly. He had no reason to doubt what his eyes told him. I'd seen the bricks firsthand and I couldn't have made them as fakes. No one I knew could tell the difference. Verde was every bit the artist he claimed to be.

The broker and Verde quickly shook hands and left in different directions. As fast as he'd fallen into the fire of suspicion, Verde was clear. He would take a hiatus for a few weeks in Arizona. With a small luggage rolly in his truck, Verde would be on Highway 5 headed south to the state border in minutes, the melodic voice of Chalino Sanchez blasted in his truck. He vanished happily as a pig in mud.

The broker had another day of really bad luck. A surveillance plane and a dozen surveillance vehicles were on him the moment he got the backpack. He couldn't have lost us if he'd tried. To make magic happen, we had to make sure: (1) we didn't lose actual sight of the faux cocaine bricks, and (2) we didn't pinch him immediately, as that would have given up the game and the illusion. It had to look like the hapless broker had yet again screwed himself in what was simply another really bad day due to his stupidity and carelessness.

As the broker got onto southbound Highway 101 headed to King City, our prayers were answered. As he was driving down the clear uncongested freeway, he must have felt a sense of relief, jubilation, and freedom as he took in the expansive views of the roadway and open countryside. The day was bright and clear, and both sides of the freeway were lined with farms to the horizon. In the distance, he had a lovely view of the Pinnacles to the east and the foothills of the Big Sur State Park on the west.

Surely the day was looking better by the minute.

As he enjoyed the pastoral beauty and solitude, he did what every motorist do on that stretch of Highway 101. He let his foot gradually depress the gas pedal, increasing the truck's speed past 70 to just this side of 80 mph. Of course he was far from alone—about ten miles south of Salinas, right on cue, a marked CHP unit dropped off an overpass and slipped in behind him. The officer carefully clocked the broker's speed for another mile before lighting him up. If the broker had tried to contest the speeding ticket, he'd have lost with God as his lawyer. Then again, he'd have much bigger things to worry about than the speeding ticket. For the second time in ten days, the broker was pulled over, this time for speeding. He still had no license, and thus his vehicle was towed . . . again, with two kilos of what his own eyes assured him was prime quality cartel cocaine.

Magic is in essence misdirection. With Verde, we'd become Masters of Misdirection, making our targets see, feel, and hear what we wanted. We forced them to look at what we wanted them to look at and rely upon the one thing they never doubted—their own eyes. We could make them believe whatever we desired as long as it met squarely with what their senses told them. We became the artists and Verde was the fine brush with which we painted masterpieces.

Upper-level cartel managers never accept coincidence as an explanation. They do believe the simplest answer that adequately and fully explains what happened is probably correct. To them, the simplest reason why the broker got pulled over twice was his monumental stupidity and carelessness. That was the explanation they would ultimately buy.

Cartel upper management also believes anything they don't understand should be avoided, killed, or destroyed. They favor the last two approaches. Avoidance only saves an incomprehensible thing to be faced later. Killing everything and anything they can't understand provides that critical stitch in time. Job done. Problem solved. Permanently.

Unfortunately for the broker, the same approach is true for anyone the cartel can't rely upon due to laziness, arrogance, stupidity, carelessness, or any other reason. Not long after his second bout of really rotten luck, the broker disappeared. We never saw or heard of him again. Some said he must have gone back to Mexico. The average person who hears that imagines the broker on a sunny beach in Cozumel drinking mojitos, dancing with warm beautiful Mexican women. Slow days and fast nights.

But going back to Mexico most likely meant the cartel peeled the skin off his chest from his neck to his navel, tossed it in his lap, and watched him die from shock and blood loss. Then they dumped his body in a shallow gravel depression in the desert and let the coyotes chew his face away. That's a more accurate translation of what probably happened.

You can hope he got a quick death.

But that's not likely.

PART EIGHT

O death, where is thy sting?
O grave, where is thy victory?

1 Corinthians 15:55 (KJV)

CHAPTER

41

I loved everything about being a narc. I loved the magic we made a little too much. I got addicted to triggering all-out havoc anonymously. I craved drug dealers fearing the mention of my name and the power I exercised in negotiating sentencing deals. I lived to blast Johnny Cash's "God's Gonna Cut You Down" as we drove down quiet streets with a dozen fellow narcs on the way to hit a house.

Like many cops who come to love the work, I couldn't imagine doing anything else. The intensity of our work is unrivaled as well as the adrenaline surge. Coming home on time was a luxury Hope and I learned to live without. The Chief had warned me that time years before in his office. I didn't care then and now I cared even less.

Off work, my days off were composed of scattered bits of normal life constantly interrupted by informants I had working around the clock. Phone calls and text messages from friends and families got returned later. Much later. They were never that critical.

When an informant called, I answered no matter the time. A phone call from an informant always meant something important just happened: a murder suspect was in town, a hit is about to go down, a shipment of dope just got delivered to a tire shop, the informant just spotted a cache of weapons in a storage unit. All my informants had simple clear instructions. They were to call me, day or night, whenever a high-value target presented itself. Informants didn't call to chat or describe how their day went at the office. It was all go-time.

All the time.

My waking and sleeping hours revolved around fighting crime. Every call, every operation, every suspect put behind bars, would save countless unknown victims' lives down to the road. People I'd never see or know. I was taking out the trash in the form of dope dealers who flooded neighborhoods with whatever vile stuff he peddled. I hunted down drive-by shooters, child molesters, strong-arm robbers, and every other kind of really serious criminal my informants lit up for us to nail. Often as not, we didn't actually nail them, rather patrol officers, the CHP, or other federal agencies took them off the chessboard. But we called the tune. Every breath I took went towards justifying the time and energy I dedicated to the Fight.

Everything else in my life took a distant back seat—especially my wife, family, friends outside of law enforcement, the youth ministry, and even my faith. The narc lifestyle is inevitably destined to ruin marriages and normal relationships.

The CNET office was the boy's treehouse for relationship ruptures. It had been that way for years before I joined the club. It was common to find someone sleeping on the couch who'd been booted from their home. Everyone on the team went through some relationship issues at one level or another. Most were serious issues and many were ultimately fatal to the relationships. The CNET couch was almost always occupied at night. The occupant wasn't working late or taking their handsome lessons. They had nowhere else to stay.

The youth ministry was my last stand. I'd seen lives transformed week after week. About eight years into youth ministry, Hope and I were seeing students we'd known since they were in middle school now enter college, and it was one of the very few exhilarating experiences left in my life outside of work. As the ministry thrived and grew, I slowly phased myself out. Constant 24/7 narc-related callouts meant I missed most services. Even when I was there, I wasn't fully present. I wasn't dedicated to the craft as I had been. I didn't attend leadership seminars and workshops, effectively rendering me insignificant in the lives of the congregation.

Hope was the de facto youth pastor. She maintained the love and passion for students as mine fell away. Every student in the ministry deserved a spiritual leader worthy of the calling. I didn't have it to give at home or anywhere else. My passion for the ministry was dwindling day by day.

In the summer of 2007, it died.

CHAPTER

42

Camelia Solorzano was probably the youth ministry's greatest success story. She came from an unchurched family riddled with drug abuse and random violence. She'd grown up in a disenfranchised neighborhood with all the odds stacked against her. She'd attended the youth ministry since middle school, joined the police cadet program for two years, and thrived in the program. She was the poster child for the youth ministry.

I'd spotted her at the department's annual formal inspection ceremony, where she proudly showed me her sergeant chevrons. Her eyes were bright and full of life as she shared her plans to attend San Jose State University, major in criminal justice, and become a police officer.

Camelia walked across the stage as she received a service award for all her volunteer work in the cadet program. Her light-blue uniform was immaculately pressed and her boots polished to a perfect shine. She was a student-leader in youth ministry and a sergeant in the cadet program. I couldn't have been prouder. Her life was full of promise.

• • •

As #1 in the stack through the front door of 445 Landis in Watsonville, the entry rule is: The first guy in is never wrong. He goes right, the next guy goes left. If #1 goes left, the next guy goes right. Always.

"Clear left."

As #1, I'd just cleared the couch on the left side of the living room.

"Clear right," another voice called out.

The rest of the stack surged down the long hallway like a slow-moving freight train giving me time to tap back in for entry into the next set of rooms.

As the first set of guys made entry into the first room to the right, I heard a loud commotion coming from the room.

"Lemme see your hands! Put 'em down, put the baby down!"

I recognized Briggs's voice.

It was Briggs's warrant we were helping serve. The house went silent before I heard a small pop followed by the sound of a Taser cycling. Then the muted scream I'd heard dozens of times before, followed (most likely) by loss of bladder or bowel control.

There were at least two cops in the room addressing the Taser issue, and whatever it was, they'd handled it. The remaining guys in the stack chugged down the hallway clearing the rest of the house. After every room was cleared, I went back to the Taser room out of curiosity. Cops do that a lot. They see some hilarious, interesting, and horrifying stuff as a result.

The room reeked of body odor, stale sex, rotten food, and

something akin to urine and feces but neither one. An infant lay crying on a bare mattress directly on a filthy bare wood floor. The commotion in the Taser-room kicked up a thick cloud of putrid dust, triggering my gag reflex.

"What happened?"

"Drifter. I Tasered his sorry ass."

Briggs proudly motioned for me to look at the shirtless Drifter laying on his side with the two Taser probes still embedded in his chest. Based on the proximity of the barbs, Briggs fired the Taser at point-blank range.

"You good?"

Normally calm and collected Briggs was in a quivering rage.

"Yeah. Can you believe he used his own kid as a shield? Who does that? What a piece of shit!"

The more Briggs talked, the more his blood got up. The glare he was giving Drifter told me he'd like to tear the norteño's head off and piss down his neck.

Abraham "Drifter" Cisneros was the complete scumbag. If you looked up the word in the dictionary, you'd find Abraham's picture. I hated the guy.

Despite being on opposite sides of an endless struggle, most criminals and cops had a mutual understanding and basic mutual regard. They did what they did. It was our job to catch them. If they were disciplined and difficult to catch, I respected that. Dedication to your craft is commendable even if your craft is the dark art of criminality.

Drifter was everything I despised. A sloppy, careless dope dealer, he got high on everything he sold—heroin, methamphet-amines, shrooms, random pills. He wasn't even a successful dope dealer, making just enough money to stay high on his supply, while he wrecked the lives of countless others with his products.

The moron was also a full-fledged Landis Street norteño, and a high-ranking one at that, his status undoubtedly the byproduct of being a Cisneros. His two cousins were bona fide NF hermanos, a position that carried terrifying weight and authority. Drifter could never make it in the NF but he didn't have to.

Drifter's loyalty to anything, including the Cause and all the NF stood for, was skin deep at best. Where most norteños considered it an honor to spend some time in prison, Drifter despised prison. I'd kept a letter from Drifter the last time he was busted for a parole violation, stating in writing that he'd work for me to avoid going back. The letter outlined all his ties with the Nuestra Familia, his familial connections with the shot callers in the organization, and his willingness to betray them all. That letter dropped on the floor in the right taqueria would have instantly resulted in his quick and cruel execution. Despite the apparent quality of the targets Drifter willingly offered up, I never worked with him. I just couldn't.

"Briggs, I got this," I said, stepping into the room.

It was clear that Briggs was looking for an excuse to physically mess Drifter up and make it look legit. All things considered, I wanted him to, and if he had, I would have covered Briggs in whatever use-of-force report needed writing.

As Briggs left the room, I reassessed what needed doing.

Job-1: Get the crying baby out.

No sooner had the idea of removing the baby crossed my mind, I noticed a female seated on the floor with a black hoodie sweatshirt pulled tightly over her head, and her hands cuffed behind her back. She had to be one of Drifter's several soon-to-be baby mommas.

"Hey, what's your name? Hey . . . look up . . . look at me . . . what's your name?"

As her face appeared from under the hoodie, it took a full three seconds to recognize Camelia. With her head up but her gaze averted, she was almost unrecognizable as the person I'd seen four months prior at the police inspection. Ten pounds lighter, her eyes were sunk deep in her skull. Her face was deathly pale and lifeless. Her pupils were completely blown out crowding the color of her light brown eyes. It reminded me of a doll's eyes made from shiny black buttons.

As my heart froze, the pit of my stomach turned and acrid bile entered my gorge.

I gotta get out of here . . . .

Camelia's life was crushed.

She would never recover. She could never be in law enforcement. Any dreams of going to college were a long shot at the very best. Not even a *sancha*, she'd most likely be Drifter's girlfriend for a minute until he found a younger, stupider stand-in. She'd run dope for him, get arrested for him, and probably bear him a couple of kids. Then he'd dump her and the kids.

I thought about how I could maybe shoot Drifter then and there. His baby, whom he'd just used as a shield in case we fired a shot, would be better off with the worst family in the foster system. A pack of wolves would have made better parents. A lone she-wolf would have been a better mother.

Any place outside of Drifter's orbit was heaven.

Drifter hadn't missed the moment. Living a few houses from

Camelia, he'd watched me pick up Camelia and the other kids from the neighborhood many times. He knew me almost as well as I knew him.

"How'd you like your favorite cadet now? Ehhh Pastor Danny? *Que linda no?* Maybe you wanna watch while *ella chupa mi . . . .*"

Before he could finish, I smashed his right cheek with my elbow. Pushing Drifter's contorted face into the wall, our faces inches apart, I whispered:

"You're fucking dead."

Petrossian always had a keen sense for when I needed help. Walking into the room, he instantly knew I had to get out. He clamped his fist on the fabric of my vest near my right shoulder and he pulled me out of the room.

"I got it."

Petrossian let go of my vest as soon as he bum-rushed me out of the room. I walked out of the house leaving Camelia and the baby where I'd seen them. I needed air, a change of scenery, a new brain, amnesia. I needed a vacation, an escape. A cigarette, a blindfold, and a small-caliber pistol sounded great.

Anything . . . .

I wanted to tell the team to avert their eyes while I dragged Camelia out of the house and took her somewhere safe to try to recover everything she's lost. But there was nowhere safe for her. Not anymore. And there was no recovering what she'd lost. No do-overs. Nothing would change. It was too late. Her death spiral had begun. Everyone knew the cycle: Camelia would commit every kind of small-time illegal act to support her habit. She'd steal mail, deal dope, have sex with random dealers and random johns, all for a single hit. Eventually, she'd slam into rock bottom and end up in a recovery program if she survived.

That was the best-case scenario.

But her old life had burned to the ground. It wasn't ever coming back. Ashes remained in place of what she could have been.

CHAPTER
43

Two weeks after the warrant raid, Petrossian and I drove down Landis. We had no business there, but it was a habit. We never drove near Landis without driving through it. The second we pulled in front of Drifter's house, we saw ten gangsters posted up on the driveway. Half were kids fifteen and under, ideal, perfect impressionable bodies for the meat grinder. Their minds primed to accept the BS gangs sell.

Two veteranos stood out in the group. One was Doughboy. I'd chased him a couple of times over the years and I liked him. He hated cops but maintained basic working respect. In his words:

"You caught me fair and square. That's on me! Mark my words, you'll never catch me again."

I loved the challenge. Doughboy was a worthy opponent.

Doughboy was a freshly minted NF member, a hermano, and one of the highest-ranking NF in Watsonville. His word was law in the streets superseding any other. He had direct-line comms with top NF leaders in prison.

Just the guy I was looking for.

We passed the house and made a U-turn at the end of Landis. As we pulled up to the house, all ten gangsters put on the hardest looks they could carry on. In the middle of the bubbling tussle was Drifter running his mouth at max volume. Sporting a white tank top tucked into tan Dickies, socks pulled up to his knees, and a red cloth belt, Drifter was modeling the perfect cholo ensemble.

"Bro, stop a second."

Petrossian pulled the unmarked to the side of the street blocking Drifter's driveway. Some cops never stopped on Landis without cavalry with them or at least in the wings ready to swoop. Several of the youngsters undoubtedly had cuetes tucked in their waistbands. It was one function of underage gangbangers. They carried the guns and if caught got virtually no serious jail time. We were in plain clothes, an unmarked car, no radios, with two compact 9mm pistols to our names. Undermanned and outgunned was our specialty.

I exited the car and nodded to Doughboy.

"What's up, bro? Can we talk a second? Alone?"

"What about? Whatever you gotta say to me, you say in front of my homies."

Doughboy was maintaining his frame per classic NF protocol. No way would anyone ever be able to say he had private words with la chota excluding his people.

"I don't know . . . man . . . *de veras?* I think maybe you're gonna want to hear this *solito.*"

Before I could finish, Drifter was running his mouth at Petrossian and me. He had to be the center of attention, show everyone who the badass was.

"Mira! Look at this *pinche cabron. El enano* . . . hey! Maybe little man's gonna preach to us?"

Drifter got chuckles all around. Even Doughboy smiled. It was a good one.

Petrossian and I both laughed. Me because I knew what I was about to do, and Petrossian because he saw me laughing and backed my play even though he was clueless.

It was the perfect green light. I turned my eyes to Doughboy, meeting his gaze.

"Homie, you're respected, so I thought you should know who you got in close to you."

"Say what you got to say, Bautista."

Doughboy still held frame with a hint of curiosity.

I took out Drifter's folded letter to me from a year ago where he'd begged to work as an informant to avoid prison on a parole violation. I glanced over at Drifter as I unfolded the letter. He knew what I had.

"So, bro, this . . . this here's a letter I got. It's from Drifter. Says here how he wants to work for me. How he's willing to snitch out anyone. How he can give me *los grandes*, you know, the big ones? Like Sinbad, Carlito, and wait . . . oh yeah, where is it? Yeah, here . . . Doughboy."

I pretended to scan the letter with my index finger struggling to find key lines like my memory had gone bad. I could recite the letter's contents word for word, forwards and backwards.

"Maybe, yeah, bro, you should probably come. Take a good look."

Doughboy reached out to grab the letter. I pulled it away.

"You can look, but you can't have it."

The entire group fell dead silent. Petrossian was playing

total catch-up. I hadn't told him my plan because I wasn't sure the opportunity would ever come up. As I held the letter so Doughboy could read it, his attention narrowed and focused like a laser. He scanned each page intently. When he reached the bottom of the page, I turned the letter over to reveal the pièce de résistance—Drifter's signature and Santa Cruz County Jail inmate number. Dead-bag proof the letter was genuine.

"Satisfied? You seen enough, bro?"

"Yeah . . . we're . . . I'm good."

Doughboy's face betrayed nothing. He stared directly into my eyes, as I folded the letter and tucked it away in my pocket.

"Sure I can't get a copy?"

"Can't do it, homie. Your word is gold though, eh? That's a fact. Nobody gonna question what you say you've seen."

"See ya around, Bautista."

"Later, bro."

I extended my hand and surprisingly Doughboy shook it. Drifter, standing ram-rod stiff on the driveway, looked like he'd swallowed an entire popsicle in one gulp.

Petrossian and I jumped in the car and roared out of the blighted neighborhood in twenty seconds.

"Bro, I can't believe you did that. Dude . . . that's a major party foul. That's . . . so nasty. So badass. I loved it!"

"Boy messed with the bull and got the horns," I muttered. "Turd's bought and paid for it a dozen times over."

Petrossian pulled a hard left merging southbound into bustling rush hour traffic.

. . .

On Friday afternoons North Green Valley Road traffic crawls. With one lane in each direction feeding several residential streets, traffic at the end of the day barely moves. That's how the three young shooters got up on Drifter. The tan Mitsubishi Galant easily blended into the plug of eastbound traffic. Drifter had just parked to pick up his kid from daycare at the intersection of Little Way Lane and Green Valley Road. As he exited the car, seven bullets from two different guns came buzzing his way. Three found their mark.

As is so often the case with gangsters, especially the most despicable ones, Drifter survived. A few days after he could breathe just fine as long as nobody unplugged him. Within a week he was wide awake and sitting up on his own.

But he'd spend the balance of his life sitting up. There was no more walking for Drifter. He was done with that. In his new electric wheelchair Drifter cruises around town at a blazing 3.7 mph with a tailwind. Drifting. Fully equipped for extended cruising, the wheelchair doubles as a rolling porta-potty where he can relieve himself into the colostomy bag taped to the stoma on his abdomen.

Por vida.

CHAPTER
44

Three years in CNET fully submerged me in the dark world of gangs and dope. Clandestine assignments can't be neat and tidy. It is probably the dirtiest work in law enforcement. J. Edgar Hoover deliberately kept the FBI away from narcotics work for decades because he feared it would corrupt and destroy the Bureau. But the work *has* to be done.

It's impossible to immerse yourself in such a corrosive atmosphere and not be changed by it. The gang and dope world brings you into intimate relentless contact with gangsters, dope dealers, and everyone they touch. You begin to think the way they do. You end up acting like them if nothing and no one intervenes to stop you. Watching Camelia and Joaquin utterly destroyed, I was eager to do anything to put bad guys away.

Anything.

Time in jail wasn't important to me anymore. I wanted vengeance, to mete out destruction. I wanted to make them suffer and see them suffer.

I was slipping.

I'd drifted far away from the mahogany beams of the chapel

at Bethany University. A chapel where I got married and where I attended morning worship services in between classes. The days of diving into Pauline literature, Hermeneutics, the Greek Bible dictionary, were gone.

I missed bright and hopeful days. As hard as I tried, I couldn't remember how it felt to not be angry and vengeful. Most of all, I missed the deep conviction that God had a plan for everyone's betterment, and I could be part of it, somehow.

• • •

Bird watchers flock to Moss Landing. It is one of the richest estuaries in the United States for wildlife of all kinds. It features dozens of trails that meander through woodlands, salt marsh, freshwater ponds, and upland grass. An amazing array of wildlife, especially birds, swarm over the terrain including herons, egrets, red-shouldered hawks, barn owls, ducks, geese, several species of quail, and swallows.

A bird watcher, hoping to film exotic wildlife at dawn, stumbled upon the Silverado parked to the right at the dead end of Via Tanques Road, surrounded by impenetrable lush uninhabited marsh.

Verde lay slumped against the truck's door frame, his head almost resting on his left shoulder. The left side of his face had a massive gaping exit wound. He'd been shot once to the right side of his head, execution-style. His ID, wallet, and $800 in cash were still in the Silverado. The bullet passed through Verde's head and lodged in the truck's frame. No shell casings were found indicating the shooter had professional cleaning skills or used a revolver. The coroner estimated that he was shot with a .38 caliber revolver or a 9mm pistol round.

There were no signs of a struggle. No mess. Verde didn't duck to avoid the shot or fight with his assassin. From all we could tell, he'd looked straight ahead and accepted his fate.

El Pulpo had reached out yet again. This time to have Verde killed.

I knew it.

The Monterey County Sheriff's Office detective who investigated Verde's shooting later told me they found a cell phone that belonged to a cop in the Silverado. The cop had reported it stolen days before the shooting.

Had a dirty cop killed Verde? Was the phone planted to implicate an innocent cop? Or was it all just a massive coincidence?

I had no idea. But like the cartel, I no longer believed in coincidence either.

I wanted to hammer El Pulpo more than ever, but that chapter was over. We took our shot when we went up on the wire and he walked. The balance had shifted in his favor.

In the dark narco-world, Verde was a bright light. I'd hoped to see him live out his days in the sun, happy and free. All of us, including Verde, knew that wasn't gonna happen. He was predestined to die a violent death the second he scribbled his name on the informant packet. His refusal to go into witness relocation cinched it.

A deep nauseous feeling came over me as I realized his murder would go unsolved, his death unavenged. Despite the life he'd lived, I find myself hoping we'll see each other again. I'm not sorry I feel that way. I hope we meet up again. He was my friend.

PART NINE

This is what the Lord says:
"Stand at the crossroads and look;
ask for the ancient paths,
ask where the good way is,
and walk in it, and you will
find rest for your souls."

Jeremiah 6:16 (NIV)

CHAPTER
45

A motivated confidential informant is a finely honed scalpel for use against a criminal enterprise. An informant who can take the stand to testify coolly, calmly, convincingly, and competently is an industrial-grade wrecking ball.

• • •

Carillo positioned the video camera on a tripod at the end of the conference table. I drew the blinds not so much to hide what we were doing from the other officers in the building, but to keep Pequeño from daydreaming while he looked out the window. I needed him to hang on to every word of our conversation.

As Pequeño's official debrief, this was his opportunity to tell us his life story in exquisitely bare-ass detail: crimes he committed, murderers he could implicate, drug dealers he could buy from, and every weapon he could lay his hands on.

"State your name and date of birth?"

"My name is Hernan Ochoa. My date of birth is November 2, 1985."

Pequeño didn't know where to focus his gaze and glanced suspiciously at the camera's red light. He knew well enough what was at stake and couldn't hide his nervousness. This conversation would be made public. His statements would be memorialized, then relentlessly and endlessly scrutinized in court.

"Tell us about yourself. Where you were born. You know, things about your childhood."

"I'm from Watsonville . . . born and raised. I was born at the old hospital on Holohan Road. I grew up in Watsonville. All my life, I . . . ."

"Which neighborhood were you from?"

"What do you mean? Like which 'hood? Like City Hall?"

"No I mean, where did you grow up as a kid?"

"Oh yeah, on Stewart Avenue, when I was young. Then later we moved to Maple Street. Honestly, man . . . we like . . . we lived everywhere when I was a kid. I think we moved like every two years, all over town. We never really stayed in one place. Know what I mean?"

"How old were you when you first became involved with gangs?"

"Like . . . I don't even know. I've been running around the hood since I can remember. It's all I ever knew. I've always been around it, gang life. Like if you wanna call it that. It was normal for me. They're not gang members, not to me. They're bros. We all came up together. We all have been running around Watson since we were kids. All of us . . . everyone."

Carillo's gang history question triggered Pequeño and he

spent the next thirty minutes talking about gang life with little to no prompting. It was like breathing, and he was comfortable describing it. In his own way, Pequeño had organized his approach to this briefing.

Overall, Pequeño's story was typical of Watsonville gang members:

His mother had her first child at sixteen. He'd never known his dad. Never finishing high school, his mom supported herself and the kids by working several low-wage menial jobs.

With his mom working at least twelve hours non-stop, Pequeño became independent as a small child. He could always do whatever he wanted any time he wanted. This free time gave him endless opportunities to hang out in the streets.

At fourteen, Pequeño stood in the middle of a group of City Hallers who'd surrounded him near the end of Coolidge Road in a wooded area on the banks of the Pajaro River. Three of the biggest City Hall gangsters stepped up and attacked him while the rest watched. For thirty seconds, Pequeño stood in the middle of the group as the three viciously punched and kicked him. It was a beat down. He wasn't supposed to fight back. One City Haller threw a solid blow to the head wobbling Pequeño and sending him to the dirt. He lay curled up for the final ten count, barely conscious. Then they stopped beating him.

Pequeño's eyes glistened talking about it. He was still proud. Pequeño had officially jumped in as a City Hall gang member. He'd spend the next decade doing everything for the City Hall gang—he'd move drugs for the big homies, stab rival gang members, rob stores, and get into countless fights. He did whatever had to be done.

Deep resentment set in while he was in prison for a robbery to raise funds for the Cause. Nearly half the money went to the big homie, who would then, in turn, send part of it to NF leadership as required.

Pequeño figured he'd earned thousands of dollars for his hood and the NF, yet while he sat in prison unable to earn money, his wife and two young children had to live in a car for months as they waited for temporary housing.

At this point in his story, Pequeño paused, his eyes misted over and his tone shifted from resentment into anger.

"Not one of them homies helped my wife and kids. Not one! Nobody gave them nothing. No money. No place to stay. No food. No help at all. Nothing! My wife and kids? They got left out in the goddamn cold. They slept in a goddamn car. My young kids and my wife . . . no one gave a shit."

Pequeño's voice became so shaky he paused and when he continued his tone carried a new resolve.

"From that day on, I knew I'm never doin' nothin' for them again. That was it."

"It's okay, man. You're doing the right thing. We'll take care of you and your family."

"*Claro*, Bautista? *Mira* . . . I gotta tell ya, it's not like that. You don't know nothin'. You got no idea what you're talking about."

"How . . . what'd you mean?" I said, trying hard to not take his attack personally, hanging on to an adage youth pastors lived by—hurt people, hurt people. I wanted to punish Pequeño there and then for being disrespectful. But he had all the leverage. At some point, things would shift and I won't forget.

"You can't protect me bro. You, Carillo, nobody. If these guys want me dead, I'm dead. I ain't doin' this for you guys or anybody else. I'm doin' this for me and my family. Understand? I know the risk. I don't give a shit about you."

"Okay. Fair enough."

"I don't need you to survive. I'm a grown-ass man and I've lived through damn near everything. But I need you to take down my hood. And you need me to take it down. *Es todo* . . . that's it."

"So, we're on the same page."

"Yeah . . . we are now."

Be patient. We're playing chess not checkers.

I could see from his expression that helping us was his way of sticking it to the family that abandoned *his family*. Maybe we were his ticket out of the gang life, maybe not. Most importantly for Pequeño, we were the instrument of his revenge and maybe the tool he'd use to clean up in the process. But first, he was gonna put the big hurt on some people.

Lots of people.

Pequeño spent two hours methodically identifying every gang member from whom he could buy drugs, stolen vehicles, and guns. He carefully described the ranking structure in all the hoods, naming every individual gang leader in Watsonville, Santa Cruz County, and a few in Salinas.

Before he was done, Pequeño described three unsolved murders where the murderers had confessed to him directly and whom he was confident he could get to confess to him again. Those gems alone were a cold-case investigator's wet dream.

He readily agreed to wear a wire, an inconspicuous camera sewn into a shirt, whatever, to make it all happen. After two hours, Pequeño was spent. I quit taking detailed notes after an hour. No sense in trying. I knew I'd just have to go back and watch the video for the details and nuances anyway. To me, the case looked like it had a near limitless upside. No telling how far it could go and it'd be a massive undertaking, with historic, epic results.

We'd found our wrecking ball.

Pequeño had found his.

CHAPTER
46

The final month working with Pequeño was the toughest. The DA's office arranged a solid week's worth of case presentation to the grand jury, in which Pequeño was the main witness. Once the grand jury deliberated and issued indictments, we'd be done with Pequeño. Although ideally, he'd testify during the jury trials, the DA's office assured us they could try most of the cases without him.

For his part, Pequeño sensed his superstar status and our aim-to-please attitude were both coming to an end very quickly. Predictably, his comfort parameters and associated demands became more and more absurd—more money, better cars, and luxurious hotel rooms.

Then an extraneous factor strained the relationship to the snapping point. Pequeño's girlfriend hit the silks, bailing on their relationship. Since she was unwilling to relocate with him, Pequeño's children would be staying in Watsonville. It was a devastating development for him.

There were many times I genuinely felt sorry for Pequeño. His decision to work with us was predicated in part on starting a new life with his family. As time went on and the operations he'd triggered became an ever greater success, what had been his secondary motivation was now clearly his primary one. Revenge was an old and cold done deal, but the real prospect of a vibrant new life hung there in his mind like a permanent trip to Tahiti. Now that entire dream-come-ever-so-close-to-true was gone.

But my empathy came and went. Like so many witnesses in big operations, he'd become a petulant prima donna. The weekend before the grand jury hearing, he threatened that he wouldn't testify. Perfect, I thought. I'll just lock him up until we need him in court. After all, given what an entitled prick he was, it'd be cheaper and easier.

"This piece of paper is a subpoena. And I just served you. You have no choice but show up and testify," I said.

"I ain't doing anything for you . . . the goddamn DA . . . for Petrossian. You'll just use me up and spit me out."

"This was part of the deal. We're not paying for your relocation unless you do this."

"You . . . you arrogant piece of . . . do you really think I need you? Like, I can't survive on my own? I've survived in places you'd never last a night."

"You think we're just going away? You think we're not going to file the charges? We're going to file every charge. And guess what every defense attorney will get? Every video. Every report. Every photo of you making the deals. I've got news for you, you've been used up and I'm about to spit you out. Everyone's gonna know you snitched whether you're testifying or not."

Chess not checkers.

"You know what, Bautista? Go . . . ."

The liquid fertilizer finally hit the forge. I grabbed his arms, spun him around, slammed him onto the side of my car, and cuffed him. He'd gotten on my last nerve and I was going to take him to jail. Instead of going hard, Pequeño broke down and cried, apologizing for how everything was falling apart and he no longer had anything to live for. He promised to show up for court but I didn't believe him.

Despite my lack of faith, in a weak moment, I uncuffed Pequeño and let him walk. I was worn out from a long and increasingly corrosive relationship with a high-value informant whose currency was coming to an end.

Surprise surprise, Pequeño testified on time and on target. It was, after all, the best option for him and offered at least the possibility that he could glean a new life from the ashes of his old one. We picked him up at 1600 hours every day for a week so he could speak in front of a closed hearing in the evenings. Just like the first big debriefing with us, Pequeño was composed, well-spoken, and professional on the stand.

The first massive swing of the wrecking ball went off perfectly.

Pequeño spent his first two nights' worth of testimony laying out his background as a City Hall Watson gang member and hashing out the ranking structure in all the hoods. He broke down exactly how meetings happened monthly and explained to the grand jury the actual dynamics in the meetings. He identified who collected the monthly $50 fee from each gang member, how it all got funneled back to the street commander, and ultimately got kicked up to the NF leadership in CDC. We periodically introduced covert videos of these meetings into evidence to bring Pequeño's testimony into sharp focus.

A grand jury was the perfect medium for Pequeño. There was a judge there to listen to him. Not the other way around. There were no defense attorneys to cross-examine him or anyone else. It is often said a good prosecutor can get a grand jury to indict a ham sandwich, but here the prosecutor had bupkus to do. The jury asked Pequeño some questions, but overwhelmingly his testimony went unchallenged. No one questioned his motivation or credibility and nobody pushed his buttons.

He had 'em all on the edge of their padded chairs.

Even the judge.

CHAPTER
47

Carillo and I walked into a room filled with two dozen law enforcement department heads. Commander Royce, the gravel-voiced but ever-amiable leader, worked the room welcoming all the chiefs and high-ranking officials. Carillo and I had zero time or energy for a meet and greet. But for things to get done some *pressing of the flesh* had to happen.

While I was focused on making sure that Pequeño's testimony would go off as planned, Carillo prepped the search warrants. After the indictments were issued, we had hundreds of charges on fourteen unlucky Watsonville based norteño gangsters. We'd charge more suspects later with additional crimes stemming from the investigation, but on Red Bull Day, we focused on taking off the fourteen Watsonville targets. In a nice dollop of irony; fourteen is the number norteños claim, given "N" is the fourteenth letter in the alphabet. This symbolism didn't escape our notice.

As with any rubber chicken presentation, Commander Royce gave brief welcoming remarks, expressing gratitude for the resources and support of all the allied agencies. WPD's chief, the acting head council member for CNET, expressed similar sentiments. With the backslapping-hail-fellow-well-met crap over, everybody wanted the real meal served.

I was next and gave a brief overview of the case. Surprisingly, the room was genuinely captivated. Carillo batted cleanup, handing out packets for each team with all the intel we had on each target, a copy of the search warrant for each residence, and an arrest warrant for each target.

There were twelve entry teams from various agencies, ranging from county SWAT teams, CHP, and BN&E teams from all over California, to ATF who deployed two entry teams at two locations.

In all, just shy of two hundred law enforcement officers wet their beaks on Red Bull Day.

By design, Carillo, Petrossian, and I had nothing to do. We'd charted, designed and plotted Red Bull Day for weeks. It was our day to enjoy the fruits of thousands of hours of effort.

We set in motion and unleashed forces that brought a new kind of living hell down on Watsonville.

On Red Bull Day, Carillo and I sat courtside first row across from the Sixth Street raid. I despised the city I'd once loved and felt betrayed for all the prayers on its behalf. The gang and drug elements had ruined hundreds of lives directly and indirectly, including several very close to me. I wanted everyone linked to any of it to get burned down. Red Bull Day was the day that pipe dream came true.

•   •   •

A week after Red Bull Day, I signed the lease for a single bedroom apartment on North Miami Beach on the thirty-seventh floor. It had panoramic views of the Atlantic coast from the balcony, with amenities that included an oversized pool, laundry service, workout facility, and a courtesy shuttle to take residents to major locations throughout Miami. It was the best really bad idea I'd had recently. There were so many things that could go wrong I'd stopped counting. With great hesitation, I handed the keys to Pequeño. The lease agreement listed Pequeño as a guest resident in my apartment.

I'd called grown men idiots for less.

PART TEN

The Lord is my shepherd;
I shall not want.

Psalms 23:1

CHAPTER
48

Seven years into my law enforcement career, my relationship with Hope was in tatters. Long hours away from home relentlessly degraded our communication and every form of intimacy. Four years into the narcotics assignment, I wasn't the person Hope married, with scattered exceptions at certain times. When she'd agreed to marry me, we were on the path to a relatively peaceful life.

Our life together became the complete opposite.

The terrible addiction in narcotics work comes from getting so used to living on the edge that you can't function without it. It is a drug squirted into your body by your body. Before becoming a cop, confrontations and conflicts were unwanted, culturally mitigated events, never sought, and invariably finessed with the lowest possible level of strife.

Most cops live and breathe life's most ghastly moments—gruesome, decaying dead bodies, heartbreaking sexual abuse of young children, armed gangsters puffed up and itching to shoot you. Downtime on the job consists of periods of Olympic-class boredom with your ass planted to the seat of a car and numbing physical inaction behind a desk. You eat bad food at odd hours on good days. Average people go to superhuman lengths to minimize exposure to traumatic events. A cop doesn't have that luxury. Periodic, random, and often senseless terror and trauma permeate our waking hours and haunts our dreams. You cannot experience this kind of trauma for long periods without being changed by it.

It's impossible.

Usually, I managed to peel off my "cop-death-face" around non-law-enforcement friends. To them, Hope and I *seemed* to be the same people they'd always known. When the topic of police work came up, I'd keep it to traffic tickets or the big stories that were already on the news. On the surface, the lake of our lives was placid and nothing had changed.

But Hope and I lived entirely other than how we appeared to others. I was hypervigilant 24/7, laboring under the constant foreboding that someone—a gang member, a shooter for a drug-trafficking operation, or a pissed-off dealer I'd busted—was hunting me, or worse, my family. My personality changed drastically. The longer I was a cop, the more pessimistic about people and their intentions I became.

All the people, all the time.

Since I thought I was *saving the city* while upholding truth, justice, and the American way, everything else took a distant backseat. I couldn't find joy or meaning in anything but police work. That made me insufferable all the way around. The worst part was I knew it and couldn't or wouldn't stop. What I thought I was doing was largely egotistical, self-righteous crap I'd built up in my head. It was the byproduct of reading my press clippings and lots of lore that never made the press.

Hope had a belly full and no longer wanted to live with the person I'd become. I didn't want to be who I was, but I couldn't find my way out of the emotional house of mirrors where every reflection told me the whole system would collapse if I wasn't there to tend it. In short, I'd started believing my lies.

Hope and I had once been youth pastors. Real ones. Now only she could claim that distinction. We'd had a clear joint calling and purpose for what we did in life. I'd suppressed and finally strangled that calling to work in another field that demanded ever more ruinous levels of dedication.

Being a great cop and a great investigator is a true calling and a profession every bit as exacting as any other profession. It's both an art and a science that can only be practiced but never mastered. Not in a lifetime. There's too much to learn. I'd experienced a lifetime's worth of adrenaline highs in a frightfully short amount of time. It's the kind of job where if you're good at it, you run out of time long before you run out of dreams. I was privileged to work with a ton of incredible cops. There was a kinship in our dedication to a job that offered zero notoriety outside the clan and could never be appropriately compensated.

As much as I loved it, being a narc wasn't what I was made to do. I was losing something. I could feel it. I knew if I let go all the way, it wasn't coming back. Part of that was Hope and part of what I was losing was me.

I missed being a pastor.

Either I had to permanently become a wolf who doesn't eat lamb or become a real shepherd.

Most cops proudly identify with sheepdogs. But great cops

are wolves. They just don't eat lamb. Most of us identify with guard dogs that watch over their flock, and it's a nice, politically correct analogy. But to truly guard a flock, we become wolves who hunt and kill other wolves. We take pride in stopping other wolves by any means necessary from destroying *our flocks*. We know extreme violence is sometimes necessary to protect our fold.

We understand that the flock doesn't like us, but they need us and tolerate our strange existence to keep the other wolves at bay. We do this because we understand at the visceral level exactly what wolves think, feel, and do. The flock can't ever befriend us and we can rarely rely on them. Our solace comes from camaraderie with other wolves in *our pack*, who understand our purpose and live it without compromise every day.

It's a difficult calling and few are cut out for it, especially in a violent town like Watsonville. The difference between an excellent cop and an arch-criminal is as fine as the cutting edge of a new razor. The deciding factor either way ultimately being *the will to do good* or the decision to give oneself over to insensate evil in a regular way.

As Alonzo Harris said in the movie, *Training Day*: "To protect the sheep, you gotta catch the wolf, and it takes a wolf to catch a wolf."

Alonzo was right, but it's not politically correct to publicly say so.

Although overly dramatized, the movie is one of the few times that kind of truth has escaped into the public realm. You can be sure it is courtesy of one or more technical advisors who told the writers to drop the normal formulaic crap and then proceeded to tell them *how the cow really eats the cabbage.*

Cops wage psychological and physical war against people just like themselves. These people are often keen to out-think cops and take countermeasures to beat them. If you're trying to catch a burglar, you need to think like a burglar: Why *this* house? Why *this* neighborhood? Why *this* time? What's your approach? What about your escape path if cops roll through? How will you move the loot you've stolen? Everything in a burglar's mind has got to be in the forefront of the cop's head if you're gonna have any chance of catching the thieves.

That's the mindset for a *simple* burglary. As the magnitude of the crimes worsens, so does the need to get into the criminal's head. The FBI Behavioral Analysis Unit is the institutionalized application of the process an individual investigator may need to go through. There is no shortage of careers, marriages, and family ties destroyed by getting inflow from the bad guy's head. Alcoholism, drug abuse, and suicides among law enforcement personnel who've become obsessed with horrific crimes they investigate is now a popular subject for TV and movies.

It's no joke.

Pastors identify with shepherds. The term shepherd is often used to refer to God. Jesus referred to himself as the Good Shepherd. Many of the Biblical figures, ranging from Abraham to King David, were shepherds. Shepherds lovingly care for their sheep as they travel through pastures, across streams, and through valleys.

In Psalms 23, the Psalmist takes great comfort in the fact that the Shepherd carries a rod and staff. The staff is long and slender with a crook on the end to pull a sheep back into the fold.

The shepherd also uses the staff to free the sheep from brush and pull them out of physical trouble.

A rod, usually made of a shorter piece of wood, is used to protect the sheep from predators and occasionally to reprimand unruly sheep. It is an offensive weapon the shepherd prefers not to use.

The shepherd cares for the quality of life of the sheep—their pasture, their diet, their health, their wounds, and the trauma that follows. Being a shepherd stems from a desire to nurture and care. The shepherd is focused on the sheep's well-being, driven by his affection for the sheep. He treats each sheep like it's his own—obsessing about their behavior, their energy, their happiness.

Real police, like wolves, have a transactional relationship with the flock. Cops live to keep the predators away and or destroy them. They've trained for it, and ultimately if they're good at it, they come to love it. Their howl (not unlike a siren) warns of impending threats, and their bite can be firm, intimidating, or fatal, depending entirely on the circumstances. Real police protect the flock unto their death when necessary. Because at heart they're wolves and not dogs, they can go to that place where dogs cannot and do what dogs can never do. The things they come to love and rely upon most in the entire world are the other wolves they serve with and not the flock they guard.

Actually, it works better that way.

One good measure of a cop's greatness is how they perform in conflict, the battles they wage, and the predators they vanquish. The wolf that guards a flock will gladly rest once the flock is safe from other wolves.

You can be a wolf who hunts wolves.
You can be a shepherd.
You can't be both.

CHAPTER
49

My last year in CNET was the most epic. As usual, Carillo pulled us into another long-term investigation targeting Salinas gang members. The City of Salinas with some 150,000 residents was a hub for gang violence. For a small town, it usually had over twenty homicides a year, not counting all the murders thoughtfully committed just outside the city limits.

Carillo, Petrossian, and I were excited to finally work Salinas because all of our previous work indicated the city was a job that needed doing sooner or later. Our operation was based out of an auto body shop in Prunedale, often called *Prunetucky,* owing to its white cowboy population and large rural properties, a few minutes from Salinas. (Yes, California has cowboys, and the Salinas rodeo is still one of the more important rodeos on the national circuit.)

The location was perfect. Only 1,200 square feet in total, the shop featured an office separated by thick walls from the actual workshop and a loft in the back. The office was a perfect place to hide the rescue team in case something went haywire. We plastered the walls with TV monitors for all the covert cameras installed inside and out.

My favorite covert camera was the one embedded in the thermostat. Right above the thermostat was the obligatory large poster of a scantily clad, voluptuous woman. All auto shops of a certain vintage have them. Even the most pious males couldn't help but glance momentarily but longingly at the poster, thus giving the camera beautiful, clear shots of their faces.

Petrossian was the primary undercover officer who contacted all the suspects, completed the transactions, and negotiated upcoming deals. I was overwhelmed at the thought of buying contraband from multiple suspects but he made it look easy. Petrossian spent his high school years working at his dad's auto body shop in San Jose. He was in his element. The shop was *his perfect cover.* In no small part because of this, the operation would become a perfect storm of criminal activity.

Carillo, ever the *master delegator,* coordinated all the cash for purchases, scheduled the rescue team, and wrote the reports. In time, this became a huge undertaking because of the size and scope of activity at the shop. All three of his main functions were strained to the breaking point by the explosive increase in business.

I was in charge of the surveillance team. My team had to identify every person who walked into the shop. We needed to know who they *really* were, where they went, and where they laid their heads at night. Once people started to stream in, it was like identifying all the shoppers on Black Friday at Target.

Almost every day.

Operation Money Train launched quietly and with no fanfare. After a few quiet days, our first car theft crew brought a 1997

Honda Civic in and Petrossian paid $1,100 for it.

That set it off. Business detonated like a fuel-air bomb.

The crew brought three more stolen Hondas in the next two days. Word spread like wildfire, and soon it was common for Petrossian to open the shop and find several stolen cars lined up outside waiting for him. When *business* exploded, we loved it, but everyone knew that it was dangerous. In the gang community, anyone busy *makin' bank* is both an opportunity and a target for gangsters.

With the operation dialed in, we became the most popular chop shop in town. But it didn't end with stolen cars. A few weeks into the operation, Petrossian diversified and we were buying guns and narcotics. The phone rang continuously.

Carillo struggled to keep the money flowing to buy the river of contraband flowing into the shop. CHP paid for the cars, ATF for the guns, and FBI for everything else. The only thing we didn't have was an online store. That would have totally swamped us.

My surveillance team struggled to identify all the people coming through the shop. Nobody flashes ID. Almost nobody uses their real name. We had to tail suspects, mostly Salinas residents, then find an opportune time to have them wall-stopped by Salinas PD or CHP so we could identify them based on the documents produced during the traffic stop.

Operation Money Train lasted eleven months.

In the end, we arrested over fifty suspects for charges related to their direct sales of contraband to Petrossian *the Super Salesman.* We arrested entire auto-theft crews, norteño gang members, sureño gang members, and major narcotics dealers.

It was a monumental operation, one of the largest in Monterey County's history. Dozens of law enforcement personnel helped in the operation, but the pillar supporting it all was Petrossian. He had criminal enterprises fawning and catering to him, never suspecting he was a cop. He negotiated with suspected murderers, bought guns from heavily armed nasty types, and at one point, talked his way out of an impending robbery.

As usual every politician and department head vied to wet their beaks and get their names associated with the operation. But the bottom line was Petrossian stole the show and carried it. His masterful, totally natural, undercover performance made the sting roar.

CHAPTER

50

The buy-in and buy-out tradition is a long-standing practice in narcotic units. At the beginning of his or her career, a narcotic agent buys alcohol for everyone, and by extension, his or her way into the unit.

The buy-out tradition is the more involved of the two, and it comes at the culmination of the narc's career. It's the time-honored way of recognizing a narc for the years of service. Previous agents and narcs from the area all gather for the buy-out. Although chiefs and sheriffs also attend, the buy-out tradition is really for the investigators who form the tight-knit community of clandestine police officers.

Petrossian, Carillo, and I decided to have our buy-out together since we were all leaving the unit within a month of each other. We worked extremely closely for years, and it was fitting for us to close the task force chapter of our careers jointly.

Ever the affectionate drunk, Petrossian started us off.

"Love you guys."

"Bro, stop touching me." Carillo, feigning annoyance, picked Petrossian's hand off his shoulder like it was a smelly dead bird.

"Yes, yes, I love you too. Jeez . . . ." I said.

"There's never gonna be nothing like this . . . never! N-F-F-N! Narcs forever . . . forever narcs." The buy-out hadn't started and Petrossian was a hot mess.

"Alright. So . . . okay . . . bro . . . you gotta pace yourself," I said.

I figured Petrossian would get wrecked and end up *driving the porcelain bus* in the bathroom long before the ceremony if I didn't talk him down now. It wouldn't be the first time narcs ended up laying in their puke, doin' lip-mambo on the bathroom floor at their buy-out.

"K . . . Dan . . . K . . . yeah . . . you're right. It's gonna be great . . . a great night! I can't believe it's all gonna be over."

"Naw . . . it's not over. Just a different chapter is all. You'll see, bro."

"Bro, I'm goin' back to *pinche patrol* . . . answering beat calls. Beat calls!" Petrossian said. "Can you even imagine that? Me? Takin' domestic violence calls? I don't even know where to start. I'll be goddamn lost. I don't wanna leave. I can't even . . . ."

"Bro . . . I'll be doin' it too . . . the same. At least Carillo gets to keep livin' the dream," I said.

Five years in a narc unit, I couldn't imagine taking beat calls either.

"Gotta admit, boys, I'm looking forward to a K-9 unit," Carillo said. "I get to work from San Luis Obispo all the way to Davenport. It's all beautiful country pretty much everywhere I go. It will be a nice break."

"Alright . . . stop it! Stop it! Let's enjoy the damn night. I really love you guys." Petrossian fumbled tilting his shot glass towards Carillo and me. *"Salud!"*

Carillo was smiling but I knew he was as unhappy as Petrossian and I.

Despite the large crowd at the buy-out, the three of us remained somber, almost stone-faced. We knew the times we experienced would never be repeated. Not even close. We'd had a once-in-a-lifetime defining experiences. We'd never work cases that challenged us like that. Worse still, we'd never work with people that driven. Not ever.

It was the end of an era for all of us.

In a flash, the identity I'd embraced for half a decade vanished.

PART ELEVEN

———

I have strayed like a lost sheep;
Seek Your servant,
For I have not forgotten
Your commandments.

Psalm 119:176

CHAPTER
51

He had a black hoodie over his head and his gray baggy Dickie pants were standard issues for vatos. The kid was walking on the right side of the street, legally. So much for Watsonville City ordinances and the California Vehicle Code as a means to make a stop.

Since it was well past midnight, I considered having a run at some violation of the curfew law for minors. The problem was I couldn't tell with any certainty if he was a minor or an adult. It simply wasn't obvious one way or another.

I tried to slowly creep up on the kid in the Crown Vic, keeping pace with his slow gait. Crown Victorias with the police package make an unmistakable noise. There's the distinct squelch from the radio and the hum of all the fans trying to keep all the computers and the vehicle cool. Even at idle the engine is doing serious work. A moving patrol vehicle just isn't stealthy. Crown Vic's huff and puff are unmistakably and when you floor one they sound like a 747 on takeoff from a short airstrip.

They just scream *COP*.

Despite the sound of the Crown Vic behind him, the kid

never glanced back to check who was following him. A major *tell* in itself. I knew from that moment *the game was afoot*. In a city with a healthy share of drive-by shootings and hit and runs, everyone was conscious of their backfield, especially any overtaking vehicle traffic. Everyone, from kids to middle-aged moms, kept their heads on a swivel. The fact that the kid didn't turn around to check made it obvious this wasn't going to end well for one of us.

He knows the sound. He knows he's being followed by a cop.

I followed him for thirty seconds as the two-lane paved roadway dipped towards the bottom of the hill. He wasn't doing anything illegal. I was following too close, but I wasn't doing anything illegal either.

I was *pushing* . . . pressuring him, waiting for a slip-up.

He was waiting for me to give up and roll by.

The game of *psychological chicken* was in full force.

As the roadway dipped towards the bottom of the 500 block of Carey Avenue, the kid blinked.

Exploding into a full sprint he shot across the street in front of me. I continued to follow him by car. Having been involved in dozens of foot pursuits, your attention locks onto certain critical movements. One common motion is the *hand to the waistband.* Both his hands were clamped on his waistband.

Maybe he's just trying to keep his pants up.

I dismissed the thought the nanosecond I had it. Maybe he was grabbing his pants, maybe he was the reincarnation of Teddy Roosevelt, and maybe he had a *gun.* No maybes. I had to assume the latter.

Hitting the lights and siren, I powered the Crown Vic within a few feet of the kid as he ran. With all the noise behind him, he broke his stride and the concentration that supports it, by looking back. You just can't run away from a threat without looking back. A million years of evolution just ain't having any.

Is it . . . it's Emilio! Ahhh Jeez . . . what's he doing?

Didn't know he was back.

Emilio was one of many students from our youth ministry. He'd attended youth services since he was a freshman in high school. I'd taken him to countless summer camps, ministry trips, and hiking trips. The last time I spoke to him was about a year ago as Hope and I saw him off for college.

As a freshman in high school, there was a brief period when Emilio dabbled with gang life. He wore a few red shirts and red shoelaces. But that ended up being the extent of his thug-life experiment. He'd focused on meeting girls, getting into college, and his spiritual life.

Now, this? Something was missing. This didn't make sense.

Here he was, running from a police officer for reasons only he knew.

At the bottom of the hill, I decided it was time to bail from the Crown Vic and treat Emilio to an old school foot-chase courtesy of a cop who seldom lost one.

I pulled up and slightly past Emilio before bailing. The moment I did, Emilio's hands came out of his waistband and dropped to his sides. Now he was running with both hands free and swinging. However, his right hand wasn't pumping nearly as much owing to the large caliber chrome revolver in it. Experience and the contours of the weapon told me it was at least a .357 magnum.

I'd say my pistol unholstered itself, but the way muscle memory works are far more subtle than that. The weapon came out because I'd been trained and had experienced this scenario many times. It came out with the muzzle pointed forwards and down in his direction but not directly at him. If I had to fire, the absolute minimum amount of time would elapse before I did so. I kept pace with Emilio comfortably, maintaining a critical safe distance of about fifteen feet. Ten feet would be too close, and at six feet anything and everything bad could and probably would happen.

Emilio darted up the driveway to Night Owl's house. Night Owl was a North Side Chico gang member well known to all the local cops and suspected of several shootings and murders. That Emilio would know Night Owl made zero sense.

Nothing made sense.

So much for Teddy Roosevelt. I just have to chase Emilio down and suss him out

He double-timed through the partially open side gate, while I slowed just enough to grab the house number before hitting my radio button.

"Going into backyard of 430 Carey Avenue"

Oops. We weren't.

I'd actually chased Emilio into the backyard of 530 Carey and I'd just sent all the backup units racing to the wrong address on the wrong block.

I was surrounded by eight gang members the second I ran through the side gate into the backyard. The gate I'd just come through was now blocked off by two menacing unhappy gangsters. There'd be no retreat. Turns out I'd run right into a *junta in progress.* It's a type of gang meeting held for various socially enriching purposes. Now I was quite literally the center of attention.

It would have been nice to wake up right about then, but this wasn't a nightmare. My admirers hosed me, screaming obscenities at such a speed and volume that I couldn't properly acknowledge and thank all my fans. A rock whizzed by my head close enough to feel the air disturbance as it passed. Surrounded and out-manned nearly ten to one, it was time to recklessly point my gun at everyone and either act completely crazed or ice-cold dead calm.

"Back up! Back up or I'll shoot every goddamn one of you!"

I was trying for *crazy* but for some reason, my voice sounded strangely calm and poised. My heart rate said otherwise, but all my fans at the *junta* couldn't hear it trying to pound its way through my ballistic vest. At least I don't think they heard it.

About then my Little Voice said:

Can't stay here. You gotta move.

Glancing past my welcoming committee, I spotted Emilio vaulting over the back fence into the backyard next door. I had one choice and that was to keep chasing after Emilio. A maelstrom was about to descend on me. Ironically, Emilio jumping over the back fence gave me an exit strategy.

Picking the least demonstrative vato in the welcome wagon encircling me, I approached with my pistol pointed directly at his forehead. Over the years, the point-blank view of my pistol barrel and especially the bore, has brought more than one antisocial person to their senses.

"Move or I'll shoot you in the head." I meant every word,

which helps if you can manage it with this sort of thing.

Surprisingly, he stepped back momentarily just enough for me to launch through the opening. As I broke through the circle, I felt a large rock pelt my right shoulder. Normally, whoever threw it would have immediately received my fullest attention. However, today was not normal.

Launching myself blindly over the fence I landed nicely and couldn't believe my luck. It was great to be on the move again considering the alternative. No matter how chasing Emilio turned out, I wasn't getting *jumped in* a gang where nobody wanted me and that I never intended to join.

Emilio had jumped right onto church property with a nice open backyard. I just love open space when it's time to chase suspects. It's a lunar landscape where I don't have to think or worry about much except running down my quarry to the ground. Although he was nearly a hundred feet away, I was closing the distance quickly.

"I'm going to catch you. You're gonna lose."

Taunting the suspects I'm chasing is a little trick I'd learned in the course of dozens of foot-chases. Taunting the guys you're chasing quite often seems to drain their physical energy. Knowing they've been going as hard as they can and I'm still on their ass like white on rice is completely demoralizing for many. Sure enough, Emilio began slowing down and I wasn't. It'd be over soon, one way or another.

Emilio slowed to a jog, and then abruptly anchored himself, turning to face me, with a chrome revolver held out and down to his right side.

I lost my footing momentarily trying to stop and dropped

to my right knee creating a stable shooting base. I clenched my body anticipating a bullet hitting my chest. Whether out of fear or an overactive imagination, I *felt* the cool breeze of a bullet whizzing past my right temple.

Emilio never fired.

"Drop the gun! Drop the gun!"

Front sight. Where's my front sight?

All the hours of training at the range were kicking in. Although the front sight was blurry, Emilio's body was somewhere in the middle of it. This would have been an easy shot.

Emilio stood breathing heavily, legs spread wide in a gunfighter stance, waiting, thinking, trying to muster the *cajones*. I waited and weighed whether to act or react. *I should shoot him.* Shooting him was completely justified. Given he hadn't already dropped the gun, he most likely wouldn't. If Dunn or any other officer were with me, Emilio would already have collapsed in a withering hail of gunfire. I would have shot him multiple times without the slightest hesitation fearing for the safety of the other officer.

The scene felt like a twisted academy scenario. A cruel elaborate ruse training officers pulled on rookie cops. But nothing here was make-believe. There'd be no do-overs with this.

I gently squeezed the trigger, felt it take up the slack, and stopped.

It's Emilio . . . .

The Little Voice got insistent:

You can't shoot 'em . . . not like this.

He'd have to point his gun at me. I knew that would give him the drop that could easily get me shot to death. But it didn't matter. I just couldn't shoot *this kid this way*. If another officer had been present, things would be terribly different no doubt, but there was no one else to protect. It was just me and it was just him—a kid I'd mentored for years, a kid Hope and I deeply cared about.

After the momentary stalemate, Emilio whipped around, rabbiting downhill. Getting to my feet I sprinted after him. So far there were no sirens.

Emilio ran behind the church building and out of sight. I figured he'd be waiting on the other side of the building, in a shooting position, waiting to ambush me. I sprinted wide to my right, away from the building, *slicing the pie* to increase the distance between us and give me a chance to react to whatever might be waiting for me just on the other side of the corner.

"We're behind the church at the bottom of the hill," I radioed.

It wasn't a wise thing to do on the radio and not a sound tactical move. But if I lost this chase and another officer found Emilio, his chances of being arrested without getting shot would be right around zero.

As I rounded the sharp corner of the building, I realized Emilio had just turned and started running towards the street. That meant he'd been waiting to shoot me behind the corner of the building for at least a few seconds.

That's it! You get a shot, you shoot. It's Emilio but that doesn't matter.

Not now.

My Little Voice reversed itself, something that didn't happen often. I ran faster and closed the gap. The chase was gonna end now.

Emilio reached the driveway leading to the church, and slowed to a walk, the revolver still in his right hand.

"Last chance, bro. Drop the gun or you're dead."

As I spoke I'd already started the two-second countdown before firing my first volley of shots. It takes approximately 26,500 years for two seconds to elapse under these conditions. It also takes a nanosecond.

Both at the same time.

As Emilio yanked the gun towards his waistband, I found my front sight picture in his center of mass and started to squeeze, again. When his arms swung open, the chrome revolver whickered through the air to his right. I couldn't believe my weapon hadn't discharged as I gingerly pointed the muzzle away from his body.

One threat instantly vanished.

But he didn't stop defiantly walking into the street towards Night Owl's nest again. For a moment I considered pulling my Taser while keeping my handgun drawn. So much can go wrong with that *mixed fruit pudding* maneuver, I rejected the notion spontaneously and holstered my handgun. Quickly transitioning to the Taser, there'd be no more *heads-up* for Emilio.

Without further ceremony I fired the Taser, its darts striking him squarely on his back below the shoulder blades. Emilio stiffened and quivered, keeling over like a king-size bologna sausage. He'd had plenty of chances to stop.

Now, I was open for business.

Normally the Taser cycles for five seconds while the recipient *rides the lightning.* There are, however, ways to modify normal operation. To prematurely end the five-second fun-cycle, you depress the safety lever down and off she goes. To extend the *lightning ride* and double the pleasure beyond five seconds, you simply keep the trigger depressed. Either way, the fun-seeker who gets "Tazed" is looking at the prospect of spontaneously urinating or defecating (sometimes both) during and after the jolts subside.

The commotion brought Night Owl and the junta out of the backyard to greet me. As Emilio lay *doing the chicken* while wave after wave of voltage coursed through his muscles, the group approached me *en masse*, screaming every obscenity I knew and a few I'd never heard. The rock throwers took up where they'd left off during our last lovefest, and rocks began whizzing past my head just as the sound of sirens started to be noticeable.

The backup was close, but no cigar.

I moved the Taser to my left hand keeping the trigger depressed while pulling the real pistol with my right hand to ward off Night Owl and the welcome wagon. The Taser cycle started to falter because I was draining every volt it had faster than it could re-energize. Emilio remained stiff and frozen as the Taser fired haphazardly. His body twitched and relaxed oddly like a guy trying to dance who simply had no rhythm and couldn't keep the beat of the music.

The first marked unit screamed down Carey Avenue to assist. It was Tony Reyes. The same rock star Tony Reyes from Operation Northern Exposure. He was the acting sergeant for the Sheriff's Office that evening. While everyone else was scouring for me at the wrong block, Reyes put the pieces together: Carey Avenue, the church, and knew exactly where to find me. People who spend time together in any battle always have a keen sense when the other is in trouble and will go through hell to find each other—even when all it means is to keep each other company while darkness engulfs what light cannot restore.

I held Emilio on the Taser cycle until Reyes cuffed him. Altogether, Emilio had ridden the lightning for almost two minutes. To him, I'm sure it seemed a lot longer.

I let the incoming units know by radio that they should feel free to place Night Owl and his friends under arrest for assaulting a police officer. Thus, the next arriving units chased the junta members who bolted scattering like hyenas facing a pride of hungry lions. The scene got even more chaotic.

When the ambulance arrived and the yelping of the fleeing vatos died down, I ambled over to Emilio who was still lying cuffed face down. The medical guys had removed the Taser barbs but I still hadn't seen his puncture wounds.

Turning him over, my heart dropped into my colon.

I was looking at Marvin Madrigal and Marvin Madrigal was blinking at me.

There's a resemblance between Marvin and Emilio, but the guy I'd been chasing wasn't Emilio from our youth ministry. Not related. Not even close. I'd screwed up from front to back repeatedly risking my life for a guy who would just as soon ambush and shoot me as he would break wind. The worst part was knowing that from that moment until the last of the stars in the universe burn out and go cold, I'll never know why he didn't.

I'd taken so many chances, putting my safety and my family's future at risk for nothing. The hesitation and refusal to shoot him, the multiple chances I'd given him, all because I thought he was Emilio. For a second I wondered if neither Madrigal nor Emilio was worth the risk.

Madrigal was a violent gangster. He was a suspect in several shootings and takeover armed robberies. I should have recognized him immediately. He was dangerous and I'd stared at his booking mugshots many times. It hit me standing there that I didn't recognize him because I couldn't. My brain wouldn't allow it. My subconscious mind had decided it was Emilio. Endless TV shows and movies feature the cop who shoots the wrong guy. Episodes featuring this scenario are almost obligatory in every cop series or movie. I'd repeatedly refused to shoot the right guy for all the wrong reasons. Life had become too goddamn ridiculous to even begin to try to understand it.

In due course, Marvin Madrigal graduated to become the designated shooter in the murder of a rival gang member. During the shooting, a six-year-old girl died from a stray bullet Madrigal fired. For that little girl's sake, if for no other reason, he was the last guy I should have afforded a second chance or any chance at all. He wasn't worth it then and he only got worse with time.

I was lucky to walk from the chase without injury. I'd given Madrigal multiple opportunities to kill me because I thought he was one of my favorite students from our youth ministry. In fact, I'd often seen the faces of students from our youth ministry in my police contacts. I'd seen Camelia's face in every young lady with eyes sunk deep in her skull from a meth binge. I wanted to snatch them out of the trap houses and drive them to a rehab. I'd seen Joaquin's face in every fourteen-year-old boy with fresh gang tattoos, on the fringe of being jumped into one of the dozens of gangs in the county.

The deep instinct to care, counsel, nurture, and minister was still alive. It had refused to die and was now forcing its way to the surface of my being. I realized I couldn't bear weapons designed to produce pain, injury, and death while caring, counseling, nurturing, and ministering. It just wasn't meant to be done that way. Maybe another man could do it. I don't see how. But either way, I knew I couldn't.

Conversely, I couldn't patrol the streets with the eyes of a youth pastor. That made me hesitant, contemplative, vulnerable, and dangerous as hell to other officers. Something had to give.

I could be the wolf who hunts wolves.

I could be a shepherd.

I couldn't be both.

PART TWELVE

Do not gloat over me, my enemy!
Though I have fallen,
I will rise.
Though I sit in darkness,
The LORD will be my light.

Micah 7:8

CHAPTER
52

I enjoyed being back on patrol, at least for a while. I liked the idea of working a ten-hour shift and coming home at a consistent time. No informants. No call-outs. No dashing here and there at 0300. Hope made no bones about how much better it and I was. It was a simpler life and a better one.

But on the streets, I started running into familiar faces over and over. Students from youth ministry, the same gangsters, the same families, same fights, same foot chases down the same alleys. The cycle looked like it would never end.

Like it could never end.

My youth pastoring days were history. I couldn't figure out how to get my wolf-genie back in the bottle and revert to the role of a nurturing shepherd. Part of me couldn't stand the idea of working so emotionally close with anyone ever again, inevitably becoming vulnerable to them. I couldn't un-see all I'd seen. There was no way to erase the heartache, deep sadness, and disappointment. I left the shepherd on the shelf and prayed someday I'd believe again in God's redemptive power. I just wasn't feeling it anymore.

I needed a new chapter. A different challenge.

I had to move on. For better or worse.

•   •   •

Passed down from the time of the Great Flood, the badly worn, genuine-imitation Hides-of-Nauga chairs ended up in the interview room where we sat. A tear in the backrest allowed a broken coil spring and stuffing that resembled fiberglass to poke through my checkered shirt. Pulling the chair's height-lever, I tried to raise the seat. The hydraulics pumped the seat upwards in a fit of optimism, held for a second, then collapsed. My seat sputtered down to the lowest setting leaving my chin barely two hands above the desktop. It was uncomfortably reminiscent of my first days in a patrol car that didn't fit me struggling to see over the steering wheel and reach the gas pedal while my T.O. howled till his eyes watered.

At 6'3", Brandon towered over me in his chair and his seat happily stayed up, no problem. The white fluorescent lights buzzed and flickered in the sea of water-stained crumbling ceiling tiles. We were seated at a small but somehow imposing table in the middle of the room. I was starting to warm up to the constant growl of a man clearly in agony coming from a bleak corner down the hallway. The hoarse voice was amplified as it boomed down the cement hallways of the administration building at Mule Creek State Penitentiary.

Maybe he's been screaming all night.

"You mind switchin' seats?" I asked. Brandon laughed.

"Of course. We want you to be able to see over the table."

"Thanks bro, I need help . . . you know? It ain't easy being me."

As Brandon and I swapped seats, we discussed the fact that neither of us had any idea what T.J. Bruce was like or how he would react to us. For all we knew, he could go berserk and lunge at us. Due to prison regs and the mandatory reports they require, any assault would make for a long day not counting somebody getting hurt. We knew almost nothing about T.J. save the description in his CDCR printout:

6'4", 220 pounds.

That info tidbit indicated that if T.J. lost his cabbage, we'd have a violent, big meat-popsicle on our hands.

Three weeks prior, my chief tossed a black three-hole binder full of disorganized copies of articles and reports laughingly called a *case file*. Ever since moving into the district attorney's office as an investigator, I'd been asking for more challenging cases. My new chief made sure my needs were met. First, he assigned me to proactively investigate human trafficking cases in the county and added a few cold cases on top to shut me up.

The case file contained a ten-page summary of an interview with T.J. Bruce in 1995. Attached to the summary was the full interview transcript.

All 416 pages.

T.J. will die in prison. The system, flawed as it is, clearly recognizes the need for this and will ensure that he does. His first murder conviction came in 1982, followed by two more murder convictions. Three murder convictions standing alone is concerning, but in the 1995 interview, T.J. claimed he had committed some thirty additional murders. The skepticism of the investigators dripped from every page of the summary.

We weren't sure what kind of horsepower T.J. had. Having the buffer of a table between us was something. I was hoping that all the time inside might have allowed him to acquire wisdom, self-control, or at least as an old man, he'd be too worn out to go full-contact batshit on two guys half his age.

"This table. That bench too. All made by inmates," Brandon said, knocking on the tabletop and then pointing to a wooden bench leaning against the wall.

"What do you mean? They assembled it?"

"No, no man. They actually built 'em from scratch. It's part of the program. You know? Like how some cons make license plates. These guys build furniture. It's part of their rehab. Look . . . lemme show you."

Brandon leaned over to check the table's edges.

"Here . . . here it is!" He said pointing to a piece of tin rectangle glued to the side of the table marked: CALPIA. "I think the program is called California Prison Industry Authority or something like that."

"I'm surprised. The . . . I'm impressed at the quality of workmanship," I allowed.

Our conversation paused just long enough for the lull to be filled with screaming.

"Bro, is it always like this with the voices?"

"It never stops. There's always someone screaming," Brandon said.

"I couldn't . . . dude, I can't imagine. That screaming every day? All damn day?"

Brandon had been a CDC corrections officer at San Quentin

State Prison, so the screaming didn't seem to bother him. The prison world was alien to me. I admit it was comforting to have Brandon with me. He knew the language, the people, and the protocols inside out from years of experience.

During his time in corrections, San Quentin housed almost seven hundred inmates on death row. It was the only place in California that executed inmates on the very rare occasion it happened. Brandon worked at point-blank range in extremely confined spaces with the most violent killers in California and lived to tell the story.

"How do you wanna play this?" he asked.

"I was thinking about that on the drive here. Let's keep it simple. Just a meet and greet. No pressure. No agenda. Let's try and suss him out. Introduce ourselves and hope he doesn't decapitate us both. I hate it when that happens."

I chuckled as I said it but it was a nervous chuckle.

"I like it. We make him feel all nice and comfy with us. As best we can. I think that's about all we can do. He's been in Ad-Seg for a hundred and eighty days, so I'm betting he's a happy guy right now. Damn happy just to be out. Probably love to talk about a cold drink on a hot day," Brandon said.

The guards briefed us earlier that T.J. was accused of sexual battery of a prison staff member and got six months in administrative segregation, aka *the hole,* for his trouble.

"So . . . he'll either be one way or the other. Like happy to see us or coming at us like a rabid dog on a rocket sled!" I said.

We agreed we'd go into the meeting offering T.J. nada. We couldn't get this guy leniency, better prison digs, more crap for his commissary, and definitely not parole. We were working without a net, hoping to elicit a confession from a three-time convicted killer concerning other murders he'd committed.

And we were offering him squat.

We had one shot at a confession. We'd appeal to his conscience. That sounds like a contradiction in terms when you're dealing with a multiple-murderer and possibly an epic serial killer. But you'd be surprised sometimes. We'd ask him to help us bring closure to the victims' families, and maybe in the process, find some semblance of peace in not taking his secret murderous past to the grave. We were asking him to do a piece of mercy and maybe feel some in return. Believe it or not, it can work for a variety of reasons, the most disgusting of which is some killers' bottomless need for attention.

After an hour, we heard metal chains jingling and crinkling on hallway tiles.

"That's gotta be him," Brandon said.

The CDC guard opened the heavy steel door to our room and escorted T.J. to his seat. T.J. didn't sit down. Another guard stood outside the room as a backup.

"You guys want us in here?" the guard in the room asked.

"Naaah we're okay," Brandon said.

Both guards looked at us like we were nuttier than T.J. Turns out they were right.

Six months in Ad-Seg had turned T.J.'s skin the color of Crisco shortening. It'd been a long time since I'd seen skin that white. We'd stood up as he walked in, and I was surprised, and a little alarmed. He was taller than Brandon. Despite wearing a baggy, short-sleeve jumpsuit, T.J.'s muscles were well defined. Since he hadn't had access to the weight pile, that meant he'd kept a rigorously disciplined exercise program going his entire stay in the hole. Varicose veins bulged on his forearms and neck. For doing 180 days in Ad-Seg, he had zero signs of muscular atrophy.

T.J. had several small, extremely old facial tattoos and both arms were covered with crude prison tattoos acquired during his long incarceration. He'd come out of the hole agitated and jumpy. He glared at us suspiciously, finally sitting across the table. His manner dripped disdain.

"You guys okay?" The other guard standing outside the room decided he'd give us one last chance to change our minds and chicken out.

"We're fine. We're good," I replied.

I took great comfort in the memory that Brandon had trained in jiu-jitsu for years. I'd spent hours grappling in mixed martial arts mats, which might help me survive a minute or two before T.J. could really hurt me. A minute or two should be all we would ever need with the Bobbsey Twins outside taking bets on how soon we'd piss ourselves and start screaming for help. The younger guard slammed the door, and we were on our own with a triple murderer who had nothing to lose. He was sitting close enough to lunge, bite a hole in my throat, and spit my larynx out on the tile.

"What *THE HELL* YOU WANT?" T.J. screamed, slamming a massive fist on the table, his heavy belly chains clanking.

I was already missing the guards and visualized them just outside our door bent over laughing as they waited for us to start mewling like poisoned puppies. T.J.'s manic state settled me. He could have said nothing and done something vicious. Guys who are good at hurting and killing people, and like it, don't always talk much. They just do what they do. But he was running his mouth—a good sign. It was his power play, his attempt at intimidating us. He wanted us to show fear.

I leaned back unfazed by his play, respectfully listening like I might want to order another latte-mocha. Brandon looked like the Sphinx. We were veteran investigators who'd both seen plenty of high-profile investigations. We knew what worked and what didn't. I'd picked Brandon to talk to T.J. because most investigators would have peed themselves, called the guards, and buggered off by now. But he and I were just gettin' started.

"Lemme guess . . . you pigs are from Santa Cruz?" Before we could say anything, he continued. "You're the last people I wanna talk to! You're a bunch of snakes! You have any idea what your office did to me? Huh?"

I had no clue what he was on about or if he even knew. But I could feel he had a load to drop that was gonna come out.

"No . . . no . . . I don't."

"That's the problem, you ain't got no clue! No idea! You have no idea what you're getting into. You have no idea what this shit does to me!"

T.J. focused on me like a raptor on a field mouse. Maybe it was because I was the smaller, easier target for his verbal power play. Brandon was just as big as T.J. and could give as good as he got in a nanosecond if T.J. said or did the wrong thing.

It was all good. I didn't mind. The man was talking. That's always a start.

"Tell me, T.J. I wanna know."

"You don't have any idea! I couldn't even begin to . . . to . . .

to open your eyes. You're wastin' your time and mine."

T.J. jacked his eyes as wide open as possible to cement the crazy-ass-killer-gonna-get-ya visual effect.

T.J.'s tall frame bent over the table so he could literally talk down to me. This was getting good. I wasn't giving him anything and he was running out of moves.

"Ya think you can just come in here and start uncovering wounds then drive back down to Santa Cruz. You got no idea what happens to me. You're wasting my time."

Now T.J. was screaming, and I noticed he was missing almost all of his upper front teeth. With no upper choppers to stop it, his tongue was flopping out and lashing around inside his mouth like some kind of exotic animal. I just couldn't place which one. It's strange what you think about at times like that. I also noticed the left arm to his black-framed reading glasses was crudely wrapped with black electrical tape.

He went on screaming for over ten minutes. I lost track of what he was talking about but remained cool as a well-digger's behind. I focused on maintaining the appearance of being engaged and unphased by every word he spoke.

Eventually, he just seemed to be running out of energy. I had thought he had a dump to drop and maybe this was it. Having vented his spleen on me, T.J. went eerily quiet and sat down. Slowly, I perked up and moved to the edge of my seat. This is one of the strongest psychological *tells* to whomever you're talking to, that you are utterly captivated with them. I had a handful of chances to turn him. I couldn't be nonchalant. Most likely, we'd never get this chance again.

"Okay. T.J., listen, you may not like us. I get that. I don't know what happened between you and our office. There's only one reason we're here. We want to bring closure to the victims' families."

"Bullshit! And you know it."

T.J. stayed seated as he spoke, another great sign. He had cooked off something that was eating him. Now we could talk.

"No. No, man, it isn't."

I replied quickly and calmly to make sure that he didn't get over on me but careful to not rouse him out of his new relative calm.

"Look, Brandon and I are here for one simple reason. We're here for the victims' families. We got no other agenda. I mean zero. You don't have to believe us. We don't have to do anything. You didn't ask for this, to talk to us. We *asked you*. We don't get anything more for closing any of these cases. We ain't gonna get promoted. We won't get famous. Been there, done that. We volunteered to work this. We asked for it . . . that's it!"

Sometimes the truth is impossible to swallow. Other times it's so plain under the circumstances it's impossible to reject. Brandon and I had graduate degrees. We were promoted to sergeant at one point with WPD, with prospects of promoting up the chain of command. We both knew that wasn't what we wanted to do for the rest of our careers. We both genuinely loved investigations and the DA's office was the only place in the county that allowed you to work the investigative bureau for the rest of your career.

T.J. visibly shrunk into his chair, signaling that he'd lowered his physical guard. I sensed he was receptive and knew we had to seize the moment.

I slo-mo'd my response, adding: "We know that . . . like . . . we've got nothing to offer to you. We can't hurt or help you. I'm just askin . . . if . . . whether you're at the point . . . you know? Where you wanna help some of the victims' families? If you are, we're here to hear you out and make that happen. No pressure. We're not trying to make a name for ourselves or anybody. It's just a piece of mercy man. At this point, that's all it is."

"Ahhh, man!" T.J. looked down shaking his head slowly. "You're really messing with my head. You caught me at the right time."

Bingo.

We'd struck just the right key on the piano. I wanted to glance at Brandon and share a nod of exhilaration, or better yet, get up and get a massive high-five. But I couldn't risk the slightest *tell*. Any movement could snap T.J. out of his reverie and destroy his spasm of honesty.

"I've been . . . ." T.J. began, "I've been wanting . . . to do this . . . you know? Talk to some . . . like you guys. Do something good before I'm gone."

I couldn't believe it. I wanted to interject *something* between his long pauses, but I remembered a homily used by guys who set chokers on massive trees once they're logged and before they're towed up steep grades to the logging deck. The job is considered one of the deadliest occupations in America due to the many ways one can be killed by trees that get loose or sweep you up in their wake. They'd say: "Never say 'whoa' on a go-ahead show." Something extremely good was happening on its own and building momentum as it went. It wasn't broken. I didn't need to mess with it or get in the way.

"Look, I don't know if there's a God. Don't know if there's a heaven. I goddamn don't think any of that BS is true. But if there is, I just wanna shot at making it in. I want to get square with the house and pay up for my sins."

God. Heaven. Forgiveness. Redemption. Hope.

I couldn't believe T.J. went the way he had. He was in my old wheelhouse, sitting there in one of the worst places on earth.

"T.J. . . . so this is what I believe . . . ." I was struggling to remain calm. "In the end, we're not judged by what we've done in the past. We're judged by what we do when there's a chance to try to make things right. You got the power . . . all of it. You're the most powerful man in this room. You got the keys to bringing closure to a lot of families. They're waiting on answers to what happened to their loved ones. We're just here to carry out your actions if you wanna act. It's all up to you. It's all with you. This is *your* show. This is *your* gift to give."

He slumped in his chair and fell dead silent.

Brandon, ever the consummate professional, hadn't said a word in almost thirty minutes. He knew all about never saying "whoa" on a go-ahead show. He knew something had clicked between me and T.J. that had to be allowed to go on. Brandon had long since mastered the martial art of submissive gesture. By comparison, cracking heads was easy.

T.J. stared at the ground, wheels spinning. He might never make it to an altar confessing his sins and asking God for forgiveness. This was probably as close as he'd ever get.

"K . . . okay, let's do this," he whispered.

"You tell us what *you* want, T.J. We will do it the way *you* want it done," Brandon added.

I slumped back into my chair, physically and emotionally exhausted. It was a massive breakthrough even though we haven't cleared a single cold-case murder. But we were on the path.

Brandon walked T.J. through all his demands:

1. No media coverage.

2. No death penalty.

And third: "I'll only mess with you two. Nobody else! If anyone else walks through that door, I'm done! Deal is dead."

Brandon and I nodded slowly, careful to cloak our enthusiasm.

T.J. said he'd confess to two murders to start and named the victims. I'd done my homework and knew both murders went unsolved, with no known suspects and zero leads. His confession and other corroborating evidence were the only possible way to clear these killings. Then he calmly confirmed in generalities that he did commit all thirty of the murders he'd talked about in 1995 and cautioned us to not get excited or get ahead of ourselves.

Over thirty killings! Maybe.

"Let's try these two cases. See how you two boys do. I'll think about the other ones. Don't mess it up," T.J. cautioned. "This'll be your *only shot*."

Made in the USA
Las Vegas, NV
24 July 2021

26966330R00215